The Work and Lives of Teachers in China

By bringing together a distinguished group of scholars who have deep, extensive and complementary knowledge and expertise of the Chinese education system, *The Work and Lives of Teachers in China* engages in detailed discussions on contemporary issues about teachers and teaching in China. It locates teachers' work and lives in a critical analysis of the political, socio-cultural, ideological and educational reform contexts, and through this, demonstrates how teachers in different professional life phases and in different schools are able to retain their vocational strength and commitment for learning and development.

Using rich illustrations from real teachers in real primary and secondary schools, this book represents a collection of scholarly writings which build research and practice informed new knowledge about the nature of teachers' work and lives in China. Through these comprehensive case studies, the book illustrates to policy makers, head teachers and training and development organisations the importance of sustaining teachers' commitment and wellbeing in their efforts to improve quality and standards in today's Chinese schools. *The Work and Lives of Teachers in China* provides valuable insight for policy makers, educators, researchers, teachers and students in education and beyond.

Qing Gu is Professor of Education in the School of Education, University of Nottingham, UK.

Routledge Research in Asian Education

This is an interdisciplinary series focusing on education in Asia. Open to established and emerging scholars with a focus on the region, it aims to inform readers of the latest research and contribute to the growth of scholarship on Asian Education.

Books in the series include:

General Education and the Development of Global Citizenship in Hong Kong, Taiwan and Mainland China: Not merely icing on the cake
Edited by Xing Jun, Ng Pak-sheung and Cheng Chunyan

Higher Education Choice in China: Social stratification, gender and educational inequality
Xiaoming Sheng

The Work and Lives of Teachers in China
Edited by Qing Gu

The Work and Lives of Teachers in China

Edited by Qing Gu

Routledge
Taylor & Francis Group
LONDON AND NEW YORK

First published 2015 by Routledge

2 Park Square, Milton Park, Abingdon, Oxfordshire OX14 4RN
711 Third Avenue, New York, NY 10017

Routledge is an imprint of the Taylor & Francis Group, an informa business

First issued in paperback 2018

British Library Cataloguing in Publication Data
A catalogue record for this book is available from the British Library

Library of Congress Cataloging in Publication Data
A catalog record for this title has been requested

ISBN: 978-0-415-84413-0 (hbk)
ISBN: 978-1-138-58019-0 (pbk)

Typeset in Galliard
by RefineCatch Limited, Bungay, Suffolk

Contents

List of contributors vii

Introduction x

QING GU

PART I

The changing landscape of teaching in China 1

1 Tensions and dilemmas for Chinese teachers in responding to system wide change: new ideas, old models 3

JUNJUN CHEN AND CHRISTOPHER DAY

2 Ideological, social and cultural forces influencing teacher education and development in China: a critical analysis 22

SHIBAO GUO

PART II

Developing teachers in times of change: contexts matter 39

3 The impact of reform policies on teachers' work and professionalism in the Chinese mainland 41

LESLIE NAI-KWAI LO, MANHONG LAI AND LIJIA WANG

4 The honourable road and its impact on teacher practice: an analysis of China's national honour system in cultivating professional development 63

HUAN SONG, XUDONG ZHU AND LAURA B. LIU

5 Dilemmas of teacher development in the context of curriculum reform 85
HONGBIAO YIN

6 China's quest for world-class teachers: a rational model of national teacher education reform 105
JUN LI

PART III
What keeps teachers going: identity, resilience and commitment 123

7 Professional identities and emotions of teachers in the context of curriculum reform: a Chinese perspective 125
JOHN CHI-KIN LEE, YVONNE XIAN-HAN HUANG, EDMOND HAU-FAI LAW AND MU-HUA WANG

8 Sustaining resilience in times of change: stories from Chinese teachers 145
QING GU AND QIONG LI

9 How principals promote and understand teacher development under curriculum reform in China 165
HAIYAN QIAN AND ALLAN WALKER

10 Teachers' beliefs and practices: a dynamic and complex relationship 180
HONGYING ZHENG

Index 195

Contributors

Junjun Chen is an assistant professor in the Department of Education Policy and Leadership, the Hong Kong Institute of Education. Her research focus is on teacher effectiveness and school improvement through measuring teachers', school leaders', and students' attitudes, and how these attitudes link to student achievement. She is experienced in managing large-scale surveys and analysing quantitative data using techniques such as exploratory factor analysis (EFA), confirmatory factor analysis (CFA), effect size, and structural equation modelling (SEM).

Christopher Day is Professor of Education at the School of Education, University of Nottingham. His particular concerns centre upon the continuing development of teachers, teacher effectiveness, teachers' lives and work, successful school leadership and the management of change. He has extensive research and consultancy experience in England, Europe, Australia, South East Asia, North America and with the OECD in the fields of teachers' continuing professional development, school leadership and change.

Qing Gu is Professor of Education in the School of Education, University of Nottingham, UK. Her research interests are teacher professional development, school leadership and school improvement, and university internationalisation. She is Vice Chair of the *British Association of International and Comparative Education* (BAICE). She is author of *Teacher Development: Knowledge and Context* (Continuum, 2007), and co-author of *Teachers Matter* (Open University Press, 2007), *The New Lives of Teachers* (Routledge, 2010), and *Resilient Teachers, Resilient Schools* (Routledge, 2014).

Shibao Guo is Associate Professor in the Werklund School of Education, University of Calgary. His research interests include comparative and international education, citizenship and immigration, social justice and equity in education, adult education and community development. His recent work appeared in *COMPARE*, *Comparative Education*, *Globalisation, Societies and Education*, *International Review of Education*, *International Journal of Lifelong Education*, and *Journal of Education and Work*. Currently he serves as president of Canadian Ethnic Studies Association and co-editor of *Canadian Ethnic Studies.*

Yvonne Xianhan Huang is Lecturer in the Faculty of Education, The University of Hong Kong. Her published and forthcoming papers appear in *Higher Education Review*, *Tsinghua Journal of Education*, *Research in Educational Development* and *Global Education*.

Manhong Lai is an associate professor in the Department of Educational Administration and Policy, the Chinese University of Hong Kong. Her research covers educational development in Chinese societies, academics' work lives in higher education, teacher development, and teacher professionalism.

Edmond Hau-Fai Law is Associate Professor at Hong Kong Institute of Education. His recent published papers appear in *School Leadership & Management*, *The Curriculum Journal* and *Educational Management Administration and Leadership*. His recent co-edited book includes *Schools as Curriculum Agencies: Asian and European Perspectives on School-Based Curriculum Development* (with N. Nieveen, 2010).

John Chi-Kin Lee is Vice President (Academic) and Chair, Professor of Curriculum and Instruction at Hong Kong Institute of Education. His recent co-edited books include *Changing Schools in an Era of Globalization* (with Brian Caldwell, Routledge, 2011) and *New Understandings of Teacher's Work: Emotions and Educational Change* (with Chris Day, 2011).

Jun Li is an associate professor of international education policy at the Chinese University of Hong Kong, and is the past president of the Comparative Education Society of Hong Kong (CESHK) and a Congress Standing Committee Member of the World Council of Comparative Education Society (WCCES). He has expertise in policy studies in comparative and international higher education and development, teacher education, citizenship education and civil society, Chinese and Asian perspectives on education and diversity in the context of globalisation, regionalisation and localisation. His authored books include *A Comparative Study of Educational Theories of the Schools of Metaphysics, Confucianism, Buddhism and Taoism* (1994), *A History of Chinese Thought on Education* (1998), *Portraits of 21st Century Chinese Universities: In the Move to Mass Higher Education* (co-authored, 2011) and *The Chinese Model of Policy Implementation: Multiple Perspectives on Teacher Education Reform* (2015).

Qiong Li is Professor of Education at the Institute of Teacher Education Research, Beijing Normal University. Her research interests focus on teacher cognition and professional development. She is a member of the Chinese Psychology Association, and Director of the Institute of Teacher Education.

Laura B. Liu is a Doctor of Education at the Faculty of Education with Beijing Normal University's Center for Teacher Education Research. Her research areas include teacher educator international professional development, teacher wellbeing and assessment, aesthetic pedagogies and narrative inquiry.

Leslie Nai-Kwai Lo is Senior Research Fellow in the Centre for Teacher Education Research at Beijing Normal University.

Haiyan Qian is an assistant professor in the Department of Educational Policy and Leadership at the Hong Kong Institute of Education. Her research mainly focuses on understanding school leadership and educational change in China.

Huan Song is an assistant professor and Vice-Director of the Institute of Teacher Education Research of Beijing Normal University. His research areas cover teacher education, teacher professional development and professional learning community.

Allan Walker is the Joseph Lau Professor of International Educational Leadership. Dean of the Faculty of Education and Human Development and Director of the Asia Pacific Centre for Leadership and Change at the Hong Kong Institute of Education. His research focuses on school leadership in East and Southeast Asia, and particularly the influence of culture on school leadership and organisational behaviour.

Lijia Wang is a lecturer in the Department of Education at East China Normal University in Shanghai, China. She specialises in educational policy and teacher professional development.

Mu-Hua Wang is an associate professor at Southwest University. His research interests focus on curriculum studies.

Hongbiao Yin is Assistant Professor in the Department of Curriculum and Instruction at the Chinese University of Hong Kong. His research interests include curriculum reform, teacher change and teacher emotion. His recent publications appear in *Teaching and Teacher Education*, *Educational Management Administration and Leadership*, and *Journal of Educational Change*. He is the co-editor of *Curriculum Reform in China: Changes and Challenges* (with John Chi Kin Lee, 2012).

Hongying Zheng is Professor of English as a Foreign Language Teaching in Sichuan Normal University. She has published in both English and Chinese academic journals and her publications focus on issues related to language teachers' beliefs and teaching and learning in primary and secondary schools in China.

Xudong Zhu is Professor of Teacher Education and Director of the Centre for Teacher Education Research at Beijing Normal University. He is also the deputy editor of the *Teacher Education Research Journal*, and the General Secretary of the Teacher Education Experts Committee of the Ministry of Education in China. His research focuses on theory, policy and practice of teacher education in China, comparative teacher education and the history of education.

Introduction

The work and lives of teachers in China

Qing Gu

This book is about the work and lives of teachers in China. It will examine what it means to be a teacher and what it is that enables or challenges Chinese teachers to sustain the quality of their commitment and effectiveness in times of change. Over the last three decades, research on teachers and teaching has produced an empirically-informed rich evidence base on why many teachers across the world enter teaching, what keeps them going and how they contribute to pupils' learning and achievement (e.g. Hansen, 1995; Day and Gu, 2010; Leithwood *et al.*, 2006; OECD, 2005, 2011). However, the widely debated theories and practices regarding teachers and teaching tend to find their roots in western dominated political, social and cultural contexts. As yet, the work, lives and effectiveness of teachers in schools in China appear to be largely missing.

The importance of understanding the work and lives of this sizeable group of teachers in the world's teaching force cannot be justified in quantitative terms alone. The potential impact of China on global economic and social change has attracted social scientists from around the world to study the history and modernisation of this 'Rising Power'. This is not least because the Chinese education system is recognised as one of the world's most improved school systems which 'have registered significant, sustained, and widespread student outcome gains' (McKinsey, 2010: 10); nor is it simply because the desire to outperform Shanghai in the Organisation for Economic Co-operation and Development's (OECD) Programme for International Student Assessment (PISA) has almost become a global obsession. Essentially, it is because research tells us the education system has to look to its front line teachers to ensure that the improvement journey is long term and sustainable (e.g. Day and Gu, 2014; Gu, 2007; Hargreaves, 1994, 2003). For educationalists, it is perhaps also about time that we extend our understanding of the challenges, tribulations and rewards that many Chinese teachers experience in contexts which, compared to those which have been widely discussed in the educational literature, have distinctive historical, political, social and cultural features.

The aim of the book is to provide state-of-the-art knowledge of the values, qualities and practices of primary and secondary school teachers in the context of educational change and reforms in China. As schools in many other countries across the world, over the last ten years Chinese schools have experienced a series of government interventions in the form of new national curricula, national tests, external inspections and standardised criteria for measuring the quality of schools to raise standards (MoE, 2010). With regard to the teaching profession, since the early 1990s particular attention has been paid to increasing its social status and building a qualified, stable and caring teaching force (MoE, 1993, 1995, 2010). However, whilst these large-scale system reforms are well-intentioned, they pose significant challenge to teachers' professional identity, emotional stability and existing notions of professionalism (Dai *et al.*, 2011; Day *et al.*, 2007; Lee and Yin, 2011; Paine and Fang, 2006). Moreover, they emanate from a deficit view of teachers, often result in an increased workload for them, and fail to acknowledge the importance of teacher wellbeing and commitment (Gao, 2008).

Teachers' sense of wellbeing is deeply connected with how they define themselves as professionals, and how they see their professionalism being defined by others. Where there are differences, there are likely to be tensions. Thus, understanding variations in the conditions for teachers' professional learning and development that enhance their sense of positive professional identity and wellbeing requires more than a consideration of the functional needs of organisations and needs arising from teachers' personal lives. It requires, also, a consideration of how tensions within and between these interact and how they might be managed by organisations and teachers in ways which build, maintain and enhance, rather than drain the commitment and resilience that are essential if teachers are to teach to their best in the new environment in which they work. This book provides rich illustrations of different scenarios in which teachers in different professional life phases and in different schools are able (or not able) to retain their vocational strength and commitment for learning and development in contexts of challenge and change, and through these, contribute to wider national and international debate about how teachers live their lives in teaching, what keeps them going, and why it matters for the improvement of quality and standards in schools. In order to address these issues effectively, the book has been divided into three sections.

Part I The changing landscape of teaching in China

The two chapters in Part 1 demonstrate how the social and intellectual status of the teaching profession has changed dramatically since the founding of the New China in 1949. The Chinese society is known to be proud of its long-standing tradition of respecting teachers. Such a tradition can be traced back to the time of Confucius (591–479 BC) who devoted his life to teaching and education in the hope of restoring social and moral harmony. However, dramatic and sometimes turbulent changes in the country's political, economic and socio-cultural environments over the past six decades have posed profound challenges to the traditional images of teachers and, more importantly, how teachers themselves perceive their professional identity, commitment and effectiveness in the light of these changes. In the opening chapter of this book, Chen and Day provide a detailed examination of the ways in which traditions, changes and innovations have intertwined to influence and shape both the professionalism and professionalisation of teachers and teaching over time. Such an analysis leads them to argue that: 'It is impossible to understand teachers' experiences of educational policies and reforms in China without positioning these in the context of its history and current changes in society by embedding them in their social, socioeconomic and political contexts.' Reviewing the impact of current curriculum reforms on teachers' work and lives in such contexts, they conclude their chapter with five challenges of change that many Chinese teachers experience in their attempts to implement and enact intended policy initiatives in their classrooms. They argue that these challenges cause unnecessary turbulence and are a consequence of the implementation of change through inappropriate top-down models. Chen and Day call for a more thoughtful, inclusive model of systems reform which places teachers' intellectual, emotional and wellbeing development in the centre of the policy and practice concern.

In the second chapter, Guo focuses on the development of teacher education since the founding of 'The New China' in 1949. He provides a close examination of how different ideological, social and cultural forces have influenced and shaped the practice of teacher education and ultimately, the professional identities and capabilities of generations of Chinese teachers. His analysis considers traditional Confucianism, Deng's pragmatism, Maoism, and Dewey's progressivism and crystallises how these 'insider' and 'outsider' forces, although often theoretically exclusive of one another, have in practice been woven into the tapestry of the Chinese system at all levels. China is thus seen as '*a contesting ground for ideologies*' and Chinese teachers are viewed as products of a history that is replete with competing and shifting political and ideological paradigms and priorities. Such a history, Guo argues, largely contributes to the construction of 'hybrid models' (Paine and Fang, 2006) of teacher education and professional development in China.

Part II Developing teachers in times of change: contexts matter

In Part II of the collection, the authors attempt to demonstrate how the wider policy and educational environments and the social and cultural workplace conditions in Chinese schools and the interactions between and within them encourage or inhibit teachers' capacity to learn and to teach to their best. The purpose is not to document exhaustively how teachers learn and develop in such contexts, but to explore connections between context and practice. Lo, Lai and Wang (Chapter 3) explore such connections from the perspective of teacher professionalism. The authors argue that competing demands engendered by reform measures have altered the nature and direction of teachers' work lives. They argue that, rather than fostering their professionalism, such policies have fostered accountability and performativity. Thus, the irony of reform is evident in a policy direction that purports to enhance the professional quality of teachers and yet leaves them little room for professional exploration and autonomy.

In Chapter 4, Huan Song, Xudong Zhu and Laura Liu provide a critical examination of the benefits and pitfalls of the national teacher honour system in relation to the professional development of Chinese teachers over a career span. Their examination shows that this multi-dimensional, complex system has established clear and transparent parameters, which provide consistent guidance to Chinese teachers for their learning and development in a country which is vibrant and diverse in many ways. Thus, in theory, this centrally controlled honours system should point teachers to a clear career progression path which leads to State recognition of their achievement. They argue, however, with Lo *et al.*, that in reality, it contributes to persistent tensions embedded in teachers' work which are caused by two conflicting elements inherent in the system: (a) the rigidity of external control over what teachers should do irrespective of differences in context; and (b) the attempt to increase their self-efficacy and professional autonomy concurrently.

The following chapter by Yin (Chapter 5) should be read in tandem with the previous two. It also examines the connections and disconnections between teacher development and educational reform and initiatives. Yin positions teachers as dilemma managers and brokers of conflict solutions in classroom teaching (Lampert, 1985). He argues that such a way of conceptualising teachers' work is of particular value in exploring 'the tension between the reform initiatives and the existing educational settings which is both the context where the reform initiatives unfold and the condition that the initiatives aim to change'. Four distinctive categories of dilemmas were reported by teachers in Yin's study: cultural, structural, professional and instrumental – each pointing to certain degrees of mismatch between what the reform initiatives demand and the practical realities in which teachers work and live.

Jun Li (Chapter 6) takes a different, and rather more positive, view of the role of national initiatives in building and nurturing 'a world-class teaching force' in China. Methodologically, his work is also different from that of the previous authors – which is essentially concerned with how universities (i.e. organisations at the meso-level) mediate the effects of policy reform (i.e. influences at the macro-level) in the training and education of future teachers (i.e. individuals at the micro-level) for Chinese schools. Li's analysis, in contrast, focuses upon aspects of institutional transformations that a case study teacher education university has experienced. Through this, he argues that China offers an alternative and promising model of teacher education which is socio-culturally embedded and which demonstrates how teacher education institutions may build and transform their capacities in order to produce an effective teaching workforce that is resilient to the often radically changing social contexts.

Part III What keeps teachers going: identity, resilience and commitment

The chapters in this section present detailed accounts of the qualities and school-based conditions that enable many teachers to keep going in their classrooms and schools in China. These accounts bring me back to my own original motivation for bringing together this collection. Over the years, my work with many outstanding teachers and schools nationally and internationally has led myself and my close colleagues to believe that

> teachers and schools *can* change the worlds of their pupils and that many of them *do*! They are not simply survivors but committed and competent professionals and organisations that are proud of being at the centre of a profession which is charged with making a difference to the learning, lives and achievement of all children and young people.
>
> (Day and Gu, 2014: 140)

Chinese teachers are no exception. This is not to deny the negative effects of imposed, top-down reforms that many have experienced on their professional identity, emotions and sense of professionalism. However, such negative accounts should not overshadow the 'professional capital' (Hargreaves and Fullan, 2012) and 'everyday resilience' (Day and Gu, 2014; Gu, in press) that many teachers and schools continue to exhibit on an everyday basis.

The chapters by Lee, Huang, Law and Wang (Chapter 7) and Gu and Li (Chapter 8) describe such teachers. The former (Chapter 7) is concerned with the ways in which externally imposed curriculum reforms affect the emotions and professional identity of Chinese teachers. Whilst acknowledging that continuous participation of teachers in the implementation of reform activities can be constrained by personal, administrative and cultural obstacles, the authors observe that teachers can formulate and maintain positive professional identity if there is a learning and development focused professional culture in their schools. Such cultures prepare, develop and support them, individually and collectively, to become competent professionals who are confident in managing persistent top-down neoliberal reforms in China's educational system and who are committed to making a difference in their classrooms.

In Chapter 8 Gu and Li call these teachers 'resilient teachers'. Drawing upon evidence gathered from 568 primary and secondary school teachers in Beijing, Gu and Li's observation supports earlier work in England that the uncertain and unpredictable circumstances and scenarios that are inherent in the reality of teaching require teachers to 'maintain equilibrium and a sense of commitment and agency in the everyday worlds' in which they teach (Gu and Day, 2013: 26). Thus, this resilience is beyond 'bouncing back' from adversity and setbacks. It is shown by teachers in their study to be driven by their educational purposes and moral values and *nurtured* by the organisational (i.e. leadership and structural), social and relational conditions in which they work. In a country such as China where teacher dropout rates are low, building and sustaining teachers' resilience and commitment in schools is an important quality retention issue. The good news is that the large majority of teachers reported in this study that they were vocationally committed to their work and that they were able to enjoy a sense of job fulfilment from the achievement of their pupils – irrespective of their age, gender and years of experience. Gu and Li conclude their chapter with a reminder that 'for resilient capacities to be sustained, they will need to be nurtured by the social and intellectual environments in which teachers work and live'.

The final two chapters by Qian and Walker (Chapters 9) and Zheng (Chapter 10) provide further evidence that who teachers are, what teachers do in their workplaces and how well they do it are influenced by the social and organisational contexts and systems in which they work and live. It reaffirms the observation made in the previous two chapters that building teachers' capacity to meet the requirements of the curriculum reform is not and should not be a job for individual teachers alone. Rather, it is essentially a collective and organisational responsibility because, as evidence in the final two chapters show, it is school leaders and school principals especially who mediate the effects of externally initiated policy reforms in their context of use. As in schools worldwide, organisational systems, structures and cultures that are created and built by school leaders shape how reform initiatives are integrated into the existing practice and how they can be used to *serve* (rather than contradict) the values and visions of the school. Creating and building favourable and responsive conditions which promote and enhance teachers' professional capacity to effectively manage and enact change is, therefore, an integral part of the process of building and retaining committed and resilient teachers.

Three observations

This book represents a timely collection of theoretical reflections, historical perspectives and empirical evidence to contribute to the debate on the work, lives and effectiveness of Chinese teachers. So far as I am aware, this book is the first of its kind to build research and practice informed new knowledge about the nature of teachers' work and lives and routes of their professional development and progression in China, providing a close examination of the extent to which the Western theories of professionalism, teacher and school development may be applied to the Chinese educational contexts. China, in this sense, is used as a *country case* to demonstrate the importance of social, cultural and political factors in shaping and influencing our understanding of the everyday worlds of teachers. Interestingly, whilst the chapters illustrate the distinctive policy and reform histories and contexts of China, they also demonstrate that there are considerable similarities between the challenges faced by teacher educators and teachers and head teachers in China and those faced by Western teachers in Western countries. Taken together, the chapters in this book celebrate the quality and commitment of Chinese teachers, and also, point to three key observations for all concerned with enhancing quality and standards in Chinese schools.

First, the rise and fall of the social and professional status of teachers and teaching in China reflects the history of the country's political, social, cultural and economic turmoil, development and transformation over the past sixty years. The professional status of teachers has been *officially* and *legally* recognised for two decades only. Irrespective of some popular perceptions that the longstanding scholarly image of Confucius has much to contribute to teachers' enjoyment of high esteem and prestige in Chinese society, the data collected by authors in this book appear to convey a rather different and a more complex message. Today the market-driven, neoliberal social and economic reforms challenge the ways in which teachers perceive their professional standing and conditions of work and lives in society; and, are argued by some authors in this book to have contributed to their increased sense of professional vulnerability. The mismatch between the intended outcomes of policy reforms which target at improving the entry standards and qualification profiles of the teaching workforce, increasing their statuary salaries and supporting their continuing professional development and the tangible outcomes in terms of how many Chinese teachers view themselves, their work and their professional status does not seem to have diminished, but widened. Moreover, the roles played by geography and economics in determining teachers' sense of professionalism, status and esteem in society must not be ignored in any systemic consideration of policies, strategies and practices of teacher recruitment and retention. The increased disparity in teacher quality and conditions of work between urban and rural areas and between different regions in China, identified by Chen and Day in the first chapter, points to the need for a more differentiated and decentralised approach to policy reform in education.

Second, the much criticised performativity agenda is not really new to today's Chinese teachers. This is because, at least in part, almost all are living products of a long-standing educational system and culture which is inherently driven and measured by test-based accountability. A common theme that runs through the chapters is that one has to understand the determining role of examinations in teachers' work and in students' lives in order to understand the architecture of teaching and the nature of teachers' work and lives in Chinese schools. However, as the chapters in Part II of this book show, the intensity of the national drive for accountability, assessment and standards is qualitatively different in today's testing times. There is a greater push from government to ensure that teachers are accountable not only for their pupils' learning and outcomes, but also the productivity and outcomes of their own professional learning and development. Such a push coincides with a concurrent curriculum reform requiring Chinese teachers to reconstruct their pedagogical principles towards more creative and more student-centred teaching and learning. Evidence from this book suggests that the mentoring and coaching approach and the research and lesson groups in Chinese schools have played a significant role, both in nurturing the professional capacity of new teachers and developing a professional culture which connects the moral purpose and responsibility of individual teachers and builds what Hargreaves and Fullan (2012) call 'professional capital' for improvement in schools.

The third and final observation is that irrespective of the exigencies and uncertainties caused by intensified accountability and performativity agendas, many of the Chinese teachers cited by authors in this book have managed to maintain their hope, optimism, commitment and resilience in the profession and continue to enjoy the fulfilment of being able to make a difference to the learning and achievement of their pupils. However, building and sustaining the capacity for commitment and resilience is clearly more than an individual responsibility.

Whilst it is the responsibility of individual teachers to teach to their best, it is also the responsibility of each individual school and the principals of these schools to create the conditions and opportunities that are necessary to enhance the effects of 'professional capital' (Hargreaves and Fullan, 2012) and through this, enable their teachers to grow, sustain and renew their individual and collective capacities to teach to their best.

Finally, I conclude this Introduction with an insightful observation from Elmore (2004) which goes some way to explaining what schools can do in the context of increased external accountability and performativity in order to achieve and sustain improvement:

> At the heart of this piece is the idea that improvement is a developmental process, not an act of compliance with policy. Schools 'get better' by engaging collectively in the acquisition of new knowledge and skills, not by figuring out what policymakers want and doing it. The development of human knowledge and skills – both individually and collectively – is not a simple, linear trajectory, as models of external accountability would seem to suggest. Development is often a ragged, uneven process characterised by significant gains in knowledge, skill, and performance, followed by fallow periods in which people confront the limits of their existing knowledge and try to discover the next set of problems that will lead to the next level of increase in performance.
>
> (Elmore, 2004: 227–228)

The chapters in this book provide evidence from Chinese teachers and Chinese schools that supports his observation. In many schools in China, the average contact time of teachers is 10–12 hours per week (Grattan, 2012). They spend most non-teaching hours each week in classroom observation, team teaching and active collaboration in school-based research which is shown to have a 'proven impact on learning' (Grattan, 2012). What we have learned from the committed and resilient Chinese teachers and teacher educators in this book is that schools and leaders that know how to 'balance accountability and support' (Payne, 2012: 139) can provide intellectual, relational and organisational environments which nurture their teachers' individual and collective capacity for continuing professional learning, empowerment and renewal.

References

Dai, D.Y., Gerbino, K. and Daley, M. (2011) Inquiry-based learning in China: Do teachers practice what they preach, and why? *Frontier Education China*, 6(1): 139–157.

Day, C., Sammons, S., Stobart, G., Kington, A., and Gu, Q. (2007) *Teachers Matter.* Maidenhead: Open University Press.

Day, C. and Gu, Q. (2010) *The New Lives of Teachers*. Oxford: Routledge.

Day, C. and Gu, Q. (2014) *Resilient Teachers, Resilient Schools: Building and Sustaining Quality in Testing Times.* Oxford: Routledge.

Elmore, R. (2004) *School Reform from the Inside Out.* Cambridge, MA: Harvard Education Press.

Gao, X. (2008) Teachers' professional vulnerability and cultural tradition: A Chinese paradox. *Teaching and Teacher Education*, 24: 154–165.

Gu, Q. (2007) *Teacher Development: Knowledge and Context.* London: Continuum.

Gu, Q. and Day, C. (2013) Challenges to teacher resilience: conditions count. *British Educational Research Journal*, 39(1): 22–44.

Gu, Q. (2014) The role of resilience in teachers' career long commitment and effectiveness. Special Issue of *Teachers and Teaching: Theory and Practice* (in press).

Hansen, D. T. (1995) *The Call to Teach.* New York: Teachers College Press.

Hargreaves, A. (1994) *Changing Teachers, Changing Times: Teachers Work and Culture in the Postmodern Age.* London, Cassell.

Hargreaves, A. (2003) *Teaching in the Knowledge Society.* Maidenhead: Open University Press.

Hargreaves, A. and Fullan, M. (2012) *Professional Capital: Transforming Teaching in Every School.* New York: Teachers College Press.

Lampert, M. (1985) How do teachers manage to teach? Perspectives on problems in practice. *Harvard Educational Review*, 55(2), 178–194.

Lee, J. C. K. and Yin, H. B. (2011) Teachers' emotions and professional identity in curriculum reform: A Chinese perspective. *Journal of Educational Change,* 12: 25–46.

Leithwood, K., Day, C., Sammons, P., Harris, A. and Hopkins, D. (2006) *Seven Strong Claims.* Nottingham: NCSL.

McKinsey (2010) *How the World's Most Improved School Systems Keep Getting Better.* London: McKinsey.

Ministry of Education of China (1993) Jiaoshi Fa (Teacher Law). http://www.moe.edu.cn/edoas/website18/info1428.htmS. Retrieved on 4 November 2006.

Ministry of Education of China (1995) Jiaoshi Zige Tiaolie (Stipulations of teacher qualification). http://www.moe.edu.cn/edoas/website18/info1428.htmS. Retrieved on 11 April 2006.

Ministry of Education (2010) Outline of China's national plan for medium and long-term education reform and development. Beijing: MoE.

Paine, L. and Fang, Y. (2006) Reform as hybrid model of teaching and teacher development in China. *International Journal of Educational Research*, 45, 279–289.

Payne, C. (2012) Turning around on turnarounds. In R. Elmore (ed.) *I Used to Think, and Now I Think.* Cambridge, MA: Harvard Education Press, pp. 135–140.

OECD (2005) *Teachers Matter: Attracting, Developing and Retaining Effective Teachers.* Paris: OECD.

OECD (2011) *Building a High-Quality Teaching Profession: Lessons from Around the World.* Paris: OECD.

Part I

The changing landscape of teaching in China

1 Tensions and dilemmas for Chinese teachers in responding to system wide change

New ideas, old models

Junjun Chen and *Christopher Day*

Introduction

China has the largest education system and the largest teaching force in the world. According to national educational statistics, the government employs 5.64 million full-time teachers in 271,804 primary schools and 5.08 million teachers in 81,755 secondary schools in 2011 (Ministry of Education (MOE), 2012). It is also mindful to note that the physical and professional conditions in which the 10.7 million teachers work differ substantially across the country because, at least in part, the social and economic urban-rural and east-west divide in China continues to widen (Wang and Piesse, 2010; Whyte, 2010). Thus, changing education systems and the mindsets and practices of all teachers in such a vast and diverse country is likely to be particularly challenging. Understanding Chinese teachers' experiences of educational changes not only would enhance knowledge of how change at macro-levels might carry through or be mediated at meso- and micro-levels in order to ensure their effectiveness in China, but would also expand our understanding of effective models of centrally initiated change as applied to large and diverse teaching populations elsewhere (Guo et al., 2012). In this chapter, therefore, the authors discuss what teachers' personal and professional lives look like against the background of the current contradictory, uncertain and rapid educational changes in China.

These changes mirror the neo liberal agendas of governments in many other societies in which, in the last few decades, social, economic and political changes have been challenging traditional forms of educational practice in many societies. Governments, including China, have initiated educational reforms to improve their educational practice so that their citizens can meet the needs of national economic, social, and political developments, in particular so that their countries can become more competitive in international markets (Brandt and Rawski, 2008; Cheng, 2009; Hannum et al., 2008; Li, 2012). The chapter is divided into three sections: (i) a brief history of educational traditions, policies and reforms in China; (ii) a discussion of the demands on teachers caused by outmoded models of system change in the new reform; and (iii) variations in the work and lives of Chinese teachers: challenges and tensions of change.

A brief history of educational traditions, policies and reforms in China

It is impossible to understand teachers' experiences of educational policies and reforms in China without positioning these in the context of its history and current changes in society by embedding them in their social, socioeconomic and political contexts (Cheng, 2009; Lin, 1993; OECD, 2010). China is marked by a collectivist culture emphasizing interdependence of self and social harmony and social obligations and responsibilities (Qu and Zhang, 2005). To maintain such social harmony, it is necessary, at least in public, to suppress one's own desires and define oneself in terms of the needs and wishes of the majority within a community (Lee and Yin, 2011; Mascolo et al., 2003). Chinese teachers in such a society may, therefore, feel that they cannot draw attention to their needs and feelings, which may eventually hold back the educational change process (Hargreaves, 1998). Moreover, China is a hierarchical society. Thus, the central government has traditionally been responsible for policy development, law enactment and implementation, and partial educational finance at the macro-level. Local government is responsible for partial financial investment, monitoring and supporting educational reform implementation at schools. It is also a supporting organization for teachers.

In China, the social status of teachers has changed in the last three decades, though within a continuing tradition of extremely high cultural expectations. In traditional Chinese cultural discourses, teachers enjoy high social status and are regarded as being in the same league as other key cultural figures, including heaven, earth, the emperor and parents (Fwu and Wang, 2002; Schoenhals, 1993), although this has not always been the case. During the Cultural Revolution, for example, teacher status was extremely low. Teachers were allocated into one of the 'black five classes' – Right-wingers which are opposite to the working class. The other four include Landlords, Rich farmers, Anti-revolutionists, and Bad-influencers. During that period, Chinese teachers had a social status much lower than many social groups such as government officials and entrepreneurs.

In the government's ideological propaganda as well as in public discourses, teachers are consistently portrayed as 'the engineers of the human soul', who are responsible for cultivating moral qualities among students (Hu, 2002; Ouyang, 2003). They are also described as 'silkworms', who diligently spin silk thread till death, and 'candles', who selflessly burn themselves to light others (He, 2002). These metaphors underscore the traditional perception of teachers and depict the teaching profession as altruistic and self-sacrificing. The government-controlled media repeatedly urged all members in society to respect teachers. In 1985, to preserve teacher status, a national 'Teachers' Day' was fixed for 10 September of each year, hence, the status of the teaching profession took a step forward during the 1980s to 1990s. The teaching profession during this period was deified. However, such high cultural expectations made their professional role highly demanding, placing individual teachers under great pressure to conform to society's moral norms, and making them more vulnerable to 'being shamed, and feeling shame, if he fails' (Schoenhals, 1993, p. 199). They were also subject to even closer scrutiny, leading to potentially disruptive tensions between teachers and the public (Gao, 1993).

Since the late 1990s, further changes have occurred which have resulted in new sets of demands being placed upon teachers. As a result of decentralization in education, together with increased competition internationally (e.g., PISA, TIMMS) the concepts of performativity and commercialization began to dominate the educational agenda of government. As with teachers in many other countries which have witnessed the rise of bureaucratic accountability and increasing State interventions, Chinese teachers also feel tremendous pressures of test and examination driven external accountability. For a significant number, it has been reported that this has placed limitations on their ability to exercise autonomy in their classrooms; and, as teachers elsewhere, and a reported failure by some to find satisfaction in their work (Guo et al., 2012). Moreover, parents and the public now regard teaching as a marketable service rather than an honourable vocation (Gao, 2008). More recently, because of some teachers' unprofessional behaviour (e.g., receiving money or gifts from parents, asking money for assigning seats, or abusing students), negative professional images of the teacher have appeared in the media and on the Internet and the new metaphors assigned to teachers are 'incompetent pedagogues', 'wealth-collectors', 'abusers' or 'demons' (Li, 2004). These often virulent criticisms of teachers have diminished public trust and increased the vulnerability of the teaching profession (Gao, 2008; Gordon, 2005; Kelchtermans, 2005; Yang, 2004).

It is no exaggeration to say that China had to rebuild the entire education system in the late 1970s from the ruins left by the Cultural Revolution (Cheung and Pan, 2006). The death of the former Chairman Mao Zedong in 1976 marked the end of the Cultural Revolution which was started by Mao in 1966 as a national-scale political and social campaign in which intellectuals including teachers at different levels were the most vulnerable. One consequence of this was that most schools were closed and the curriculum was totally revamped to reflect the essence of class struggle. In 1978, the former Chairman Deng Xiaoping promulgated the 'open door' policy which transformed the Chinese economy from a centrally planned economy to a socialist market economy. This policy also stressed the importance of education as the foundation for modernizing science and technology and paved the way for a series of educational policies and reforms (Brandt and Rawski, 2008; OECD, 2010). Over the last 60 years, then, the conditions and status of teachers in society in Modern China, as in many other countries, have fluctuated as the political agendas have changed.

There is no doubt that all educational policies and reforms have influenced teachers and teaching. However, four of them, namely Decentralization, the Teacher Act, Regulation of Teacher Qualification and Curriculum Reform, are considered by the authors to have had a more direct and stronger impact on teachers' professional and personal lives. (i) The central concept of educational reform, decentralization of education, was the first of the reforms in modern education in 1985. It established a framework for decentralizing school orientation, financing, curriculum and management to the local government (Zhao, 2009). (ii) In 1986, China enacted the Law of Compulsory Education, which required every child to complete nine years of formal schooling – six years of primary school and three years of junior secondary school. In contrast to Mao's lawlessness (*wufa wutian*), this marked a new era in which Chinese education would be governed according to the rule of law (*yifa zhijiao*) as part of educational reform (Cheung and Pan, 2006). To assist Chinese education on its lawful way, the release of the Teacher Act in 1994 was a second crucial event. It identified teachers' positions and responsibilities from the perspective of law. (iii) In the following year, the release of the Regulation of Teacher Qualification refined the system of teacher professional qualification and promotion. The Ministry of Education (MOE) in 2001 initiated Curriculum Reform which currently dominates basic education in China. (iv) Curriculum Reform provided guidelines and standards for the majority of subjects across primary to secondary schools (Dello-Iacovo, 2009; Jiang, 2009). It is the nature of this reform and its consequences which form the focus of this chapter.

Curriculum reform: new ideas, old models of change

Within this last reform was the intention to reform classroom pedagogy. This was to prove perhaps the most problematic reform to implement since it would, by definition, challenge both the existing purposes, practices and professional identities of many teachers, the continuing prioritization of examination success required by the highly competitive Chinese secondary education and higher education system and, therefore, the expectations and aspirations of many parents. We will discuss this in more detail in the third section of this chapter. The latest initiative is a major national comprehensive campaign to improve education in the next decade up to 2020 – the Outline for Medium and Long-term Development and Reform of Education in 2010. It is also worthwhile to note that the concept of quality education (or quality-oriented education, in Chinese *suzhi jiaoyu*) was first formally used as the antithesis to 'examination-oriented education' and has become a guiding principle of education policies in China until now (MOE, 2010). The quality rhetoric has endured and continues to act as a broad framework for the major goals of many current reforms. The increasing emphasis on quality also signals that the reform focus has shifted to the improvement of schooling, teaching, and student qualities from teaching and learning for examination (Li, 2004; Walker and Qian, 2012). This educational concept has gradually found its place in Chinese education.

Before examining the impacts of these changes on Chinese teachers' work and lives, it is necessary to understand the major features of the management of Chinese educational reforms. Many of these have been characterized by a top-down, centre-periphery model, which has been described as 'brutal restructuring delivered in ignorance or defiance of teachers' beliefs and missions' (Goodson, 2003, p. xiii). Policymakers formulate reforms and policies that represent the interests of central government. The central government controls the content of the reform and the manner of its delivery so that they can monitor progress. The nature of this kind of reform is that it is initiated by central government without consulting teachers and schools and is directly pushed down to schools with little input and contribution from practitioners. This centre-periphery model certainly has the advantage of authority and speed of initial efficiency, in that schools are required to adopt the proposed reforms or can be made to see a good reason to accept them (Hoyle and Bell, 1972). However, a major flaw of this change model is that it tends to ignore 'the power that teachers have to mediate changes' (Priestley, 2005, p. 1). Indeed, recent international debates about educational changes suggest that centrally initiated curriculum reform is unlikely to be successful over the medium and long term unless it actively engages the teachers 'who are the foot-soldiers of every reform aimed at improving student outcomes' (Cuban, 1998, p. 459).

Closely associated with the centre-periphery model, the research, development and dissemination model (R. D. & D.) represents a perspective that reform initiatives have an empirical basis and this is considered to provide a rationale for the change (Havelock, 1971). In this model, the initiatives will have been taken by researchers, developers, and disseminators with the receivers, the teachers, continuing to remain passive (Priestley, 2005). To a certain extent, the recent initiatives, modifications of curriculum reform and quality education, could be said to align with this model. For example, some researchers (e.g., Jiang, 2009; Lee and Yin, 2011; Tao, 2006) have investigated the implementation and effects of curriculum reform in schools. Based on these empirical findings, educational officials from the central government modified curriculum reform syllabus documents to better fit school settings. As with curriculum reform, educational researchers (e.g., Dello-Iacovo, 2009; Pang, 2004) and officials have continued to update the concept of quality education based on the empirical research since it was first proposed in 1994. The modifications of the reforms can be seen in each version of national outlines issued by MOE. However, this R. D. & D. model still assumes a passive diffusion of innovation to teachers, and has proved to be ineffective in initiating and sustaining change. Those who do not comply by adopting the change are regarded as resistant and dysfunctional (Priestley, 2005). Scott's (2001) three institutional pillars, regulative, normative and cognitive perspectives, might be more appropriate as a framework to interpret why the current Chinese reform models failed to engage teachers into educational reforms. The regulative perspective refers to 'surveillance and sanctioning power' of the state to regulate and constrain behaviours (Scott, 2001, p. 51). As aforementioned, the central government in China is a dominating and coercive force to regulation and policies of education reforms. There is very limited room for teachers to make changes or engage in dialogue about changes. The normative perspective includes 'values and norms practiced under obligations, appropriateness, conformity, and expectations' (Scott, 2001, p. 54). The cognitive perspective involves 'the consideration of the power of commonly shared conceptions and meanings among members and social actors' in the same institutional field (Scott, 2001, p. 57). Chinese teachers are shaped by values and social norms in Chinese cultural, organizational and daily practical contexts (Yin, 2013). Because of greater power distance, Chinese teachers are more likely to accept what more powerful people and organizations impose on them (Hofstede, 2001). This may restrict teachers' willingness and sense of agency in engaging with and mediating educational reforms.

It should be acknowledged that even though these educational change models have appeared to accelerate the development of Chinese education and its influence, they also have posed threats to teachers' professional practices and to their sense of professionalism (Gao, 2008). Helsby and McCulloch (1997) present an alternative version of the change processes. They argue that reform initiatives should be developed in a dialectical fashion to reflect a dynamic two-way relationship between the initiative in question and the context for enactment, including local practitioners. According to Cuban (1998, p. 455), 'schools change reforms as much as reforms change schools'. However, it seems that the Chinese central government has not yet heeded such messages, since reform initiatives in China are still dominated by the two top-down, flawed change models.

China has a long tradition of respecting education highly as an important means of acquiring social capital and achieving advancement on the socioeconomic ladder (Gao, 2008; OECD, 2010; Schoenhals, 1993; Turner and Acker, 2002); and, at least in theory, in China teachers are acknowledged to be crucial to the success of the change process (MOE, 2010), since the reforms and policies in education are eventually assigned to them for implementation (Lee and Yin 2011). Yet system wide change efforts of the kind described above mean, for teachers, that different parties such as policy makers, administrators, and parents have high expectations, and make increasingly high demands without taking into account the experiences and views of teachers themselves. Yet, paradoxically, they rely for their success upon teachers' participation, whether or not they agree or do not agree that these are in the best interests of their students (Dello-Iacovo 2009; Kwo, 2004; Lin, 1993). Moreover, they do not always provide the necessary support for managing the change:

> Just when the very most is expected of them, teachers appear to be being given less support, less respect, and less opportunity to be creative, flexible and innovative than before. Teachers, in other words, are caught in a dilemma. They are expected to be leading catalysts of the informational society, yet they are also one of its prime casualties. This is a daily challenge for teachers themselves and a policy challenge for those who want to reform and improve teaching.
>
> (Hargreaves and Lo, 2000, p. 2)

In this chapter, we take as an example the current government policy to make education more student-centred and classroom teaching more creative. This continues to cause tensions for teachers and parents. Although many parents may accept that more student-centred education is a better choice for their only child, they still would like their children's teachers to continue with didactic, exam-oriented practices (Lee and Yin, 2011). No matter how convincing the curriculum reform initiatives and changes promoted by policymakers or reformers, many stakeholders simply do not believe that a reduction in drilling will enhance the quality of learning (Law, 2006). The media continue to report on anxious parents who have forced schools to remove certain teachers from teaching their children out of fear that these teachers might not help their children to achieve the best exam results. Whilst such cases may be rare, they are certainly psychologically unnerving for teachers (Gao, 2008). These phenomena have tested teachers' professional confidence, practices and traditional educational values, and certainly help to increase teachers' professional vulnerability. It seems evident that expectations of teachers and, therefore, how they are defined as professionals, are once again changing.

Variations in the work and lives of Chinese teachers in contexts of reform: challenges and tensions

Research has shown connections between teachers' personal and professional lives and how these intersect and shape their professional thoughts and actions (Day, 1999; Goodson, 2003; Woods, 2001) and affect their effectiveness as teachers (Hargreaves, 1999; Day et al., 2006; Kwo, 2004). For example, Day and his team (2007) conducted a large empirical study investigating influences upon and between teachers' professional and personal lives and relations between these and their effectiveness in terms of pupil attainments over a three year period of continuing educational policy changes in England. They found that teachers' perceived and relative effectiveness are influenced by variations in their work and lives and their capacities to manage these. The findings indicate that one feature for greater effectiveness may be how well the teachers are able to sustain their sense of commitment, positive stable professional identity (Day and Gu, 2012; Day, 2011) and capacity to be resilient (Day and Gu, 2014).This research illustrates the importance in educational reform of a developing awareness of the need to understand and take into account teachers' personal lives together with their professional life phase in relation to their effectiveness. This is acknowledged by policy makers and reflected in recent Chinese educational policy (MOE, 2010) which states that it is 'essential to improve the status of teachers, safeguard their rights and interests, raise their salaries and benefits, and turn teaching into a respected occupation' (p. 36).

Successful educational reform hinges on schools and teachers being given both the opportunity and capacity to learn, grow, and expand their repertoires as professionals. These ambitious goals imply that teachers must be continually learning about content, pedagogy and learning theory if they are to develop students as flexible, responsive and active thinkers in a rapidly transforming world (Kwo and Intrator, 2004). Educational reforms in China have undeniably made new demands on teachers, but also offered new opportunities for teachers' professional development (PD). Access to PD is crucial to ensure quality education (Jiang, 2009). Based on the Teacher Act, it is also the teachers' right. PD opportunities include training workshops, seminars, and presentations offered by district school boards, university experts, and curriculum developers; school-based teaching and research activities; model lesson sharing by excellent teachers, and local, national, and international study tours. These opportunities are, however, focused almost exclusively on fulfilling the aims of the reforms, enhanced understanding of the reforms, for example, by introducing a new educational philosophy, new curriculum content, and learner-centred pedagogy, and enlarging teachers' educational views in different situations. Teachers also have opportunities to get training on practical skills such as computer skills, and Putonghua, lesson and unit planning (Dello-Iacovo, 2009; Guo et al., 2012; Lee and Yin, 2011). Whilst these provide important positive support at system level, they do not address issues of individual teacher change. Rather, they (implicitly) assume that the change processes which are, for many teachers, difficult and emotionally costly, are unproblematic. We move now, therefore, to presenting five challenges of change.

While the literature (e.g., Guo et al., 2012; Lee and Ying, 2005; Li, 2012) shows that educational changes have improved Chinese teachers' lives at one level, the changes have also brought some challenges to teachers as they strive to manage their workplace lives in increasingly complex and testing times. Research reveals at least six major tensions between the rhetoric and realities of the implementation of educational reforms.

Tensions between aims of educational reforms and school assessment system

The most discussed challenge is the conflict between the aims of the reforms and the continuing dominance of the school assessment system (Dello-Iacovo, 2009; Guo et al., 2012; Lee and Yin, 2011). One of the major aims of the reforms is to promote students' skills and creative abilities through more student-centred activities and pedagogies, and so to reduce the huge academic pressure on students. As the former Chinese Vice Premier Lanqing Li stated, the current situation of Chinese students is 'buried in an endless flood of homework and sit[ting] for one mock entrance exam after another, leaving them with heads swimming and eyes blurred' (Li, 2004, p. 337). It seems that, although reforms such as Quality Education and Curriculum Reform may have arrived at the right time, they conflict with the school assessment system in which many teachers' core identities and sense of professionalism are located. To a large degree, the Chinese educational system is still examination-oriented, and educational practice is driven by university and secondary entrance examinations. Yet now teachers are asked also to meet the demands of reforms for innovative teaching and prepare for evaluation of the reforms by school leaders and educational bureaux. They still have to focus on examination-oriented practices in the classroom to help students do better in examinations. Teacher participants in one study (Guo et al., 2012) indicated that lack of change in the exam-based evaluation system was the biggest barrier to a shift towards student-centred teaching and learning. From this perspective, reforms have created even heavier burdens on, and challenges for, teachers.

Challenges of transition to new teaching pedagogies

During educational reforms, teachers are always expected to be change agents (Fullan, 2006; Lee and Yin, 2011). Under the latest reforms, they are expected to promote a paradigm shift from teacher-centred to student-centred teaching pedagogies in their classrooms. However, together with commitment to the current assessment system, real-life school situations such as class size, increasing workload, and insufficient support, challenge the abilities and opportunities for teachers to implement more student-centred pedagogies.

Class sizes are generally large in China normally ranging from 55–65. Class sizes are even larger in rural schools and key schools in urban areas (OECD, 2010; Lin and Zhang, 2006). Teachers claim that, in order to align with the goals of educational reforms, they would like to utilize more student-centred activities such as group work, games, hands-on activities, field trips, and individual instruction. However, it is difficult to utilize these preferred pedagogies in a large size classroom within a 40–45 minute lesson in most situations (Dello-Iacovo, 2009; Guo et al., 2012; Jiang, 2009).

Additionally, the increasing workload is claimed to be another barrier to implementing student-centred teaching. Curriculum reform has not only changed curricula standards and content, but also curricula structure and textbooks. Teachers have to understand the new content and create new teaching pedagogies using new teaching materials (Dello-Iacovo, 2009). Workload for lesson preparation has been increased substantially. Teachers need extra time to prepare for their lessons, especially for highly-specialized lessons. However, the routine work for teachers has not changed. They have to squeeze in time during working hours or use their spare time for lesson preparation. According to the study by Guo et al. (2012), out of 102 teachers in the study, 60.8 per cent reported preparing for lessons in the evenings and 36.6 per cent on weekends. Tao (2006) also reported that the new textbooks lack cohesion with many changes in topics, which prevent teachers organizing their teaching and increase teacher workload and stress. Each of these has challenged the existing stability of teachers' working lives as well as their competencies in learning and applying new practices.

Challenges to educational beliefs

Another challenge for teachers is the gap between their existing teaching ideologies and those advocated by the reforms (Lee and Yin, 2011). Teachers claimed that their professional teaching beliefs, accumulated through prior educational practices, are disconnected from those in educational changes. Some teachers felt that they had to abandon their prior knowledge and skills in order to accept the new educational philosophies and skills. During this process, teachers needed to rebuild their professional identity and professional confidence to formulate their new teacher role. However, many teachers, especially experienced teachers, reported resistance to such changes or disagreed with the philosophies grounded in the educational reforms and policies. This led to problems because they were in conflict with their own professional ideologies which were rooted deeply in their traditional professional practices. This phenomenon has been caused by insufficient communication between policymakers and front-line teachers before the implementation of educational reforms (Li, 2012). Teachers have, therefore, had difficulties in moving out of the comfort zone of their professional practice and embracing the uncertainties of reform (Lee and Yin, 2011; Jiang, 2009).

> Whatever the specifics of the complaint, the process has caused dissonance and perplexities. The complexities of the unlearning-relearning process have brought much uncertainty and ambiguity to teacher lives.
>
> (Guo et al., 2012, p. 71)

Tensions between educational reforms and the quality of associated professional development

Many studies have surveyed teachers' attitudes towards PD training during educational changes and most of them reveal positive feedback. However, teacher participants in some studies have complained of inadequate teacher training marred by the faults of the traditional education it was meant to replace, with large groups of teachers listening to theory-based lectures (Dello-Iacovo, 2009). Another common complaint has been that the training is divorced from reality and does not address their needs during the transition from teacher-centred to student-centred education (Tao, 2006). Some teachers claim that only selected groups of active teachers are given the chance to attend PD training, whilst the rest of the teachers have to digest the policies and materials mainly by themselves or with the help of those who attended the training (Tao, 2006; Guo, et al., 2012). The time and volume of PD was also a concern for the teachers. Some teachers have reported that it was compulsory to attend PD activities organized by both the local education bureau and the school. While some PD activities took place in school hours, some of them were offered during out-of school hours such as in the evenings, during breaks, or on weekends. Teachers report feeling constant pressure to find extra time to participate in these kinds of PDs which are normally not paid (Li, 2012). Some teachers have also reported that their personal lives have had to be sacrificed to their professional lives. For example, a teacher reported that she sent her 2-year daughter back to her parents' home since she and her husband did not have the time to take care of the girl (Guo et al., 2012). This shows that teachers' personal and professional lives are imbalanced. Based on the study by Day et al. (2007), this situation affects teacher effectiveness. Therefore, it is time for developers and organizers to consider the relevance and quality of the PDs, selection of teachers, and teachers' capacity to accept these PDs.

It seems clear, then, that teachers experience tremendous pressures from heavy workload, unprepared working conditions and an unchanged system structure, to struggling with personal stress and facing conflicting personal teaching ideologies. The curriculum reform innovations imposed on Chinese teachers have forced them to try to change their philosophy and practices in a high pressure system while existing structural elements and traditional cultures of many schools have remained unchanged. If teachers are expected to act as change agents for educational reforms, it is crucial to recognize challenges which these pose for teachers' lives and to provide support wherever relevant (Dello-Iacovo, 2009; Guo et al., 2012; Harfitt and Tavares, 2004).

Equity: variations in working conditions and professional development opportunities

One of the consequences of financial decentralization in education has been that the gaps between the 'haves' (urban teachers) and the 'have nots' (rural teachers) in China have increased. The professional and personal conditions of teachers are particularly challenging in remote and less developed regions (Guo, 2010; Guo et al., 2012; Wang and Li, 2009; Zhang, 2007). The urban-rural disparity reflected in teachers' personal and professional lives is described in this section with respect to income, teacher qualifications, student characteristics, teaching resources, and distribution of opportunities for PD training.

Variations in personal conditions

At first glance, the salary level between urban and rural teachers is not significantly different, especially after factoring in the cost of living index of these regions. However, the addition of some 'grey' income (e.g., school bonus, school choice fee, private tutorial fee, and additional assignment fee) on top of their salary is an important factor contributing to real differences between urban and rural teachers' incomes (OECD, 2010; Yang, 2004). This kind of income may range from 15 per cent to 50 per cent of the total income of urban teachers. Rural teachers, on the other hand, have fewer opportunities to earn this income and have received it at a much lower rate when they do (Guo et al., 2012). Rural teacher salaries are lower, and their basic salary may not even be guaranteed if the financial situation of the local government is not good. In some rural areas, teachers' seniority pay may not be guaranteed. Moreover, urban teachers can be provided with additional housing, pensions and medical subsidies, which rural teachers may receive or not receive depending on their local government (Jiang, 2009; Li, 2012; Singh, 2012; Wang and Li, 2009).

The situation of rural substitute teachers is even worse than that of rural public teachers. As reported by the education line, a rural substitute teacher's payroll was only RMB500 (USD79) per month in 2012 (Guo et al., 2012). This is inadequate for them to live a decent life. Some schools try to pay their salaries, but typically offer meagre amounts held in arrears, as countryside schools are almost always in deficit, or replace salaries by goods that the village produces (Liu, 2010; Shang et al., 2008). This inadequate payment causes teacher movement from rural to urban areas, especially by those teachers with a higher qualification and/or more educational experience. This has created a domestic brain drain and an imbalance in teacher qualities between the rural and urban areas (Niu, 2009). The national government and provincial administrations are acutely aware of this situation and have over time enacted policies, legislation and regulations to address these problems. Teachers have, by the Teacher Law in 1994, been given a status equivalent to civil servants and other professionals in terms of pay and remuneration. However, this has not yet been uniformly applied in all regions of the country (Guo et al., 2012; Jiang, 2009; Wang and Li, 2009).

Variations in professional conditions

As with the gap in personal conditions between urban and rural teachers, educational reforms also enlarge the discrepancy in working conditions between rural and urban teachers from the perspectives of school resources, student population, teaching force, and PD opportunities. School equipment and teaching resources for rural teachers are considerably less, especially when compared with key schools in well-developed urban areas. Remote rural schools either have no computers or only a few old donated ones with limited Internet service or even no internet (Cheng, 2009; Li, 2012). Yuan (2005) highlighted striking urban-rural disparities in the physical conditions of schools. The study reported that 82.0 per cent of primary school buildings that were in a dangerous condition across the nation were located in rural areas. The difficulty in providing quality rural education lies in the unsettled financial relationship between the central and the local governments, resulting in a shortage of educational funding and resources in rural areas (Fu, 2005).

Rural teachers are also facing more diverse student populations and smaller teaching forces (China Development Research Foundation, 2005; Ren, 2007; Zhou and Shang, 2011). In some areas, such as Gong County, Yunnan province, there are over sixty village schools with only one or two teachers who are responsible for teaching all subjects at all grade levels using the one-school teaching approach (Yang, 2012). Many rural teachers have to teach subjects that are not consistent with their expertise, while such a phenomenon in town and city schools is rare. In addition, Curriculum Reform requires finding new resources for a variety of new courses and electives such as computing, technology, music and art or finding the specialist teachers needed to teach them. These specialist teachers are normally unwilling to work in rural areas, so rural teachers teach these courses without additional training in order to meet the requirements of Curriculum Reform (Pang, 2004, p. 2). In rural schools, research and teaching reforms are hard to develop and put into effect because of the reasons mentioned above (Wang and Li, 2009). Under these circumstances, it is not surprising that some rural schools are likely to be left behind through their inability to implement reforms compared to urban schools. It also has created a domestic brain drain and the imbalance of teachers' qualities between poor areas and rich areas, particularly between rural areas and urban areas (Niu, 2009; Ye, 2009).

Compared to urban teachers, PD opportunities for rural teachers are also much fewer. The further away a school is from a city, the less likely its teachers will receive PD opportunities (Li, 2012). Urban teachers, especially in big cities, have more opportunities to attend PDs offered by higher educational institutions than their rural peers (Guo et al., 2012). Urban teachers have more opportunities to attend advanced PD training taught by experts in the field. Rural teachers, in contrast, can only attend PDs offered at the local level. Consequently, these lead to differences in the understandings and interpretations of the reforms and policies. Taking curriculum reform as an example, urban teachers who show a more advanced understanding of the new curriculum and associated pedagogies are able to more clearly articulate the shift from teacher-centred to learner-centred approaches and are able to give specific examples in relevant situations, whilst rural teacher participants fail to demonstrate a deeper discussion, even with appropriate prompts (Guo et al., 2012; Wang and Li, 2009). Further, Guo (2010) examined rural Chinese teachers' experiences in curriculum reform and reported that rural teachers experience tremendous pressure, ambivalence, resilience, and pedagogical struggles during the process of curriculum reform implementation, because they lack high-quality PD opportunities and resources.

System autonomy and professional vulnerability

As a result of the decentralization in education, a marketization approach which was introduced in the mid-1990s was fully implemented by 2005. This is known as the contract-based teacher employment system (*jiaoshi pinren zhi*) (Niu, 2009). Before the reform of decentralization, most teachers were traditionally employed in permanent positions by local educational authorities across the country. The new system treats education as a huge market where schools are employers and teachers are traded based on their education background and teaching experience. The motivation of this movement is to give schools more autonomy and flexibility in employ-ment practices and to create a competitive system for teacher employment. However, the downside of this effort places some teachers, especially temporary contract-based (*linshi hetong*) teachers and rural substitute (*daike)* teachers, in a very vulnerable position (Gao, 2008; Niu, 2009). Kelchtermans (2011) argues that policy makers and school leaders are potential sources of teacher vulnerability. Achieving a tenured position in a school is a high-priority concern of almost all teachers but especially beginning teachers, since a tenured position means recognition of performance and job security. 'As long as they are not tenured, teachers are vulnerable to the decisional power of the school board. This is a kind of formal, statutory vulnerability' (Kelchtermans, 2011, p. 68). Chances are larger for the temporary contract-based teachers to be fired by school leaders even without notice being given to the local educational authority. Such teachers do exactly the same jobs as their counterparts who are in permanent positions at the schools, but the payment and status are different in terms of salary and bonus/subsidy, academic promotion, and opportunity of professional development. This kind of teacher has a lower salary payment and bonus on Teachers' Day and other Chinese festivals. They have some opportunities for promotion and PDs, but need to give way to tenured permanent contracted-based staff. As a consequence of the decentralization of administration and of educational marketization, then, teachers with a temporary contract become professionally more vulnerable (Gao, 2008).

Conclusions

In this chapter we have considered what teachers' personal and professional lives look like against the background of the current paradoxical, uncertain and rapid educational changes in China and how these impact on teachers' work and identities. We have argued that the new educational reform initiatives in China are managed and implemented through the use of outmoded and largely ineffective models of change – the centre-periphery model, with some features of closely associated research, and the development and dissemination model. These two top-down, flawed change models appear to be the most efficient 'delivery' mechanism, especially given the size of the teaching population in China. However, what appears to be efficient at whole system level, runs the risk of being ineffective at meso- and micro-levels and so, in the longer term, is likely to be inefficient. The continuing use of these outmoded and discredited change models against the backdrop of societal change and the rhetoric of increasing participation is likely to be counter-productive to the successful implementation of the intended changes. Moreover, the continued use of these change models create tensions and dilemmas in teachers' lives, pose threats to teachers' professional practice, identities and their sense of professionalism and risk the loss of their commitment.

Under the two existing flawed change models, it seems that Chinese teachers have little input into, and control over, the reform initiative implementation. As an alternative approach would involve teachers in shaping their implementation. They would be likely to extend the improvements and reduce the challenges and threats that the changes bring to them.

Although in China, the government, either central or local, is in the best position to initiate educational changes, it may need to consider improving the current flawed change models since it is responsible for educational finance and policy development and dissemination. To respond to the challenges and threats that the existing flawed change models bring to Chinese teachers, the government could try to promote a school-based change model through involving practitioners' (schools and teachers) input during the changes. In such a model, schools are normally provided with a loose framework and encouraged to experiment. A school-based change model combines impetus in the form of government policy guidance with support in the form of resources and time.

Most importantly, it fully engages teachers in the initiatives (Priestley, 2005). Thus, this inclusive model of change would take into account local factors and the institutional logics in managing and implementing curriculum reforms by paying more attention to real school contexts and teaching practices, and addressing teachers' concerns. This could decrease the tensions and dilemmas (e.g., quality of PD, transition of new teaching pedagogies and beliefs, variation in teacher conditions, fair employment system, and professional vulnerability) that teachers are facing. Day and his colleagues (2006, 2012, 2014) have found that one feature for greater effectiveness may be how well the teachers are able to manage their working lives, sustain their commitment and sense of professional identity and build their capacity for resilience.

In conclusion, this chapter has investigated the contexts for, management and impacts of educational reform changes on school teachers' identities, practices and sense of professionalism with a focus on decentralization, the Teacher Act, Regulation of Teacher Qualification, and Curriculum Reform. Based on empirical research, improvements, challenges and issues impacting on teachers' willingness, abilities and capacities to adapt their professional practices have been discussed. Further investigations are now needed to gain a better understanding of the interface between system wide models of change and their effective management and enactment at school and classroom level. The evidence provided in this chapter suggests that this interface may be improved by abandoning outmoded and ineffective change models and developing new, more effective models which are both inclusive of all stakeholders and which acknowledge the importance of attending to the vital mediating role of teachers' sense of commitment and professional identity. As Fullan (2006) has argued, the status quo is difficult to change if the designated change agents – overwhelmingly teachers – do not perceive themselves as having any stake in the process.

References

Bao, C. (2006). Policies for compulsory education disparity between urban and rural areas in China. *Frontiers of Education in China,* 1(1), 40–55.

Brandt, L. and Rawski, T. (2008). China's great economic transformation. In L. Brandt and T. Rawski (Eds), *China's Great Economic Transformation* (pp. 1–26). New York: Cambridge University Press.

Cheng, H. (2009). Inequality in basic education in China: A comprehensive review. *International Journal of Educational Policies,* 3(2), 81–106.

Cheung, K. W. and Pan, S. Y. (2006). A transition of moral education in China: Towards regulated individualism. *Citizenship Teaching and Learning,* 2(2), 37–50.

China Development Research Foundation. (2005). *China Human Development Report 2005: Development with Equity.* Beijing, China: China Development Research Foundation.

Cuban, L. (1998). How schools change reforms: Redefining reform success and failure. *Teachers College Record,* 99(3), 453–477.

Day, C. (1999). *Developing Teachers: The Challenges of Lifelong Learning.* London: Falmer Press.

Day, C., Sammons, P., Stobart, G., and Kington, A. (2007). Variations in the work and lives of teachers: Relative and relationship effectiveness. *Teachers and Teaching: Theory and Practice,* 12(2), 169–192.

Dello-Iacovo, B. (2009). Curriculum reform and quality education in China: An overview. *International Journal of Educational Development,* 29, 241–249. doi:10.1016/j.ijedudev.2008.02.008

Fu, T. M. (2005). Unequal primary education opportunities in rural and urban China. *China Perspectives,* 60, 1–8.

Fullan, M. (2006). *The Development of Transformational Leaders for Educational Decentralization.* Toronto, Canada: Michael Fullan.

Fwu, B. and Wang, H. (2002). The social status of teachers in Taiwan. *Comparative Education,* 38(2), 211–244.

Gao, X. (2008). Teachers' professional vulnerability and cultural tradition: A Chinese paradox. *Teaching and Teacher Education,* 24(1), 154–165. doi:10.1016/j.tate.2006.11.011

Goodson, I. (2003). *Professional Knowledge, Professional Lives: Studies in Education and Change.* Open University Press: Maidenhead and Philadelphia, PA.

Gordon, J. A. (2000). Asian American resistance to selecting teaching as a career: The power of community and tradition. *Teachers College Record,* 102(1), 173–196.

Gordon, J. A. (2005). The crumbling pedestal: Changing images of Japanese teachers. *Journal of Teacher Education,* 56(5), 459–470.

Guo, L. (2010). *The Meaning of Curriculum Reform for Chinese Teachers: A Hermeneutic Inquiry into Teachers' Lived Experiences in Curriculum Change.* Saarbrücken, Germany: LAP Lambert Academic Publishing.

Guo, S. B., Guo, Y., Beckett, G., Li, Q., and Guo L.Y. (2012). *Teaching under China's Market Economy: Five Case Studies.* Research report. Available from http://download.ei-ie.org/Docs/WebDepot/Study%20on%20China.pdf

Guo, S. B. and Pungur, L. (2008). Exploring teacher education in the context of Canada and China: A cross-cultural dialogue. *Frontiers of Education in China,* 3(2), 246–269.

Hannum, E., Behrman, J., Wang, M. and Liu, J. (2008). Education in the reform era. In L. Brandt and T. G. Rawski (Eds), *China's Great Economic Transformation* (pp. 215–249). Cambridge: Cambridge University Press.

Hargreaves, A. (1997). Rethinking educational change: Going deeper and wider in the quest for success. In A. Hargreaves (Ed.), *Rethinking Educational Change with Heart and Mind: 1997 ASCD Yearbook* (pp. 1–26). Alexandria, VA: Association for Supervision and Curriculum Development.

Hargreaves, A. (1999). Series editor's forward. In S. Acker (Ed.), *The Realities of Teachers' Work: Never a Dull Moment.* London: Cassell.

Hargreaves, A. and Lo, L. N. K. (2000). The paradoxical profession: Teaching at the turn of the century. *Prospects,* 30(2), 167–180.

Harfitt, G. J. and Tavares, N. J. (2004). Obstacles as opportunities in the promotion of teachers' learning. *International Journal of Educational Research,* 41, 353–366.

Havelock, R. (1971). *Planning for Innovation through Dissemination and Utilization of Knowledge.* Ann Arbor, MI: Centre for Research on Utilization of Scientific Knowledge, institute for Social Research, University of Michigan.

He, M. (2002). A narrative inquiry of cross-cultural lives: Lives in China. *Journal of Curriculum Studies,* 34(3), 301–321.

Helsby, G. and McCulloch, G. (1997). Introduction: Teachers and the national curriculum. In G. Helsby and G. McCulloch (Eds), *Teachers and the National Curriculum*. London: Cassell.

Hirsch, E. (2004). *Teacher Working Conditions are Student Learning Conditions: A Report to Governor Mike Easley on the 2004 North Carolina Teacher Working Conditions Survey.* Chapel Hill, NC: Southeast Center for Teaching Quality.

Hofstede, G. (2001). *Culture's Consequences: Comparing Values, Behaviors, Institutions, and Organizations Across Nations.* Thousand Oaks, CA: Sage.

Hoyle, E. and Bell, R. (1972). *Problems of Curriculum Innovation.* Bletchley: Open University Press.

Hu, G. (2002). Potential cultural resistance to pedagogical imports: The case of communicative language teaching in China. *Language, Culture and Curriculum,* 15(2), 93–105.

Jiang, X. (2009). Realities of education reform in China. *Far Eastern Economic Review,* 172, 50–51.

Kelchtermans, G. (2011). Vulnerability in teaching: The moral and political roots of structural conditions. In C. Day, J.C.K., Lee (Eds.), *New understanding of teacher's work: Emotions and Educational change* (pp. 65–84). New York: Springer.

Kelchtermans, G. (2005). Teachers' emotions in educational reforms: Self-understanding, vulnerable commitment and micropolitical literacy. *Teaching and Teacher Education,* 21, 995–1006.

Kwo, O. W. Y. (2004). Understanding the awakening spirit of a professional teaching force. *International Journal of Educational Research,* 41, 292–306. doi:10.1016/j.ijer.2005.08.002

Kwo, O. W. Y. and Intrator, S. M. (2004). Uncovering the inner power of teachers' lives: Towards a learning profession. *International Journal of Educational Research,* 41, 281–291. doi:10.1016/j.ijer.2005.08.001

Law, W. W. (2006). Education reform for national competitiveness in a global age: The experience and struggle of China. In K. Mazurek and M. A. Winzer (Eds), *Schooling around the World: Debates, Challenges, and Practices* (pp. 68–103). Boston, MA: Pearson.

Lee, J. C. K. and Yin, H. B. (2005). The new curriculum of senior secondary school in mainland China: Blueprints, challenges, and prospects. *Hong Kong Teachers' Centre Journal,* 4, 1–10.

Lee, J. C. K. and Yin, H. B. (2011). Teachers' emotions and professional identity in curriculum reform: A Chinese perspective. *Journal of Educational Changes,* 12, 25–46. doi:10.1007/s10833-010-9149-3

Leithwood, K. (2006). T*eacher Working Conditions that Matter: Evidence for Change.* Toronto, ON: Elementary Teachers' Federation of Ontario.

Li, L. Q. (2004). *Education for 1.3 billion – Former Chinese Vice Premier Li Lanqing on 10 Years of Education Reform and Development.* Beijing, China: Foreign Language Teaching and Research Press, Pearson Education.

Li, Q. (2012). Education under China's market economy: A case study of urban and rural teachers in Hunan Province. *Canadian and International Education,* 41(2). Available at: http://ir.lib.uwo.ca/cie-eci/vol41/iss2/5

Li, Y. (2004). Deconstructing the demonization of teachers' images in the mass media. Retrieved from http://www.culstudies.com/rendanews/displaynews.asp?id=4303S.

Lin, J. (1993). Chinese teachers' social status and authority in the classroom: A historical perspective. *McGill Journal of Education*, 28(2), 213–230.

Lin, J. and Zhang, Y. (2006). Educational expansion and shortages in secondary schools in China: The bottle neck syndrome. *Journal of Contemporary China*, 15(47), 256–261.

Liu, W. H. (2010). Substitute teachers in rural areas in western investigation and analysis: Based on empirical research in Gansu County. *Journal of Gansu Normal Colleges*, 15(3), 98–101.

Ma Y., Lam C., and Wong, N. (2006). Chinese primary school mathematics teachers working in a centralised curriculum system: A case study of two primary schools in North-East China, *Compare: A Journal of Comparative and International Education*, 36(2), 197–212. doi: 10.1080/03057920600741206

Mascolo, M. J., Fischer, K. W., and Li, J. (2003). Dynamic development of component systems of emotions: Pride, shame, and guilt in China and the United States. In R. J. Davidson, K. Scherer, and H. H. Goldsmith (Eds), *Handbook of Affective Science* (pp. 375–408). Oxford: Oxford University Press.

Ministry of Education of the People's Republic of China (MOE). (2010). *National outline for mid and long-term education reform and development 2010–2020.* Available from http://www.gov.cn/jrzg/2010-07/29/content_1667143.htm

Ministry of Education of the People's Republic of China (MOE). (2012). *Educational statistics in 2011.* Available from http://www.moe.edu.cn/publicfiles/business/htmlfiles/moe/s7308/201305/152566.html

Niu, Z. (2009). Reforms on teachers' employment system and children's rights to education in China. *International Journal of Educational Management*, 23(1), 7–18.

OECD (2010). *Strong Performers and Successful Reformers in Education: Lessons from PISA for the United States: Shanghai and Hong Kong: Two Distinct Examples of Education Reform in China.* Paris, France: OECD.

Ouyang, H. (2003). Resistance to the communicative method of language instruction within a progressive Chinese University. In K. M. Anderson-Levitt (Eds), *Local Meanings, Global Schooling: Anthropology and World Culture Theory* (pp. 121–140). Basingstoke: Palgrave Macmillan.

Pang, L. (2004). Quality education versus examination-oriented education: Which one is winning? Available from http://www.sd.xinhuanet.com/news/2004-11/27/content_3294815.htm.

Priestley, M. (2005). Making the most of the Curriculum Review: Some reflections on supporting and sustaining change in schools. *Scottish Educational Review*, 37(1), 29–38.

Qu, R. and Zhang, Z. (2005). Work group emotions in Chinese culture settings. *Singapore Management Review*, 27(1), 69–86.

Ren, L. Y. (2007). *A study on the combination system of public and private schools in Chinese elementary education* (Unpublished master's thesis). National University of Defense Technology, Changsha, China.

Schoenhals, M. (1993). *The Paradox of Power in a People's Republic of China Middle School.* New York: M.E. Sharpe.

Scott, W. R. (2001). *Institutions and Organizations* (2nd edition). London: Sage.

Shang, Y. G., Liu, Q., and Liu, Y. Z. (2008). A report on living conditions of teachers substitute in less developed northwest area-based on the study in three regions, Tongwei, Huachi and Tianzhu. *Private Education Research*, 38(5), 86–93.

Singh, A. (2012). *Taking a Stand for Rural Teachers in China*. China Daily. http://www.chinadaily.com.cn/opinion/2012-10/04/content_15796923.htm

Tao, W. Z. (2006). Teaching supervision and evaluation report on experimental subjects of Beijing basic education curriculum reform. *Educational Research,* 3, 77–82.

Turner, Y. and Acker, A. (2002). *Education in the New China*. Hampshire: Sage.

Wang, J. and Li, Y. (2009). Research on the teaching quality of compulsory education in China's west rural schools. *Frontiers of Education in China,* 4(1), 66–93.

Wang, X. and Piesse, J. (2010) Inequality and the urban-rural divide in China: Effects of regressive taxation. *China and World Economy,* 18(6), 36–55.

Walker, A. and Qian, H. (2012). Reform disconnection in China. *Peabody Journal of Education,* 87(2), 162–177. doi: 10.1080/0161956X.2012.664462

Woods, P. (2001). Teaching and learning in the new millennium. In C. Sugrue (Eds), *Developing Teachers and Teaching Practice: International Research Perspectives* (pp. 47–62). London: Falmer Press.

Whyte, M. K. (2010) Social change and the urban-eural sivide in China. In: F. Hong and J-C. Gottwald (Eds) *The Irish Asia Strategy and Its China Relations.* Amsterdam: Rozenberg Publishers.

Yin, H. B. (2013). Societal culture and teachers' responses to curriculum reform: Experiences from China. *Asia Pacific Education Review,* 14(3), 391–401.

Zhao, Y. and Qiu, W. (2010). China as a case study of systemic educational reform. In A. Hargreaves et al. (Eds), *Second International Handbook of Educational Change* (pp. 349–361). Dordrecht, The Netherlands: Springer.

Zhao, L. T. (2009). Between local community and central state: Financing basic education in China. *International Journal of Educational Development,* 29(4), 366–373.

Zhang, J. and Lu, A. (2008). Review of teachers' mental health research in China since 1994. *Frontiers of Education in China,* 3(4), 623–638.

Zhang, L. (2007). The key to promote educational equity is to improve compulsory education quality in village. *Jiangxi Educational Research,* 1, 82–84.

Zhou, H. Q. and Shang, X. Q. (2011). Short-term volunteer teachers in rural China: Challenges and needs. *Frontiers of Education in China,* 6(3), 571–601. doi:10.1007/s11516-011-0146-y

Zhou, X. T. (2002). On aiding the poor through education and strengthening the rank of teachers in ethnic minority poverty-stricken areas. *Journal of Research and Education for Ethnic Minorities,* 1(3), 65–68.

2 Ideological, social and cultural forces influencing teacher education and development in China

A critical analysis

Shibao Guo

Since the time of Confucius, teachers have had a long-honored standing in China, and teaching as a profession has been held in high esteem. Teachers historically were listed among the five classes of those most respected by society: the God of Heaven, the God of the Earth, the emperor, parents, and teachers (Zhou, 1988). As an educator and teacher, Confucius himself was venerated as a sage by generations of Chinese. In contemporary China, especially during Mao's era, circumstances changed. During the Cultural Revolution (1966–1976) teachers were criticized as petit bourgeois and were targets for political transformation. With Deng Xiaoping's rise to power in 1978 and the shift from political struggle to economic reconstruction, teachers began to be treated with more respect. Yet, despite the long and rich heritage of education in China, the formal education of teachers is a relatively modern development that emerged only at the beginning of the twentieth century. At that time the national government developed special teacher education schools, and since then a well-developed and hierarchical teacher education system has evolved. This chapter traces various ideological, social and cultural forces that have defined and guided China's teacher education and development in recent Chinese history, including traditional Confucianism, Maoism, Deng's pragmatism, and Dewey's progressivism. These forces, although often theoretically exclusive of one another, have in practice been woven into the tapestry of the Chinese system at all levels. It is hoped that this analysis will shed new light on emerging issues and challenging facing teacher education and development in the age of globalization and market economy.

Mapping the teacher education terrain in China

The development of teacher education after the "new China" was established in 1949 can be divided into four periods (Guo, 2005; Wen, 1989). The first period, from 1949 to 1965, laid the foundation for teacher education—not the least of which was a number of programs organized for the purpose of transforming "old" teachers into "new" ones through their adoption of socialist ideas. The second period, the Cultural Revolution, lasted from 1966 to 1976. Teacher education came to a standstill during this time and practically collapsed. Many qualified teachers were prevented from teaching or were sent to the countryside to be "re-educated" by preliterate peasants. A large number of new graduates from schools were recruited to replace them, and hence the problem of teacher shortages and quality became critical as a result. The third period followed the death of Mao Zedong in 1976, which also marked the end of the Cultural Revolution. Education and society recovered during this period and a number of new reforms were introduced. These reforms were generally characterized by the opening-up policy, which shifted the nation's focus from political struggle to economic reconstruction. Educational institutions were required to produce a workforce adequate to support the country's economic development. The transformation of the education system, especially in the seriously affected area of teacher education, became a national priority. Teachers celebrated the first Teachers' Day in 1984, and the Teachers' Act was passed in 1993 to protect their legal rights. The fourth period, from 2001 to the present, was characterized by remarkable progress in preparing a large number of qualified teachers and passing legislation to improve teacher education. China's opening-up policy and economic development programs have shifted to focus on establishing a socialist market economy. Having experimented with teachers' qualification regulations in selected provinces, a new national system was set up in 2001 to certify qualified teachers. According to the new regulations, only those with teaching certificates can teach. This is a major milestone in the history of teacher education in China, and the new system should be instrumental in raising the general standard of teaching in the country. Its effectiveness, however, needs to be proven in practice.

There are five basic routes to teachers' education in China: (1) universities, colleges, or schools; (2) correspondence education; (3) broadcast and television education; (4) self-study examination; and (5) pedagogy research. Formal educational programs are the most prestigious of the five avenues listed above, and play an important part in Chinese teacher education. A number of programs are available. Normal universities or colleges offer four-year first-degree programs that prepare students to teach in senior secondary schools. Junior normal colleges provide two-year certificate programs for junior secondary school teachers. The entrance requirement for both these programs is the successful completion of senior secondary school by the age of 18 or 19. Below these programs are secondary normal schools. These offer two- to three-year teacher education programs for those who wish to be kindergarten or elementary school teachers. Admission requires the successful completion of junior secondary school, usually at the age of 16. The Chinese government has plans to upgrade the secondary normal schools to colleges or to eliminate some of them; as a result, their number has declined. Finally, there are education colleges and teachers' training colleges that provide in-service teacher education programs. These offer both two-year and four-year courses for teachers. Those who attend are expected to have completed their initial teacher education and to have some practical experience in teaching. With the exception of secondary normal schools for elementary grade teachers, which are considered part of the secondary professional training system, all these programs are considered part of the higher education system.

In addition to these conventional teacher education institutions, there are four other types of programs. Northeast China Normal University began to offer correspondence courses for teachers in 1953, and since then about sixty higher education teachers' institutions have followed suit (some secondary normal schools are doing the same). Courses have been offered via radio and television since the 1960s and in recent years the internet, and large cities like Beijing and Shanghai have established broadcasting and television universities to provide higher education; the majority of their students are secondary school teachers. In recent years the Internet has been introduced to help with this mode of delivery. Another route to teacher education is "self-study examination." As the name implies, teachers study independently and take national examinations at a particular time of the year. Once they have accumulated sufficient credits, they receive their certificates or degrees. In reality, however, self-study examination is an assessment of teacher proficiency rather than a means of providing formal teacher education. Finally, there are professional development programs (usually organized by "pedagogy/teaching research sections") set up under education departments at the provincial, prefectural, and county levels. These help teachers to understand the teaching syllabi and textbooks and attempt to improve their teaching methods.

As discussed above, teacher education offered through normal universities, colleges, and schools is foremost among pre-service training options. Correspondence courses, broadcasting and television programs, and self-study education may be economically attractive, but they are not ideal. Teacher-learners mainly study by themselves and are isolated, depriving them of the chance to exchange views and experiences with others. While teachers may be able to learn their subject matter this way, they are unlikely to improve their teaching skills through reading books at home. Pedagogy research is thought to be a more popular, direct, and practical type of education for in-service development. Consequently, while it seems that there are many ways to educate teachers, in fact only a couple of these options have proved to have practical value for most educators. A recent development has been the merging of postsecondary institutions in China under the auspices of a socialist market economy. The government's goal is to reduce operating costs as well as increase competitiveness through these mergers. Many smaller teacher education colleges and schools have become part of larger universities or colleges as a result of this restructuring. Their unique position as specialized teacher education institutions is under threat, and they also have lost many of their special advantages. In the long run, these changes likely will do more harm than good for teachers' education. On a positive note, recently there has been an increase in the number of teachers who hold master's degrees—an encouraging new phenomenon.

Researching teacher education

A number of studies have documented challenges facing teacher education in China (Guo, 1996, 2005; Li, 1999; Manzar-Abbas and Lu, 2013; Paine, 1990; Wan, 2012; Yan and He, 2010). One such challenge involves attitudes toward teacher education. Some teacher education students believe that good teaching is innate, and that some teachers will never teach well despite formal teacher training (Guo, 1996). A second problem relates to the focus of teacher education. Many researchers maintain that current teacher education programs are narrowly designed, with a rigid curriculum, excessive focus on subject training, and insufficient emphasis on teaching methodology and educational practice (Manzar-Abbas and Lu, 2013; Paine, 1990). Furthermore, current teacher training courses have been criticized as being overly theoretical and abstract, with teaching practica that are too short to provide adequate preparation for the field (Chen and Mu, 2010; Guo, 1996, 2005; Yan and He, 2010). Often teacher-instructors whose focus is subject teaching methodology were taught by those who could not teach a specialized subject very well. Other lecturers may not have had training themselves, in spite of being assigned to teach methodology—since pedagogy has a low status, some think that anyone should be able to teach it.

Many, however, see professional competencies as the core of developing quality teaching (Cochrane-Smith and Zeichner, 2005; Zeichner, 2006). The above mentioned factors have led to China's teacher-education programs neglecting to teach their student teachers actual teaching skills, and many teachers arrive in the classroom with little instructional experience (Guo, 2005). The current philosophy of teacher education is also reflected in the little time given to reflective and collaborative practices, and the social foundations of education. The pre-service teacher is seen simply as an apprentice to the master teacher (Li, 1999). Zhou (2002) has pointed out the outdated system of postsecondary education built on the Soviet model, and has called for more internships and new curricula. Qi and his colleagues (2004) have seconded this call, arguing for new models based on three or four years of basic postsecondary schooling followed by one year of teacher education. Paine (1990) sees the need for teaching to become less teacher-centered and more interactive. Curriculum and program changes are not the only solution, however. The social status of the teaching profession—once so highly thought of and respected (Li, 1999)—needs to be reclaimed through renewed professionalism (Guo and Pungur, 2008; Zhou, 2002).

Social and ideological forces influencing teacher education

The preceding discussions have examined the historical development, current provisions, and ongoing challenges facing teacher education in China. To help us better understand its past and present, the next section will trace various ideological, social and cultural forces that have influenced China's teacher education and development in recent Chinese history. Given the limited space, the following analysis will focus on traditional Confucianism, Maoism, and Dewey's progressivism.

Traditional Confucianism

Traditional Confucianism was one of the most influential forces in providing philosophical vision and guidance to teachers and teacher education in China. As stated earlier, as an educator and teacher Confucius himself was venerated as a sage by generations of Chinese. Confucius (551–479 BC) was the greatest and most highly revered of all traditional Chinese philosophers. He was not only a great philosopher but also a great educator, who has greatly influenced the Chinese education since the Han Dynasty (207 BC–220 AD). It is beyond the scope of this chapter to discuss Confucius in detail; however, it is necessary to introduce some of his most important political and educational ideas as a way to understand traditional Confucianism.

During Confucius' life 3000 disciples studied with him, 72 of whom became very distinguished. One of Confucius' most important principles was *rén*, or benevolence. Its fundamental meaning is "to love others," but it also meant "self-cultivation." Benevolence also includes filial piety and loyalty. The precept of *rén* requires teachers to be caring toward their students and students to be loyal to their teachers in return. Confucians as a group regarded education as the most important thing in life. Confucius said: "[i]n teaching there should be no distinction of classes" (Legge, 1960, p. 305). This is one of Confucius' greatest educational thoughts. He advocated that people should have education whether they were rich or poor. However, this tends to be a contemporary interpretation of his philosophy. Galt (1951) argues that during Confucius' time, there was no conception of real democracy in China. The primary goal of traditional Confucian education was to prepare the ruling elite and to mold the character of the citizenry (Zhou, 1988).

Confucius taught the "six arts": rites, music, archery, chariot driving, calligraphy, and mathematics. His curriculum exhibited a kind of intermingling of moral and intellectual education (Zhu, 1992). According to Confucius, rites (norms of proper social behavior) and music were the most important subjects. He compiled his own texts, including the *Classic of Poetry*, the *Classic of History*, the *Classic of Rites*, the *Classic of Music*, the *Classic of Changes*, and the *Spring and Autumn Annals*. Unfortunately, the *Classic of Music* was lost. The other five books were revered as the Five Classics by Confucian educators and students who came later, and were recited by thousands of scholars in preparation for civil service examination (*kējǔ kǎoshì*). What is particularly interesting for this discussion is not so much the finer points of its content, but the overarching ethos and values of Confucianism. Since the Han Dynasty, Confucian philosophy and educational ideology has played an essential role in shaping the Chinese educational system in general and teacher education particularly. P. W. Kuo (1915), Dewey's first Chinese doctoral student at Columbia University Teachers' College, pointed out that this high veneration for Confucius and the principles he represented had an important bearing upon the subsequent history of Chinese education. From the Han Dynasty forward, Kuo argues, Chinese education became less liberal than it once was, and the content of education became narrowly confined to the Confucius classics, which excluded the natural sciences and social development.

For centuries, Confucian education emphasized rote learning. The whole process of learning was geared towards the memorization of ideas of antiquity, by way of the Five Classics and the Four Books (i.e., *The Analects*, *The Great Learning*, *The Way of the Mean*, and *The Mencius* compiled by Zhu Xi—a neo-Confucian scholar in the Song Dynasty [960–1127]). These works constituted the content that had to be mastered for the Civil Service Examination. Success in the Examination marked the end of learning (Cheng et al., 1999). This form of teaching tended to suppress the spirit of free inquiry, and did not encourage any initiative on the part of students. It was assumed that they would be submissive. The passivity of the learner was further compounded by the status and power of the teacher. For centuries Chinese education followed the Confucian model, so the history of Chinese teacher education has been influenced greatly by Confucian teaching until the visit of John Dewey and the birth of communism in China.

Dewey's progressivism

Widely regarded as the chief exponent of progressive education, John Dewey (1859–1952) may well be the single most influential philosopher of education the United States has produced (Elias and Merriam, 1995). He is also one of the most influential philosophers in Chinese teacher education, who visited and lectured in China from 1919 to 1921. During his stay he traveled extensively in China and lectured on philosophy in general and the philosophy of education in particular, including the goal of education, the relationship between school and society, moral education and democracy, and experiential learning. He was among the first to challenge Confucianism. It is necessary to first review the major theories of progressive education as presented in Dewey's *Democracy and Education* (1916) and *Experience and Education* (1938).

Dewey (1916) believed that personal growth is the ultimate aim of education. Growth is possible because human beings possess plasticity, or the capacity to retain and carry over from prior experience factors that modify subsequent activities. This plasticity signifies our human capacity to acquire habits or to develop definite dispositions, and by extension the capacity of a thoughtfully constructed educational environment to shape these. Dewey rejected the idea that education is preparation for work. Instead, he believed that schools should focus on the present lives of children. Dewey (1916) also believed that education had a role to play in social reform and reconstruction. In his view, education has both a conservative and a reconstructive function. In *Democracy and Education* (1916), he placed education at the very heart of social reform. He argues that education would flourish if it took place in a democracy; in turn, democracy would develop only if there were true education. For Dewey, a democratic society is committed to change and a democratic education produces a society that is in a constant and positively directed state of growth and development. The traditional or liberal philosophy of education confined the aims of education to intellectual development through a study of certain academic disciplines. Dewey's progressivism broadened the concept of education through the introduction of a practical, pragmatic, and utilitarian approach to curriculum development.

For Dewey (1916), the primary task of education was to develop the potential of the child. Dewey and other progressives contend that people are born neither inherently "good" nor "bad." Rather, we are born with unlimited potential for development and growth. Dewey argues that a person could achieve a more satisfying life through the application of the scientific method and experimental thinking, and emphasized the interests, needs, and desires of learners in forging educational experiences. The teacher's task is not just to capitalize on the interests that already exist in the learner, but also to pique his or her interest in subjects that are deemed educationally desirable. Dewey (1916) defined education as the reconstruction and reorganization of experience, which increases our ability to direct the course of subsequent experience. In 1938, he distinguished between traditional education, in which students learn from texts and teachers; and progressive education, in which learning occurs through experience. Experience was described as the interaction of the individual with the environment; interaction and continuity were two fundamental principles stated to constitute experience (Dewey, 1938). According to Dewey (1916), intelligence is developed through the solving of problems, which ideally should occur in a cooperative social context in which people can work collaboratively. Problem solving, both as an individual and a group process, plays a central role in Dewey's overall concept of education. He believed that problem-solving activities in the school not only develop intelligence and facilitate growth; they also develop problem-solving skills that transfer to life in general. According to Dewey, learning is not dictated by the teacher; rather, the teacher first attempts to help the student identify problems and then acts as a resource. Dewey (1938) argues that in traditional education, books, especially textbooks, are the chief representatives of the lore and wisdom of the past. Teachers serve as mere agents through which knowledge and skills are communicated, and rules of conduct enforced. Dewey defined education as the reconstruction of experiences through interactive processes with one's environment, and learning as the outcome of students' personal experiences. The educator's task, therefore, is to guide, direct, and evaluate these experiences.

The preceding discussion demonstrates that Dewey's progressive education differs from traditional Confucian education in many aspects. For example, he attacked the notion of teachers passing knowledge on to students as if that knowledge were ready-made and enshrined as permanent truth. Instead of learning from texts and teachers, progressive educators maintain that learning occurs through experience and solving problems. Instead of using teacher-centered approach, progressives advocate student-centered education. Dewey felt a child-centered curriculum was important, which represented a turning away from classroom emphasis on subject matter to emphasize the growth of the child. He believed that child-centered education should be a priority for China as a departure from the stratified society or authoritarian tradition that tended to promote the "pouring in" of accepted subject matter as education. Dewey's impact on recent Chinese education was intensive and pronounced, which will be discussed later in this chapter. Particularly from the 1920s to the founding of the People's Republic of China in 1949, Dewey's pragmatic education theory dominated Chinese education ideology. Researchers maintain that China was the foreign country in which Dewey exercised his greatest influence, particularly in the field of education (Su, 1995; Xu, 1992).

Maoism and its influence on education

With the birth of the new republic in 1949 came the era of Mao Zedong (1893–1976). Many people in the world know Mao as a communist revolutionary leader, but in fact he was also one of the most important social and ideological forces in modern Chinese education, if not the only one. As early as 1917, Mao started the first evening school to improve literacy for poor workers in his hometown of Hunan (Xiao, 2003). Owing to his personal belief in the transformative role of education and his preeminent power position in the Chinese Community Party, its army, and its government, his views on education influenced both the development of education theory and policy making. Cleverley (1985) called him "the single most influential figure in the creation of a distinctively different communist system of education in China" (p. 70). Under Mao the aim of education shifted from producing a scholar class well versed in Confucian classics to training new socialists who would serve proletarian politics and become part of a productive labor force.

Both Dewey and Mao challenged traditional Confucian education and teaching, and in the process helped to advance teacher education and development. Comparisons between Dewey's progressivism and Maoism, which dated back as early as the 1950s, found amazing similarities as well as many differences between these two influential figures in modern Chinese history. According to Xu, similarities between the two include their views on the significant connections between school and society, the social role of education, the role of experience in learning, and their stress on moral education. Both Dewey and Mao believed that education was not an isolated enterprise, but one "closely connected with, affected by, and achieved with and for social change" (Xu, 1992, p. 97). Dewey's "learning by doing" and Mao's "learning by practicing" ring a similar note. Both saw the necessity and significance of moral education in schooling, and placed it as the top priority before intellectual and physical development. Their similar notions about moral education and the socializing function of schooling led to an epistemological similarity. They both agreed that knowledge consists of experience and can only be developed through active human inquiry into experience.

In addition to the above stated similarities, there are a number of differences between these two great thinkers. According to Xu (1992), Dewey's educational ideas were built on modern sciences and western philosophy and pursued through academia, whereas Mao's were founded on Marxist political ideology and focused on social and political transformation via revolutionary struggle. Consequently, the two clearly had quite different visions of what constituted moral education. For Dewey, moral education bred democracy, open-mindedness, intelligence, intellectual honesty, and responsibility. Mao's moral education, on the other hand, had a strong political and class orientation; it demanded an absolute belief in Marxism and the development of proletarian consciousness. Their emphases on educational experiences also differed, with Dewey stressing natural sciences for the personal and academic growth, while Mao's passions lay with political ideology for social welfare. Thus, the emphasis each placed on educational content was also different. Deweyan schools introduced modern subjects, a variety of topics, and experimental experiences into their curricula, whereas Mao's schools assumed political study and productive labor as their main content, in place of academic courses.

Despite these differences, it is important to point out that what Dewey and Mao did share was a progressive agenda for social development; one which challenged the traditional Confucian education and the old social orders (Xu, 1992). As explained earlier in this chapter, Confucian education clung to classics as its only content, and devalued any form of ordinary experience. Both Dewey and Mao advocated change and brought everyday experience into the classroom for educational purposes and teacher training. Both strongly opposed the use of rote-learning and imperial examination by traditional Confucian educators. Instead, they guaranteed learners an active role in learning and took their interests into consideration. Both favored inductive methods, group discussions, and activities. They also focused on fostering imagination, originality, creativity, and the student's own capabilities of thinking and problem solving. However, Xu (1992) also qualifies that Mao's insistence on proletarian ideology was the only "correct" outlook undermined the freedom and originality he advocated for education. Sadly, this rigidity eventually reduced his educational methods to precisely those he had originally set out against: didactic instruction and traditional "cramming." In the end, Mao and his followers contributed to the regression of Chinese education by relying upon rote learning to cram Marxist and Maoist thought into students' minds, with no say on their part whatsoever.

The main understanding to draw from comparisons between Dewey and Mao is that despite their approaching education from completely different cultural and ideological backgrounds, both issued challenges to the principles of traditional Confucian education. To a certain degree, their efforts drew modern Chinese teacher education out of its isolated ivory tower, and situated it much more within China's current social realities.

China as a contesting ground for ideologies

The above discussion has clearly demonstrated that traditional Confucianism, Dewey's progressivism, and Maoism have co-existed in China jointly shaping China's teacher education in distinct ways. Their co-existence reveals that China is an important ground for contesting theories and ideologies: the old and the new, the indigenous and the foreign (Guo, 2004). The discussion that follows will examine how they interacted to bring China's teacher educational system to its current state, and to determine which of these forces are exerting the strongest influence today.

Evaluation of Dewey's influence on China

As mentioned earlier, John Dewey was among the first to challenge traditional Confucianism that dominated China's educational landscape at the time. During his stay in China from 1919 to 1921, he addressed Chinese audiences from some 78 different lecture forums, including several series of between 15 and 20 lectures apiece (Keenan, 1977). Dewey's series of lectures on education usually dedicated as much as one-third of their content to defining the revolution in knowledge that led to the erosion of the authority of tradition. He maintained that education could be liberated from passive learning by conceiving of knowledge not as an end in itself, but as an instrument for intelligently directing human activity. In his China lectures, Dewey felt it important to emphasize the child-centered curriculum: a shifting of emphasis from the subject matter to the growth of the child. But in Dewey's vision for a democratic China, there had to be equal opportunity for each child to develop his or her potentialities and become a participating citizen.

An evaluation of Dewey's influence on China can be categorized into three stages. The first stage covers the 1920s to the 1940s, when Dewey's pragmatic educational theory dominated the Chinese education field and when the American's influence on Chinese education was intensive and prominent. Nearly all of Dewey's educational works were translated into Chinese, and some of them were used as textbooks in teacher education. His ideas were also adopted in the transformation of China's educational system and his influence was evident in forming educational aims and principles, making educational policies, and revising curriculum and teaching methods (Clopton and Ou, 1973; Ou, 1970; Zhou, 1991). His former students and disciples in China (e.g., Chen Heqin, Hu Shi and Tao Xingzhi, among several others) played an important role in implementing Dewey's essential ideas, many of whom were already intellectual leaders in the country. Su (1996) documented how Tao Xingzhi experimented with Dewey's progressivism in Chinese teacher education, which was carried out in the Xiaozhuang Normal School near Nanjing that he created in 1927. Derived from Dewey's "learning by doing", Tao developed his own pedagogical principle in teacher education—the unity of teaching, learning, and reflective acting, a complete break from traditional Confucianism. Tao also transformed Dewey's "school as society" into his "society as school," "education as life" into "life as education." The School was forced to close down in 1930 because the experiment became a "seedbed for developing democratic, experienced-based, and community-focused education in China" (p. 149), which posed a "threat" to the Nationalist Government. Su maintains that Xiaozhuang Normal School represents the most thorough and creative implementation of the Dewey philosophy in Chinese teacher education.

The second stage was from the 1950s to the 1970s, after the new People's Republic was founded in 1949. This period of time was characterized by severe criticism and a complete reversal of Deweyan experimentalism (Su, 1995). Dewey was portrayed as "anti-Marxist," "reactionary," "a defender of American imperialism," and an "enemy of the Chinese people" (Chao, 1950; Chen, 1957). These criticisms were based on some of the arguments he made in his lectures in China and in his writings. One example was his opposition to the use of violence to overthrow the old system. While Marxists believed that Communism would win the final victory in the world, Dewey maintained that the future was highly uncertain. Because of his emphasis on children's interests and experiences in the educational process, his educational ideas were criticized as lacking discipline, teacher authority, and rigor. Critics called Dewey's theories "poisonous and harmful" to China (Su, 1995). Hence, Keenan (1977) concludes that Dewey's influence on education, though original and decisive, was not enough to overcome strong opposition from Confucian scholars and Marxists.

Critical response to Dewey shifted again in the latest stage, which began in the 1980s and continues to the present. Over this period, the political and philosophical climate in China moved from Marxism to pragmatism. As the late Chinese leader Deng Xiaoping put it, "[n]o matter if it is a white cat or black cat; as long as it catches a mouse, it is a good cat" (Su, 1995, p. 315). This famous quote proposed that if the economic theories and practices of capitalist countries had resulted in a better living for the ordinary people, then there must be something of value for the Chinese people to learn from and to apply to their own situation. Deng's political and economic pragmatism paved the way for Chinese intellectuals to become infatuated once again with western pragmatism. The new political situation sparked a serious re-evaluation of Dewey's influence on Chinese education which is in many ways drastically different from the early embrace of Deweyan education in the 1950s. Moving beyond the blanket denouncements of the Communist era, Chinese thinkers turned to more critical appraisals, seeking ways to borrow and adapt Dewey's ideas for China's educational needs. New thinking centers on the contributions that Dewey made to world education, the similarities between Dewey and some Chinese educators and politicians, and the utility of his ideas for the improvements of China's educational practices. Some efforts are underway to re-introduce Dewey's progressive theories into China's educational practices. Going back to the story of Xiaozhuang Normal School which reopened in 1950 following the founding of the People's Republic of China, the School was attacked as bourgeois reforms throughout the 1950s (Su, 1996). Since the early 1980s, the School reintroduced Tao Xingzhi's principle of the unity of teaching, learning, and reflective acting in teacher education (Su, 1996). Chinese educators often looked into the practices of Xiaozhuang Normal School for models. However, they remain ambivalent and reluctant regarding Dewey's ideas and influence on Chinese teacher education. In this view, Su concludes that Dewey's influence on current teacher education in China is "indirect and inconspicuous", largely through the manifestation of Tao's educational ideas (p. 148). Of note, in 2000 Xiaozhuang Normal School was merged with Nanjing Teachers' College and Nanjing Education College under a new entity—Nanjing Xiaozhuang University. At this point, I am grappling with the following questions: As part of a larger university, to what extent can the original progressive roots of Xiaozhuang Normal School be sustained? Two decades later, will the students of the newly formed university even know who Tao Xingzhi or John Dewey were?

Education under Deng and the renaissance of Confucianism

When Deng Xiaoping came to power in 1978, he implemented his political and economic pragmatism into a number of new reforms within the scope of a new "open door" policy and a socialist market economy. He also affirmed the special role of education as an economically "productive force" in the construction of China's new socialist economy (Zhou, 1988, p. 13). Teachers were able to reclaim their respectable status, and were hailed as "glorious engineers cultivating human souls;" teaching became "the most glorious profession under the sun (Li, 1999). With this proviso, education underwent tremendous transformation under Deng's leadership. Many schools and universities that had been shut down or moved to the countryside during the Cultural Revolution moved back to cities and resumed offering academic classes. Formal curricula with a focus on traditional academic subjects replaced those offered during the Cultural Revolution, which emphasized ideological and political study, and physical labor. Meanwhile, secondary education expanded its vocational and technical education components to generate the manpower needed to support the country's economic development. After 11 years' abeyance, university entrance examination was restored in 1977 with a strong emphasis on the students' examination results rather than their political background. In a few years, "education was brought back to the highest point before the Cultural Revolution, [and] exceeded far beyond" (Xu, 1992). According to Fouts and Chan (1995), the system began to resemble once again the Confucian model and has taken on "a more decidedly pragmatic and technological flavour" (Fouts and Chan, 1995, p. 528).

A number of studies have demonstrated that present-day education in China is still rigid and teacher-centerd and teaching and learning rely heavily on the use of textbooks, memorization, and examination (Guo, 1996, 2005; Paine, 1990; Pratt, 1992; Pratt et al., 1999). Pratt (1992) and Pratt et al. (1999) report that teachers in China are regarded as content experts and transmitters of knowledge, while students are perceived as the consumers of knowledge: Teachers give and learners receive. Teachers are expected to be thoroughly prepared and organized for lectures. Paine (1990) describes this kind of teaching as the "Chinese Virtuoso Model of Teaching," where the teacher, like a musician, "performs", students are the audience. The main intellectual thrust of this model of teaching, Paine continues, centers on the teacher's performance and minimizes or inadvertently neglects the interactive potential of classroom experience. In short, teachers in today's China remain the "sage on the stage." Obviously, this pedagogy does not draw from Dewey's learner-centerd education; the active role assigned to the learners by Mao during the Cultural Revolution is also notably absent. Learning is still widely understood as simple transference of information from teacher to learner (Pratt, 1992). Except where learning is taking place directly related to a particular enterprise, there is no philosophy of "learner involvement;" there are no "participatory techniques," no "problem-solving methodologies."

Knowledge is perceived by the Chinese as both external to the learner and stable in its movement from the teacher to learner (Pratt, 1992). Usually there is little doubt about what constitutes the "basics" or foundational knowledge that students are expected to master (Pratt et al., 1999). The major source of that knowledge usually comes from authorized textbooks. As Paine (1990) puts it, "The textbook, as the source of knowledge, and the teacher, as the presenter of that knowledge, stand at centre stage for the activity of Chinese schools" (p. 51). Criteria used to judge the effectiveness of teaching and learning is based on how well a teacher performs or transmits knowledge, and in turn, how well students memorize or master it. Textbook learning and a strict emphasis on content mastery are further aspects of present Chinese education that disregard both Dewey's inquiry-based pedagogy and Mao's focus on political study, physical labor, and students' daily lived experiences. Finally, present-day education in China is still examination-centerd (Guo, 1996, 2005). Almost a century has passed since the Civil Service Examination was abolished in 1905. The sciences, Marxism, Leninism, Mao Zedong Thought, and Deng's Theory have replaced the Confucian curriculum, but in essence, the way of testing students remains much the same.

The Chinese government launched the new curriculum reform in the new millennium; the examination system however still remains in place (Guo et al., 2013). While the content of examinations varies according to the subject and level, all emphasize the testing of facts. Formal examinations only stopped for a decade during the Cultural Revolution, but resumed soon after it was over. This is another legacy of Confucianism that remains firmly intact.

Education under China's market economy: which force drives it?

The foregoing discussion has demonstrated that, despite the opposition of Dewey and Mao, traditional Confucian traits still dominate teacher education in China today, supported in their modern iterations by of the tenets of Deng's pragmatism. However, this does not mean that Maoism and Dewey's progressivism have completely vanished from China's present-day educational practices. Fouts and Chan (1995) maintain that "elements of Mao's ideas were inculcated into the educational system" (p. 527). The authors also pointed out that Mao's aim of universal education remains relevant, and that political education remains in the curriculum alongside moral education. The core of the five aims of education (i.e., moral, intellectual, physical, aesthetic, and social) may still be credited to Mao. Although Mao is rarely quoted today, Xu (1992) predicted that his ideas have been and will continue to play a significant role in contemporary Chinese education. It is true that the influence of Dewey's progressivism on Chinese education was most profound from the early 1920s to the late 1940s. Yet like

Mao, his educational theories have not been entirely shuffled into the museums. Dewey's views on education for socialization, moral education, vocational and technical education, and the connection between school and society have been partially incorporated into the Chinese educational system (Su, 1995). In fact, Su argues, China is trying to avoid going to either extreme—"traditional education," as represented by Confucian educational theories, or "modern education," as represented by Dewey and his Chinese advocates.

In the new millennium, we witness the pendulum of Chinese education swing again, this time toward neoliberalism. Neoliberal reforms in education are redirecting China to marketization and privatization in terms of orientation, provision, curriculum and financing (Chan and Mok, 2001; Guo, 2013; Mok, 2005, 2009). Chan and Mok identify four features of education under China's market economy: the rising of private or non-government schools, funding from non-state sectors, increasing number of self-paying students, and market-driven curricula. In this process, education has adopted the fee-paying principle, reduced state provision, and been driven by revenue-generating courses and programs. As such, education has become a commodity and schools are run like businesses. As Chan and Mok argue, the "user pay" principle and the rise of non-state provision in China suggest a withdrawal of the state from provision and subsidy of public education. The recent changes in education have had a tremendous impact on all facets of teachers' lives and work, including their workload, income and benefits, wellbeing, and teaching and living conditions (Guo et al., 2013). According to Guo et al., the market economy has not improved the conditions of teachers; on the contrary, the status of teachers and their working and living conditions have deteriorated. Owing to roaring housing prices, high inflation rates, and expensive living costs, many teachers are paid less, live in poor housing conditions, face heavy workloads and greater responsibilities, and suffer from psychological disorders. To make ends meet, many teachers have to tutor outside of school hours or work a second job. Under China's market economy, the nature of teaching has also changed (Guo, 2012). Once conceived as a highly respected profession, under China's market economy teaching has become a commodity that can be traded in the market. It is evident that there is a dire need for the Chinese government to take active measure to reduce social injustice and inequity facing teachers in China.

In the years to come, it appears that neoliberalism will join traditional Confucianism, Maoism, Deng's pragmatism, Dewey's progressivism, and many other trends of thoughts in informing, defining, guiding, and challenging China's teacher education system. Since each of these theories and ideologies were developed in a completely different historical, social, political, economic, and cultural context, their implementation into practice will inevitably require interpretation, imagination, and adaptation. As Xu (1992) puts it, "the implementation of Dewey would never be pure Deweyan" (p. 62). The same could be said about many other theories and ideologies as well. Each will evolve in a new social, political, and economic context. The development of each will bring changes to the educational system in China. It is the force of these ideas together that makes the education system in China dynamic, vibrant, and fascinating. Such activity is well worth being reflected upon by teacher educators around the world who seek to learn from others and improve their own educational systems.

References

Chan, D. and Mok, K. H. (2001). Educational reforms and coping strategies under the tidal wave of marketization: A comparative study of Hong Kong and the mainland. *Comparative Education*, 37(1), 21–41.

Chao, F. (1950). Introduction to the criticism of John Dewey, Part I. *People' Education*, 6, 21–28.

Chen, J. and Mu, Z. (2010). The cross-national comparison of pre-service mathematics teacher education and curriculum structure. *Journal of Mathematics Education*, 3(1), 119–136.

Chen, J. P. (1957). *Criticism of Dewey's moral education philosophy*. Wuhan, China: Hubei People's Press.

Cheng, K. M., Jin, S. H., and Gu, X. B. (1999). From training to education: Lifelong learning in China. *Comparative Education*, 35(2), 119–129.

Cleverley, J. (1985). *The Schooling of China*. Boston, MA: George Allen and Unwin.

Clopton, R. and Ou, T. (1973). *John Dewey: Lectures in China, 1919–1920*. Honolulu: An East-West Center Book, the University Press of Hawaii.

Cochrane-Smith, M. and Zeichner, K.M. (2005). Executive summary: A report of the AERA panel on research and teacher education. In M. Cochrane-Smith and K. M. Zeichner (Eds), *Studying Teacher Education: The Report on Research and Teacher Education* (pp. 1–36). Mahwah, NJ: Lawrence Erlbaum Associates.

Dewey, J. (1916). *Democracy and Education*. New York: The Macmillan Company.

Dewey, J. (1938). *Experience and Education*. New York: Collier Books.

Elias, J. and Merriam, S. (1995). *Philosophical Foundations of Adult Education*. Malabar, FL: Krieger Publishing Company.

Fouts, J. T. and Chan, J. C. K. (1995). Confucius, Mao and modernization: Social studies education in the People's Republic of China. *Journal of Curriculum Studies*, 27(5), 523–543.

Guo, S. (2012). Globalization, market economy and social inequality in China: Exploring the experience of migrant teachers. *Canadian and International Education*, 41(2), 8–27.

Guo, S. (2005). Exploring current issues in teacher education in China. *Alberta Journal of Educational Research*, 51(1), 69–84.

Guo, S. (2004). China as a contesting ground for ideologies: Examining the social and ideological forces that influence China's educational system. *Canadian Journal of University Continuing Education*, 30(1), 55–77.

Guo, S. (1996). Adult teaching and learning in China. *Convergence*, 29(1), 21–33.

Guo, S., Guo, Y., Beckett, G., Li, Q., and Guo, L. (2013). Changes in Chinese education under globalisation and market economy: Emerging issues and debates. *Compare*, 43(2), 144–164.

Guo, S. and Pungur, L. (2008). Exploring teacher education in the context of Canada and China: A cross-cultural dialogue. *Frontiers of Education in China*, 3(2), 246–269.

Keenan, B. (1977). *The Dewey Experiment in China.* Cambridge, MA: Harvard University Press.

Kuo, P. W. (1915). *The Chinese System of Public Education.* New York: Teachers College Press.

Li, D. F. (1999). Modernization and teacher education in China. *Teaching and Teacher Education,* 15, 179–192.

Manzar-Abbas, S. and Lu, L. (2013). Student teachers' perceptions about the curriculum content: A case of a normal university in China. *Education as Change,* 17(1), 37–52.

Mok, K.H. (2009). The growing importance of the privateness in education: Challenges for higher education governance in China. *Compare,* 39(1), 35–49.

Mok, K. H. (2005). Riding over socialism and global capitalism: Changing education governance and social policy paradigms in post-Mao China. *Comparative Education,* 41(2), 217–242.

Ou, T. C. (1970). Dewey's lectures and influence in China. In J. A. Boydston (Ed.), *Guide to the Works of John Dewey.* Barbondale and Edwardsville, IL: Southern Illinois University Press.

Paine, L. (1990). The teacher as virtuoso: A Chinese model for teaching. *Teacher College Record,* 92(1), 49–81.

Pratt, D. D. (1992). Chinese conceptions of learning and teaching: A Westerner's attempt at understanding. *International Journal of Lifelong Education,* 11(4), 301–319.

Pratt, D. D., Kelly, M., and Wong, W. S. S. (1999). Chinese conceptions of "effective teaching" in Hong Kong: Towards culturally sensitive evaluation of teaching. *International Journal of Lifelong Education,* 18(4), 241–258.

Qi, W., Wei, W., Lu, S., Qiao, Z., and Chen, Y. (2004). Research on curriculum system of teachers' education and reform of teaching contents. *Journal of Shandong Normal University (Humanities and Social Sciences),* 49(6), 3–8.

Su, Z. (1995). A critical evaluation of John Dewey's influence on Chinese education. *American Journal of Education,* 103(3), 302–325.

Su, Z. (1996). Teaching, learning, and reflective acting: A Dewey experiment in Chinese teacher education. *Teachers College Record,* 98(1), 126–152.

Wan, G. (2012). The educational development in China: Perspectives from the West. *New Horizons in Education,* 60(2), 1–20.

Wen, H.J. (Ed.) (1989). *Brief Introduction to Teacher Training.* Beijing: Beijing Teachers' University Press.

Xiao, J. (2003). Redefining adult education in an emerging economy: The example of Shenzhen, China. *International Review of Education,* 49(5), 487–508.

Xu, D. (1992). *A Comparison of the Educational Ideas and Practices of John Dewey and Mao Zedong in China: Is School Society or Society School?* San Francisco: Mellen Research University Press.

Yan, C. and He, C. (2010). Transforming the existing model of teaching practicum: A study of Chinese EFL student teachers' perceptions. *Journal of Education for Teaching,* 36(1), 57–73.

Zeichner, K. (2006). Reflections of a university-based teacher on the future of college and university-based teacher education. *Journal of Teacher Education,* 57(3), 326–340.

Zhou, G. P. (1991). The spread and influence of modern western education theories in China. *Educational Sciences, East China Teachers' University,* 3, 77–96.

Zhou, N.Z. (1988). Historical contexts of educational reforms in present-day China. *Interchange,* 19(3–4), 8–18.
Zhou, Z.Y. (2002). The teaching profession: To be or to do? *Journal of Education for Teaching*, 28(3), 211–215.
Zhu, W. (1992). Confucius and traditional Chinese education: An assessment. In R. Hayhoe (Ed.), *Educational and Modernization: The Chinese Experience.* Oxford: Pergamon Press.

Part II

Developing teachers in times of change

Contexts matter

3 The impact of reform policies on teachers' work and professionalism in the Chinese mainland

Leslie Nai-Kwai Lo, Manhong Lai,
and *Lijia Wang*

Introduction

In 1978, China embarked upon a massive social engineering project when it broke out of its self-imposed isolation and rejoined the community of nations with a vision of power and prosperity. Education was placed at the core of a modernization project that was initiated by the Chinese Communist Party. It was counted on to produce the necessary manpower to drive a developmental engine that was desperately in need of a jump-start. From then on, education has become a major concern on China's developmental agenda, and systemic educational reform has been a continuous process that underlined the development of Chinese education in the last three decades.

Educational reform for "quality education" was initiated toward the end of the twentieth century. Full-scale curriculum reform was implemented only a few years later. Among the stakeholders of Chinese schooling, the teachers have felt the brunt of educational change most strongly because they were frontline workers who have to satisfy myriad demands of reform imposed top-down by the state. Reform policies were promulgated frequently by governments on the national, provincial, municipal, and county levels. Operational mechanisms that were installed to ensure their conformity became more purposeful and sophisticated. Scrutiny of their work was made more intense by the commonly shared expectation that teachers were supposed to support if not spearhead the reform endeavors. As their schools tried to keep pace with the rapid changes that enveloped the education system, stress caused by additional work and professional dilemmas was prevalent among the teaching staff of many schools.

This article is an analytical essay on the impact of reform policies on the work and professionalism of teachers in the Chinese Mainland. It attempts to address three questions:

1. What kinds of impact do reform policies have on schooling and teachers in the two schools?

2. How do reform policies, including quality assurance measures, affect the schools and teachers?
3. Why is it difficult for teachers in the two schools to transcend conventional practices and embrace the new approaches that are propagated by reform policies?

The discussion in this paper employs data collected mainly from Shanghai. The main interests embedded in the data are on two aspects of teacher development: teachers' work and professionalism, and teacher education and development. Recent field work in Shanghai yields insights into teachers' response to school and teacher evaluation. Analyses of data are based on information collected through qualitative research that combines the strengths of documentation research, interviews with teachers and principals in Chinese schools.

The focus of this article is on the dilemmas of Chinese teachers who attempt to facilitate the implementation of state reform policies as well as to ensure upward mobility of their students through academic achievement. It is divided into five sections. The first section explores the Chinese conception of teacher professionalism and its relations to teachers' work in the Chinese Mainland while delineating its difference from the western conception. The second section describes important educational reform policies that have direct impact on teachers' work. The third section explains the research method. The fourth section discusses the impact on reform policies on teachers' work and the dilemmas that teachers faced in carrying out their duties. The final section consists of concluding remarks that illuminate the limitations of systemic reform policies and the fragility of teacher professionalism.

Teachers' professionalism and work

In western literature, a broad interpretation of teacher professionalism is how stakeholders perceive the meaning of the profession. Research on teacher professionalism in the West since the 1980s has mainly examined the domains of knowledge, responsibility and authority, and autonomy of teachers (for example, Darling-Hammond, 1989; Hargreaves, 1994; Lieberman and Miller, 1999; Helsby, 2000; Furlong, 2001; Day and Sachs, 2004; Evans, 2008). Emphases on these domains suggest an orientation toward expertise, power and obligations of the teaching profession. It is widely assumed that, if teachers possess a strong knowledge base, apply their knowledge effectively in teaching, and exercise their autonomy responsibly on the job, then the stakeholders would accord them the kind of authority necessary for the sustenance and development of their professionalism. One of the main concerns over the development of teacher professionalism is the relationship between the teaching profession and the state. The influence of state policies over teacher professionalism, for example, has drawn increasing scholarly attention (for example, Gray and Whitty, 2010). One of the new trends of state policies is the installation of competitive performativity that involves the use of targets and incentives. Under the above trend, teachers' work is profoundly changed and self-monitoring is put in place under appraisal system, output comparisons, and merit pay (Ball, 2003).

Being a socially constructed concept that varies among different contexts and conditions (Helsby, 2000; Whitty, 2002), teacher professionalism takes on a different meaning in the Chinese context (Lai and Lo, 2007). To the Chinese teachers, knowledge, responsibility and authority are essential components of their professionalism while autonomy is a more confining concept with limited application. Their understanding of professional knowledge is directly related to the subject matters that they teach. The depth and richness of subject knowledge define the level of competence of teachers. Skillful application of rich subject knowledge in the pedagogy affords expertise. Teacher responsibility represents their academic and moral obligations toward their students. To enable students to learn and to perform well academically, and to mold them into persons of good character, are considered the major responsibility of teachers. It is through the application of knowledge and skills, and the demonstration of a strong sense of responsibility that teachers establish their authority among students and colleagues. Their autonomy grows in concert with authority, especially when formal positions of authority are secured. For the ordinary teachers, autonomy is confined to the pedagogy where they can have a certain degree of control over contents and methods. (Lo, 2008: 13).

A major feature of Chinese teacher professionalism is its emphasis on the students. From our interviews with Chinese teachers, we discerned a commonly shared belief that their work could affect the future of their students. Their sense of responsibility toward the students' future was particularly strong in the areas of academic performance and character building. In China, good academic performance is a ticket to upward mobility, and good character ensures harmonious social relations in the family and community. The teachers are aware of their role in preparing their students for the good life, like parents who see it as their duty to do so. Thus, there is an added moral dimension to teachers' work in China. In referring to their students as "children", the Chinese teachers actually take on a parental role in the school setting. That teaching is "work of conscience", as they so frequently surmise, reflects the kind of mindset that characterizes the teaching profession in China.

The moral dimension of teaching is equally emphasized by the state. From laws, regulations, and policies on teachers (PRCSC, 1993; MoE, 2011a, b, c), moral and political rectitude is considered the most important component of teacher professionalism. Morality and political correctness constitute the ethical base of teacher professionalism and are considered as the most essential qualities of the teaching force (Wang and Lo, 2009: 56).

The professional orientation of Chinese teachers that favors academic achievement and character building operates within a system that rewards academic success and social conformity. For all intent and purposes, the state has maintained such orientation through its policies. As academic success is demonstrated by success in public examinations and social conformity is illustrated by students actively participating in activities that enhance harmony (or reduce unrest) in society, the teachers seem willing to perpetuate a schooling tradition that is bookish and authoritarian. Indeed, preparation for tests, examinations, and academic competitions of all kinds seem to have consumed the energies of teachers and students alike. Likewise, training good boys and girls for public recognition is also high on the teachers' education agenda. Through observation of the work of their predecessors and peers, teachers learn the crafts of teaching and contribute to these longstanding practices as we know them now. Thus, when the same party-state that has been maintaining the *status quo* calls for change to their deeply-rooted tradition with novel ideas, the teachers are bewildered by the reform policies (Lo, 2000; Yin and Cao, 2008).

Reform policies

Major educational reform policies have sought have run the gamut from the decentralization of administrative responsibilities (CCP, 1985; PRCSC, 2001) to the proposed establishment of quality standards for schooling; from the reform of national curriculum and teaching (MoE, 2004) to the narrowing of the achievement gap between and within schools (PRCSC, 2006); and from setting up professional standards for teachers (MoE, 2011a; MoE, 2011b; MoE, 2011c) to introducing a performance-based salary structure for them (MoE, 2008).

In the last decade, China's educational policies have consistently reflected a direction toward strategic decentralization in resource allocation and administration, professed equity in the provision of schooling, and relentless pursuit of higher educational standards. A sample of such policies includes: orders to the local governments to plan for a steady increase in funding for education and for teacher salaries (PRCSC, 1993; MoE, 2004); elimination "key schools" as a move to equalize the quality of public schools (PRCSC, 2006); restriction on school choice and encouragement of enrolment in neighborhood schools; and accountability measures for teacher evaluation (MoE, 2008), continuous professional training, and a state-sponsored test for the re-registration of teachers (ZXXJS, 2011).

Recent reform policies indicate that educational quality and professional accountability are the chief concerns of the state. The policies that have the strongest impact on teachers' work are policies for curriculum reform and for performance-based salary reform. Implemented at the advent of the new century, curriculum reform aimed to transform the nature of Chinese schooling at the classroom level (MoE, 2001). The deeply rooted teacher-centered pedagogy was to be modified in favor of a student-centered approach. The importance of public examinations was downplayed, and alternate routes for student mobility were explored and established. Along with these changes, the quality and effectiveness of schools and teachers were to be evaluated systematically.

Reform of the teacher salary structure, introduced in 2009, presented a new way of calculating teacher salaries on the basis of their performance. The aim of this reform endeavor was to institute finer differentiation of salaries among school teachers so as to provide stronger incentives for better performance. Added to the traditional considerations in teacher evaluation – demonstrated competence in teaching, staff seniority, loyalty to school, and diligence at work – were newer criteria such as relations with colleagues and parents, views of colleagues and students, and participation in the schools' research projects and publications (Shen and Sun, 2008; Tian and Zhang, 2004). The results of performance evaluation would affect the salaries of teachers. In the salary reform, teachers would be guaranteed their basic salaries (about 70 percent of full pay), but merit pay (30 percent of full pay) would play an increasingly larger role in determining the real salaries of teachers. The adoption of a performance-based salary was introduced under the principle of accountability. It was a bold move to steer the teaching force toward a meritocratic system that would reward good performance with money. Along with changes in the teacher salary structure, a national standard for entry into the teaching profession and a required re-registration test for serving teachers were instituted in 2011 (ZXXJS, 2011).

With its frequent policy promulgation and swift implementation, educational reform has become an integral part of the teachers' work life. The hierarchical administrative structure of Chinese schooling has made teacher conformity to state and school directives seemed voluntary and natural. The multi-tiered system of policy implementation – with county level governments being responsible for offering basic schooling and for carrying out national, provincial, and metropolitan reform directives – supports a top-down approach that has provided the underlying logic of educational reform in China. Even though such an approach has allowed policy measures to reach the grassroots level quickly, it has also cost educational reform its intended effectiveness.

Research method

This study takes a qualitative research approach based on analysis of data collected by semi-structured, in-depth interviews with staff from a junior secondary school in Shanghai. The fieldwork was carried out in 2012. We employed purposive sampling to ensure collecting in-depth understandings of teacher professionalism under recent educational reforms in an ordinary school context. The sample school is a junior secondary school established in 1996 as a 'key point school"[1] in its local district. Since its establishment, the school has progressively been downgraded to an ordinary school due to its acceptance of students who had lower academic performance from two other schools in the locality. It comprised over 1100 students and 83 teachers divided into 26 classes.

Fifteen informants were selected from school leaders and regular teachers, selection being based on subjects taught and length of service. Within the 15 informants, eight teachers taught the major subjects (English and Mathematics) which received the greatest attention and resources in school. The major subjects stressed conducting formal school based teacher development activities regularly. Four teachers taught political education which was not perceived to be the key subject and did not participate in public examination. Political education teachers mainly relied on informal school based teacher development activities. Three teachers taught Physical Education which was the marginalized subject in school. Informants' length of work included within 5 years, 10–15 years, and over 15 years. As subject taught and length of service affected teachers' status and perceived autonomy, the selection of 15 informants helped to collect different perceptions of teachers with different resources and opportunities. The analysis of qualitative data employed an inductive approach. It aimed at reducing the data into a manageable number of themes that addressed the concerns of the study (Creswell, 2008).

In the meantime, this study is also supplemented by another study which was conducted in one ordinary secondary school in Beijing. The fieldwork was carried out in 2009. In this study, 20 informants included principal, head of academic unit, heads of subject panels, and ordinary teachers have been interviewed. The Beijing study investigated how the educational leaderships affected teacher development. This study mainly helped to understand the educational leaderships on the strategic planning of school development which affected teachers' work substantially.

Impact of policies on teachers' work

The impact of educational policies on teachers' work is clearly discernible in its growing complexity which is illustrated by the changing orientation of classroom teaching. Much of this change has to do with the curriculum reform, introduced in 2001, that attempted to change the pedagogy to suit a more student-centered approach. The schools' ability to follow the direction of reform would be used as a major measure in the evaluation of their quality. Teachers were expected to support the reform efforts and to help their schools to pass the quality inspections. As professionals, they were challenged in at least two ways. Firstly, they had to change their time honored practices in teaching in order to conform to the demands of reform. Secondly, they had to support school strategies so as to satisfy the interests of the assessors.

Teachers confronting curricular change

Curriculum reform required teachers to make pedagogical adjustments to facilitate the all-round development of students. The new curriculum would be based on a synthesis of knowledge to be achieved through an integration of academic subjects. Curricular content would be based on real life situations rather than abstract ideas. The kind of bookish learning for examination preparation would be replaced by a more exploratory approach to teaching and learning, where the pedagogy would be an interactive process that stressed the curiosity and initiative of students (MoE, 2001). "Explorative learning" (for primary students) and "research oriented learning" (for secondary students) were key curricular features designed to allow students to learn through direct participation.[1] In teaching and learning, the role of public examinations would be downplayed.

Teachers' reacted cautiously to the reform directives, even when the state ordered that teaching should be "inspiring, explorative, communicative, and participatory" (Yuan, 2011). Their major concern was losing control of the pedagogy. Given their time-honored tradition in "direct teaching" – direct impartation of knowledge to students – teachers were skeptical of the proposed interactive pedagogy. For a long time, "direct teaching" was commonly accepted by teachers as the most reliable way of ensuring student learning. They were unwilling to face uncertainties in their classrooms, for there was no guarantee that a more flexible, learner-centered approach to teaching would lead to higher academic performance. In the absence of convincing evidence to support the effectiveness of the new approach, the teachers were hesitant to shift from the pedagogical center. As one teacher points out, the tradition of "direct teaching" is valuable and should be preserved:

> I think traditional teaching . . . is like a very precious porcelain vase . . . this stage of curriculum reform is like breaking this precious vase into pieces and leave it to the students to glue it back together in order to create a new thing. Actually it's not worth a cent.
>
> (Interview, Shanghai, 2012: KM22-TL)

In the educational reality of China, "direct teaching" is considered to be a dependable approach to enhance students' opportunity for upward mobility through examinations. Preparing their students for public examinations through "direct teaching" has always been one of the teachers' main duties. Without a dependable replacement, alteration of "direct teaching" means risking their students' future by venturing into some unknown territories where the influence of examinations would be less discernible, and where the standards of student achievement would become more nebulous.

The role of examination preparation is the thorniest issue in curriculum reform. While few teachers can argue against reform policies that aim to free students from the bondage of examinations and to let them learn actively and creatively, their major concern is that less attention to examination preparation will lead to poorer results which will in turn undermine the students' opportunity for upward mobility. As professionals engaged in "work of conscience", teachers will earnestly try to prepare their students for public examinations, for their students' future will be determined by the outcomes of these examinations:

> I feel that being a teacher is a responsibility, doing work of conscience . . . In the senior school entrance exams, if you score a couple of marks less in math, it may affect your chance in further study and your future direction [of development]. Also when the time comes [for exam], there are so many students, and their quality varies so much. Some of them feel that they cannot keep up in class, and you have to spend more time with them and offer supplementary lessons. This kind of thing is endless, really endless.
>
> (Interview, Shanghai, 2012: AF12-MH)

Responsibility and integrity aside, another reason for the teachers' reluctance to divert their attention from examination preparation is that their schools, despite their supportive rhetoric for curriculum reform, would take the results of examinations as a major indicator in the assessment of teachers. Such assessment places great importance on students' learning outcome, which is invariably translated into examination results. Thus student examination results in the subjects that they teach becomes the determining indicator of the teachers' performance. In preparing students for examinations, teachers are under pressure to achieve passing rates set by their schools as well as to help the schools achieve "exemplary school passing rates" established by the local authorities:

> As a class teacher, of course I want them all to do well in examinations . . . The school also has its requirements in this regard, for instance, the passing rate should be such and such. Of course I'll try to my best to get a hundred percent [passing rate]. There's also the exemplary rate. I look at it this way: even if I can't contribute a lot, at least I won't drag the school's leg . . . For instance, if in my class, there is not even one student who can get into a key school on the city level or district level through examination, I would definitely feel the pressure.
>
> (Interview Shanghai, 2012: BM10-HB)

The teachers see an intimate link between the overall performance of their schools and their own performance. Some of them may even put the interests of schools ahead of their own interests:

> I have to care about the overall development of the school . . . If I work very hard [teaching] my own subject, but the overall standard of the school is deteriorating, I feel that my hard work won't have any effects. So I worry about the whole before I worry about myself.
>
> (Interview, Beijing, 2009: LA1B2009CT)

The pressure on Chinese teachers to drive their students to achieve established passing rates intensifies when their performance is now linked to salary. In a context of performativity where both teachers and schools are under pressure to achieve goals set by the state in order to qualify for better pay and more resources, the teachers seem willing to work harder to enhance the status of their schools because their own status and benefits are dependent on the overall performance of the schools:

> People judge the quality of a school by its standing in the middle and senior secondary examinations. If your school is very active in research related to teaching, but only average in teaching, no one will say your school is good. In the hearts of the people, a good school is one with high promotion rates and high exemplary rates. It's that simple . . . Why do you think leaders in

the district send their own children and their relatives' children to high ranking schools and not to those with strong research capacity?

(Interview Shanghai, 2012: WM12-TA)

School evaluation and change in teachers' work

The teachers' preoccupation with the standing of their schools reflects a substantive change in the managerial interests of school leaders who are also under pressure to perform. School evaluation was introduced at the turn of the century to assess the capacity of the schools in terms of the quality of their leadership, management, and teaching and research (Lo et al., 2011: 23). Initially designed as a self-evaluative exercise to scrutinize the conformity of schools to reform measures, school evaluation has become an elaborate undertaking that details the schools' academic and social achievements. For ambitious school leaders who aspire to higher status for their schools, such as becoming "exemplary schools" (formerly key schools), school evaluation warrants the mobilization of teachers to push the students to perform well in public examinations and interschool competitions so that exemplary merits could be earned for advancement to the pinnacle of the school system.[2]

For principals of ordinary schools, school evaluation means satisfying the quota for passing rates in public examinations and for promotion rates to the next level of schooling. Neither quota is explicitly set, for the central government has forbidden local authorities to pressure schools to pursue rigidly determined passing rates. Nevertheless, school leaders do recognize the expectations of local officials and would strive to achieve respectable passing rates for their schools in order to secure resources. For school evaluation, comprehensive inspection does not occur frequently; but quasi-official inspectors (known as "teaching-research officers") pay regularly visits to the schools.

On the whole, school evaluation taxes the energy of principals and teachers alike, not so much as a labor-intensive assessment exercise that lasts a few days but as an ongoing process of preparation for readiness. Preparatory work includes achieving the necessary passing rates and exemplary rates, but there is much more work to be done because the scope of school evaluation has reached beyond student academic achievement. Teacher performance in classroom teaching, results of student participation in competitions of all kinds, and even the general conduct of students would be taken into consideration in school evaluation. Additionally, the exceptional strengths of schools will play an important role in assessment, especially if the principals aspire to higher status for their schools. Under the influence of policies that encourage overt display of achievements, most school leaders in China are searching for an angle to demonstrate the "unique" strengths of their schools in an assessment system that embodies layers of official recognition, from the school district level to the national level.[3] The emergence of "safety schools", "green schools", and designated "bases" (*jidi*) for patriotic education and for good student conduct, to name just a few, are phenomena that attest to the spirit of performativity that prevails over schooling.

In order to distinguish themselves from others, schools are looking for ways to develop their unique strengths. While this kind of pursuits can be attributed to school evaluation, the schools' enthusiasm is also driven by the growing competition among schools to attract students. Lower birth rates have caused shrinkage in the school-age population, and schools with insufficient enrollment will be closed and merged. Even with policies forbidding publicly funded schools to select students for enrollment, those students with desirable backgrounds are always preferred by the schools (Lo and Dong, 2009). The schools' continual efforts to develop and propagate their unique areas of strength, such as academic, cultural and sport activities, are aimed to attract the enrollment of children from affluent families. "Schools of chess", "schools of international learning", and "schools of sports", to name just a few of this kind of schools, have sprouted in the landscape of Chinese schooling. The schools substantiate their declared areas of strength with accomplishments big and small, and they will be inspected regularly for their performance in the specialized areas.

That a school should have its unique strengths is very much on the mind of school principals who see school evaluation as a window of opportunity for their schools to win recognition. The ideas of school leaders, a critical mass of teachers in the specialized areas that need to be developed, and the right social connections with persons who can facilitate favorable consideration of their achievements for official recognition are some of the factors that contribute the birth and development of a specialized area. Regarding the development of the "unique" strengths for his school, a secondary school principal shares his insights:

> For the development of the school, it definitely needs to have some special characteristics. How can it develop without special characteristics, right? I can tell now that this unique strength is sports. Our physical education group is pretty good in the district. There is no lack of teachers; they are mostly middle-age. Also the group leader is a "backbone teacher"[4] in the district. Whenever the district has a big event, he'll be their commander. So the teaching force is good, and they have a lot of ideas . . . There aren't a lot of schools in Beijing doing this, and it's the same in the Eastern District [of Beijing] . . . So I thought we could develop sports as our special characteristics. We can use this to make it big, and then we could apply for a sport club. Now that [the sport club] has been approved, and we are the only one in the Eastern District that was approved, the students are very happy. I would surely follow through with the planning. For example I would say that we have so and so working in the Sports Bureau. I might not go [to these people] myself, but I'd ask the deputy principal or the group leader to go and search for social connections.
>
> (Interview, Beijing, 2009: LAIBJ2009SP)

As school principals and teachers alike are caught in the maze of competition and status enhancement, school evaluation itself seems to have lost some of its original vigor. At its initial stage of implementation, teachers have found the quality assurance inspection to be useful because they could learn from the feedback provided by the inspectors. However when observation of classroom teaching is replaced by the submission of reports and documents, certain teachers find that the overemphasis on documentation and the deterioration of the quality of inspectors has put the efficacy of school evaluation in doubt:

> But [school evaluation] has deviated from its course. It's all about taking care of documents now. Producing documents and submitting documents. It was one hundred percent classroom observation of teaching in the days of quality education inspection. Now documents are more important than the practice of education and teaching. They only look at documents. The quality of inspectors also has an impact. Those who just sit in their offices can't understand educational practice. They are not people like us who really practice. Now there's a huge amount of materials to be inspected. It's wasting time, wasting paper, and not environmental.
>
> (Interview, Shanghai, 2012: ND-CF27-PH)

Teacher evaluation and teachers' work

The changing course of school evaluation also affects the orientation of teacher evaluation which used to be a regular administrative exercise that entailed mainly the examination of work reports submitted by individual teachers. A more comprehensive effort to reform teacher evaluation was initiated in 2002 to enrich the criteria of assessment by establishing four dimensions for the evaluation: "professional morality, understanding of and respect for students, pedagogical design and application, and exchange and reflection" (MoE, 2002). A noteworthy feature of the reform policy is that it explicitly forbids "using student examination results as the sole assessment measure of teacher performance" (Hao and Wen, 2005). Since the introduction of reform, a variety of measures have been introduced to define the requirements of teacher professionalism and to enhance the performance of teachers. Some of these measures can be seen as ways to compel teachers to improve their quality, such as the requirements for mandatory continuous training and re-registration tests, while other measures use material incentives to encourage teachers to perform better by linking salaries to their performance.

In 2011, the state promulgated professional standards for secondary, primary, and preschool teachers (MoE, 2011a, b, c). The professional standards are represented by 61 indicators that are listed under three dimensions: "professional conception and teacher morality", "professional knowledge", and "professional competence". In line with the spirit of earlier policy documents on teachers, the moral aptitude of teachers is given prominence in this official articulation of teacher professionalism. Other emphases – the central place of students in education, the importance of practical competence and the expectation of life-long learning – signal a significant departure from the traditional interpretation of teacher professionalism and reflect an understanding that is more in line the assumptions of teacher professionalism that are commonly found in "advanced industrialized countries" in the West. Whether the promulgation of the teacher professional standards, which form the basis for further refinement of teacher evaluation, would alter the conception and practice of the teachers depends on how these standards could be put into practice during policy implementation. The teachers' reception of the policies that harbingered the promulgation of professional standards suggests that the tasks of transforming cardinal principles into reality will be arduous.

When the "performance-based teacher salary reform" was introduced in 2008 (MoE, 2008), speculations abound as to how the principles of "more work, more pay" and "good performance, good pay", both key features of the new policy, could be implemented effectively. Another new policy introduced in 2011 that required teachers to take a test every five years for re-registration was met with skepticism over the soundness of testing teachers for a variety of proficiencies, such as the ability to conduct school-based research and information technology proficiency, that could only represent a very partial view of teaching (for example, Peng and Li, 2011).

State policies notwithstanding, nagging problems in teacher evaluation persist within the schools. These problems include: the criteria used to assess teacher performance, the appropriate parties to conduct the assessment, and the consequences of assessment. These problems challenged the professional aptitude of the school administrators as well as their sense of equity and fairness in conducting the assessment exercise. To begin with, the diversification of assessment criteria leads to the inclusion of indicators that are hard to measure, thus making accurate assessment difficult to achieve. Moreover, the role of school administrators in teacher assessment is suspect because of potential conflict of interests, particularly when the salaries of administrators, like that of the teachers, are linked to their performance. Furthermore, the lack of procedural clarity in processing the outcome of assessment, such as possible rewards and penalties, casts doubt on the effectiveness of assessment.

Since its introduction in the 1960s and institutionalization in the 1980s, teacher evaluation was considered a matter of formality by the teachers, a kind of window dressing for accountability that legitimized the schools' decisions in hiring, selection, promotion, and salary increases (Shen and Sun, 2008). The teachers' moral aptitude, together with their devotion to teaching, is used nebulously to augment the application of student academic achievement (examination results) as the singularly important assessment criterion. Teachers' performance in teaching and learning is normally determined by the examination results of the subjects that they taught. Examination results have a tenacious grip on teaching, bounding teachers' work to the institution of examinations and deciding their future prospects in the process. The problem was so pervasive that the state had to intervene and forbade the use of examination results as the sole criterion in the assessment of teacher performance. The official guideline was issued ten years ago. The problem, however, has persisted to this day.

The continual reliance on examination results in teacher evaluation reflects the poverty of assessment criteria and tools. Teacher evaluation in China is mainly a "normative" rather than "formative" exercise. The purpose of evaluation is to see whether teacher performance conforms to certain standards, with much less attention given to help teachers improve. For the parties involved in assessment, the most important aspect of teacher evaluation seems to be identifying an approach that is acceptable to the stakeholders. Unable to loosen the bondage of examinations, teacher evaluation in some schools has moved away from the assessment of individual teachers and adopted an approach that "bundled" examination results of a whole class-level as a reference for teacher evaluation. In doing so, student examination results in various subjects would be taken as a composite score for teachers who are involved in the teaching of different classes on the same class-level. The improvement of student examination results would mean enhanced performance for the teachers concerned. The purpose of this kind of administrative maneuvers is to encourage cooperation among teachers of different subjects because the "bundled" approach encourages individual teachers to take a holistic view of examination results for their own benefits. However, such "innovative" approach continues to operate within the confines of examinations; and competition between teachers of different subjects is now transferred to the teachers of the same subject teaching at different class-levels.

As the debates surrounding the new policies have demonstrated, thorny methodological problems that are inherent in assessment of this kind have undermined its efficacy from the start. That many of the proposed performance indicators simply defy quantification is widely shared by teachers. One teacher puts the treatment of these indicators in a real assessment situation in his school:

> And then there are some [assessment] items that are subjective, not very objective, and hard to put a value on them. So the points given depend on how you feel. [The assessor] asks you, "You love your work?" Of course I love my work. And I get full marks for that. No one would give himself a zero, right? [Then the assessor asks] "Have you used corporal punishment on your students?" [The question is] "Have I?" I haven't, so I get full marks for that. So for this kind of thing . . . things in teaching are impossible to measure by things with absolute [values]. Unless in the end it's [the students'] grades. Now that's the ultimate way and method [for assessment].
>
> (Interview, Shanghai, 2012: GF19-MLB)

As for the appropriate parties to conduct teacher evaluation, the principals and their deputies are in charge of the assessment of teachers (Tian and Zhang, 2004). Annual assessment of teachers is performed by the "middle management" staff. These persons are administrators (including some teachers) who serve under the principals in a variety of capacities, including the heads of "academic affairs units" and "teaching and research units" (see school administrative structure in Hu and Liu, 2012). In schools where teacher evaluation is more formalized, an "evaluation leadership group" is established for the purpose of teacher evaluation.

Depending on the administration of individual schools, teacher evaluation can range from a bureaucratic routine to individual consultative sessions with school administrators (which are reserved for failing teachers). For assessment, teachers review their own work within their own functional groups, such as academic subject panels and class-level panels (*nianji zu*), and submit their self-evaluation:

> It's self-evaluation within the [functional] groups. It's like you put down what you've done this semester or this year, convert them into marks, and submit [the report] yourself. Then someone up there will take what you've submitted, and then work in the information that the school has about you, including the students' evaluation of you, and synthesize.
>
> (Interview, Shanghai, 2012: KM22-TL)

Certain teachers seem to view the annual assessment casually:

> Annual assessment . . . this sort of thing involves writing about small matters, and the leaders take a look at them, and that's it. This is to say, in an education unit like ours, usually, you just need to pass the annual assessment and that's okay.
>
> (Interview, Shanghai, 2012, WM12-TA)

In the past, doubts about the role of administrators being the sole assessors in teacher evaluation have been expressed. As it is normal for teachers to serve in administrative positions concurrently, the question of conflict of interests naturally arises. The problem was made more transparent when the lop-sided distribution of rewards in favor of teachers and administrators in key positions emerged in the initial implementation of the performance-based salary reform. In a Shanghai middle school, for example, the range of salary subsidies for school-level administrators is 200 percent to 500 percent higher than that for ordinary teachers.[5] While merit pay constitutes about 30 percent of teacher salaries, the salary discrepancies are clearly discernible and disruptive to staff morale. The fact that ordinary teachers have to shoulder the heaviest workload and yet receive the lowest salary subsidies has caused them to wonder about the principle of "more work, more pay". The inequitable distribution of salary subsidies serves to demonstrate the incapability of school management to deal with reform of this kind. To alleviate this problem, other support measures need to be in place to make the present reform endeavor effective.

A systemic measure to enrich the composition of assessors in teacher evaluation was introduced together with the performance-based teacher salary reform in order to enhance its efficacy. At the state's behest, teacher evaluation would take into consideration the opinions of students and parents (MoE, 2008). The diversification of the pool of assessors seems to make sense on the policymaking level: if the role of school administrators as colleague, judge and executor of performance evaluation is problematic, then add other important stakeholders to enrich the representation of assessors. Thus far, the inclusion of students and parents as assessors has not been met with teacher opposition. Perhaps this is because the expectations of students and parents are congruent with the teachers' intent, which is, to foster the upward mobility of students through academic pursuits. From the teachers' perspective, the students and parents are more detached from salary matters and their opinions are mainly used as supplementary information in teacher evaluation (Chen, 2011).

Diversification of representation in assessment may diffuse criticisms against the role of school administrators as sole assessors, but it can hardly solve the deeply-rooted problem of unequal treatment of teachers and administrators in the calculation of salaries. Within the schools, teachers' adherence to hierarchy and their understanding of power relations in the school organization lead them to be more tolerant of unequal treatment of colleagues of different ranks. As far as the performance-based salary reform is concerned, they do not seem to expect that the new policies would bring any substantial benefits to their income:

> Merit pay, to be frank, is changing the label but not changing the substance. That is to say, the teachers' salaries haven't increased, that's it. There are teachers who even get less pay . . . it's only a change in ways [of paying salaries] . . . There's only one cake here. [If the school] usually pay out more, you won't have any left at the end of the year. [If the school] saves a little each month, then there's still a little cake left for everyone to share at the end of the year. No matter what, there's only that much money to pay out.
>
> (Interview, Shanghai, 2012: WM12-TA)

At its initial stage of implementation, the ambiguous effectiveness of the performance-based salary reform leads to a larger concern over the handling of teacher evaluation results and even the effectiveness of teacher evaluation itself. Official claims that the reform will provide incentives for better teacher performance require the support of strong evidence that can be gathered only through longitudinal research. In the short run, the questions whether the assessment results will be used in the schools' personnel decisions and how they will facilitate the teachers' further development need to be addressed so as to justify the continual implementation of salary reform.

Regarding the use of assessment results, there are tangible benefits given to those teachers who receive favorable evaluation. These benefits include: slightly higher salaries; opportunities to participate in high level professional training and research; and better promotional prospects. Taken as a whole, the rewards afford opportunities for career advancement which may include access to leadership positions of the schools.

For those teachers whose performance is consistently judged to be poor, there will be certain penalties: less merit payment; less opportunity for career advancement, no chance for recognition of their work, and loss of face in the eyes of colleagues. Whereas teachers with poor assessment results will be censored by the school leadership in different ways, such as in private consultation sessions and staff meetings (usually being referred to anonymously by principals), firing of teachers is the most uncommon practice in China's school system. Once hired, the teachers can assume that they will work in the schools that employ them until retirement. A derogatory portrayal of the teachers' employment situation is that they "can come in but won't go out", and that their "positions can only go up but not come down". It has been argued that such a situation can only breed complacency because there is no pressure on teachers to improve when they can hold on to their "iron rice bowls" without any fear of losing their jobs.

In order to weed out the "failing" teachers, another remedial measure was introduced in 2011 to require teachers to prove their competence in state-sponsored tests every five years in order to qualify for re-registration. The purpose of the new initiative is clearly to carve an exit for incompetent teachers while safeguarding certain standards of professional competence as defined by the state. In defense of the new policy, the state downplays the severity of its implications and stresses the importance of ensuring the quality of the teaching force.

As skepticism and misgivings surrounding the debate on testing teachers for re-registration continue to whirl, pressing issues of teacher professionalism and their work remain to challenge policymakers to dig deeper into their chests of wisdom for more timely solutions that are relevant to the reality of teaching in China.

Concluding remarks

The impact of reform policies on teachers' work, which cumulates to the performance-based salary reform, has created dilemmas for the teachers. In their attempt to accommodate the reform initiatives, Chinese teachers struggle alongside the leaders of their schools to satisfy official demands and to make sense of the changes that the state has mandated. Calls for accountability and quality assurance in education have led to system-wide endeavors that integrated school and teacher evaluation into the school system. These initiatives fueled the anxiety of school principals and teachers who searched for ways to meet the challenges of reform, on the one hand, and to look for opportunities to get ahead, on the other.

From the foregoing discussion, several observations on the impact of reform policies on teachers' work can be made. The following concluding remarks include observations on: the dilemmas of teachers in the face of profound change; the teachers' perception of their performance in relations with the status of their schools; the conceptual confusion arising from the application of "accountability" in education; the fragility of teacher professionalism; and the limitations of systemic reform policies imposed top-down by the state.

The first observation is that reform policies have created serious educational problems which cannot be solved by the teachers alone. The teachers reacted cautiously to reform measures not because they were unwilling to work harder for change but because they encountered difficulties in trying to balance the competing demands that converged on them at different levels of schooling. The reform policies produced contradictory purposes for teacher's work while we looked at the implementation process in different levels. The central government wanted the teachers to adopt a more progressive approach to teaching by introducing novel educational ideas and practices. The local governments wanted them to maintain high achievement standards by putting pressure on the schools. The principals wanted their teachers to do both so that state demands could be satisfied. As competing demands trickle down to the classroom level, the teachers had to adjust their conception of teaching and to re-examine the approach of their work. Such adjustment was not simply operational for it entailed a profound change in the teachers' educational outlook and practices. Indeed, educational practices that were once deemed to be acceptable can no longer suffice current reform requirements. Teachers' anxiety over changes brought on by reform stems from the incongruence between their professional outlook, which is intimately linked to student academic achievement, and the dictates of reform measures, which seek to broaden the conception of education to other areas of human development. In the face of state policies that demand change in the way that they interpret the curriculum and conduct their teaching, the teachers have few tactics to navigate the torrents of change.

Secondly, the teachers' reluctance to change is closely related to their perception of how the quality of their work will affect the status of their schools. Chinese teachers take the status of their schools seriously because it reflects on the quality of their work. School evaluation, which is the most high stake quality assurance measure, is an exercise that requires school leaders to demonstrate the achievements of their schools while proving that they have satisfied the competing demands from various levels of the state. Thus high academic achievements and all-round development of students are both required as evidence to support positive school evaluation. The school evaluation exercise presents threats and opportunities to school leaders who either see it as a trial of the weaknesses of their schools or a commemoration of their accomplishments. It is the labor of the teachers to present their schools in a positive light, for they are fully aware that school evaluation is in fact an examination of the quality of their work. It is considered as a judgment that affects their reputation.

Thirdly, the dilemmas that confront teachers in the reform process are caused by conceptual confusion regarding "accountability" and the misalignment of state and school expectations. In their work, teachers seldom have a chance to explore the question "What is accountability?" This is because a related question, "Accountable to whom?" has yet to be openly debated properly. Teachers work to satisfy different sets of expectations that are generated by the state, schools, students, and parents (Lo et al., 2011: 21). The teacher evaluation system, which is established to ensure their compliance with state directives, functions as a mechanism of state administration but is operated within the schools by the principals who have their own developmental agenda and preferences. For teacher evaluation, the state's expectation is that teachers will be assessed by their ability to facilitate "quality education"; but the expectation of school leaders is that teachers should enable their students to pursue academic excellence and good examination results. When there is a misalignment between state and school expectations, teachers are faced with the difficult task of trying to satisfy both. Yet there exists the difficulties for teachers to transcend conventional practices and embrace the new approaches that are propagated by reform policies. As teachers in the two schools are fully aware, they are ultimately accountable to their students. However, it appears that factors such as external interference, hierarchical school organization, well-defined power structure in schools have made the answers to "What is accountability?" and "Accountable to whom?" much less definite.

Fourthly, the acquiescence of Chinese teachers can be attributed to the absence of a professionalization endeavor that has yet to begin (Lai and Lo, 2007). If the teachers seem passive in their response to state-directed reform initiatives, it is because they lack a cohesive voice that can be heard through an effective body of representation. Their silence on critical issues in curriculum reform, such as the need for clarification of "student-centered pedagogy" for all-round development, is an indication of unwarranted passivity. The lack of critical response to teacher evaluation being a simple normative exercise is a sign of professional unawareness. The perceived fearfulness of teachers epitomizes the current state of teacher professionalism in China and depicts its tentative development under tightly organized state control. The dominance of the state over the teachers has allowed for swift policy implementation; but it has also impeded the development of a truly autonomous profession. Therefore, it limits the possibility of establishing a professional association and there is no authentic teacher union that fights for teachers' professional authority and autonomy. In its fragile state, the teaching profession in China has very limited space for development. Yet the teachers find ways to uphold their beliefs while fulfilling their duties. Rather than fighting a battle against state encroachment of their professionalism, the teachers seem able to focus on the purpose of their work, which is on the academic achievement and character development of their students. To be sure, there is a discernible erosion of professional dedication among teachers who have become weary of the relentless demands on them. However, the dictum that teaching is "work of conscience" is still widely shared, and the hope to help students strive for greater achievement is still preserved. It is clear that teachers care a lot about their students, for they have frequently pointed out that the students' future was the core purpose of their work. It is therefore ironic that teachers have experienced such hardship in implementing reform policies that promise a brighter future for their students, and for the nation.

Finally, the trying experience of Chinese teachers and schools in policy implementation exemplifies the limitations of systemic state policies in solving educational problems which are indigenous to the schools. In adopting quality assurance as the guiding principle for the evaluation of schools and teachers, policymakers have apparently neglected to forge an understanding among stakeholders on the concepts of "quality" and "quality education." They have also overlooked important issues surrounding the application of these concepts in policy implementation. The assumption that the directives of the central government can be applied across the nation is flawed with wishful thinking; and the expectation that local governments and schools would loyally implement centrally formulated policies is unrealistic. In the school system of China where disparity and diversity are the norm rather than exception, the efficacy of centrally formulated policy is often cast in doubt. It is because the state's top-down approach to implementation defies the logic of authentic educational change which invariably takes place in the schools and classrooms.

Notes

1 During their 12 years of schooling, "activities for integrated practice" will be made compulsory for all students. The scope of this curricular component embodies a broad range of activities related to "information technology education, research oriented learning, community service and social practice, and labor and technical education" (MoE, 2001).

2 To accomplish this feat, school principals and teachers have to work to satisfy a myriad of school quality requirements. For instance, schools in the province of Guangdong which aspire to become exemplary schools would be inspected in accordance to with 77 indicators. (Lo et al., 2011: 23).

3 The schools can accumulate points gained from the "single item" assessment of their demonstrable strengths. These points are in turn used in their general assessment. Differentiation of the achievements of schools is set in a system that ranks schools by the number of stars that signify their quality. Such differentiation is further refined by the inclusion of "single item" achievements of the schools. Thus a two-star school may have a three-star status in a certain area of work, such as being a "green school" or a "safety school" (Interview, Shanghai, 2012: AF12-MH).

4 "Backbone teacher" is an officially approved title denoting sustained accomplishments.

5 The "ordinary teachers" being referred to are those teachers with functional positions in the school. Compared to the school-level administrators, they receive considerably less salary subsidies. These teachers include class-teachers (<220%), head of class-level panel (<400%), head of teaching and research unit (<500%) (Interviews, Shanghai, 2012, *passim*). For those teachers who have no administrative duties, the discrepancies are even larger. Given the fact that teacher salaries in the Chinese Mainland are not high, and that such merit pay constitutes no more than 30 percent of teacher salaries, the discrepancies are nonetheless significant and annoying to the teachers.

References

Ball, S. J. (2003). The teacher's soul and the terrors of performativity. *Journal of Education Policy*, 18(2), 215–228.

CCP (Chinese Communist Party). (1985). Zhonggong zhongyang guanyu jiaoyu tizhi gaige de jueding ['Resolutions of the Central Committee of the Chinese Communist Party to reform the educational system']. Beijing: author.

Chen, Z.H. (2011). Jinnianlai jiaoshi pingji ruogan biange pingxi ['Analysis of certain changes in teacher evaluation in recent years'], *Zhongguo gaodeng jiaoyu pinggu* ['*China Higher Education Assessment*'], 4, 42–46.

Creswell, W. J. (2008). *Educational Research: Planning, Conducting, and Evaluation Quantitative and Quantitative Research*. New York: prentice Hall.

Darling-Hammond, L. (1989). Teacher professionalism and accountability. *The Education Digest*, 55(1), 15–19.

Day, C. and Sachs, J. (2004). Professionalism, performativity and empowerment: Discourses in the politics, policies and purposes of continuing professional development. In C. Day and J. Sachs (Eds) *International Handbook in the Continuing Development of Teachers.* Maidenhead: Open University.

Evans, L. (2008). Professionalism, professionality and the development of education professionals. *British Journal of Educational Studies*, 56(1), 20–38.

Furlong, J. (2001). Reforming teacher education, re-forming teachers: accountability, professionalism and competence. In R. Philip and J. Furlong (Eds) *Education Reform and the State: Twenty-five Years of Politics, Policy and Practice.* London: Routledge Falmer, 118–136.

Gray, S. L., and Whitty, G. (2010). Social trajectories or disrupted identities? Changing and competing models of teacher professionalism under New Labor. *Cambridge Journal of Education*, 40(1), 5–23.

Hao, D. K., and Wen, J. L. (2005). Zhongxiaoxue jiaoshi pingjia xianzhuang de gean diaocha – cong cujin jiaoshi zhuanye fazhan de jiaodu ['Case study on the current situation in the evaluation of secondary and primary teachers – From a perspective that promotes teacher professional development'], *Jiaoshe jiaoyu yanjiu* [*'Teacher Education Research'*], 5, 49–53.

Hargreaves, D. (1994). The new professionalism: the synthesis of professional and institutional development. *Teaching and Teacher Education*, 10(4), 423–438.

Helsby, G. (2000). Multiple truths and contested realities: the changing faces of teacher professionalism in England. In C. Day, A. Fernandez, E. T. Hauge and J. Moller (Eds) *The Life and Work of Teachers: International Perspectives in Changing Times.* London: Falmer Press, 93–108.

Hu, H. M., and Liu, Q. Y. (2012). Woguo zhongxiaoxue jiaoxue yanjiu zuzhi de fazhan jiqi kunjing ['Development and predicaments of the teaching-research organizations in secondary and primary schools of our country'], *Jiaoyu fazhan yanjiu* [*'Research in Educational Development'*], 2, 1–8.

Lai, M. H. and Lo, L. N. K. (2007). Teacher professionalism in educational reform: the experiences of Hong Kong and Shanghai, *Compare*, 37(1), 53–68.

Lieberman, A. and Miller, L. (1999). *Teachers – Transforming their World and their Work.* New York: Teachers College Press.

Lo, L. N. K. (2000). Educational Reform and Teacher Development in Hong Kong and on the Chinese Mainland, *Prospects*, 30(2), 237–253.

Lo, L. N. K. (2008). Teachers as foot-soldiers serving cultural duties: a reflection on teacher leadership and learning community in Chinese schools. Keynote address at the Second International Education Conference, "Leadership in a Learning Society", co-organized by Beijing Normal University and Institute of Education, University of London, at Beijing Normal University, Beijing, 11–12 November 2008.

Lo, L. N. K. and Dong, H. (2009). Shenshi zhaixiao xianxiang: quanqiu mailuo yu bentu jingyuxia de sisuo ["Examining the phenomena of school selection: pondering global trends and indigenous circumstances"], *Jiaoyu fazhan yanjiu* ["*Research in Educational Development*"], 20, 1–6.

Lo, L. N. K., Lai, M. H. and Chen, S. Y. (2012). Performing to expectations: teachers' dilemmas in East Asia and in Chinese societies. In C. Day (Ed.) *Routledge International Handbook of Teacher and School Development.* Oxon: Routledge, 19–32.

MoE (People's Republic of China, Ministry of Education). (2001). Jichu jiaoyu kecheng gegai de mubiao ["Outline of curriculum reform in basic education"]. Beijing: author.

——. (2002). Jiaoyubu guanyu jiji tuijin zhongxiaoxue pingjia yu kaoshi zhidu gaige de tongzhi ["Circular of the Ministry of Education on actively advancing the reform of secondary and primary school evaluation and the examination system"]. Available at: www.moe.edu.cn/edoas/website18/05/info405.htm.

——. (2004). 2003–2007 nian jiaoyu zhenxing xingdong jihua ["Action plans to vigorously develop education during 2003–2007"]. Beijing: author.

——. (2008). Guangyu zuohao yiwu jiaoyu xuexiao jiaoshi jixao kaohe gongzuo de zhidao yijian ["Guiding opinions on the implementation of the assessment of school teachers' performance for compulsory education"]. Beijing: author.

——. (2011a). Zhongxue jiaoshi zhuanye biaozhun (Shixing) ["Professional standards of secondary school teachers (For trial implementation)"]. Available at: www.moe.gov.cn/public files/business/htmfiles/moe/s6127/201112/127830.html.

——. (2011b). Xiaoxue jiaoshi zhuanye biaozhun (Shixing) ["Professional standards of primary school teachers (For trial implementation)"]. Available at: www.moe.gov.cn/public files/business/htmfiles/moe/s6127/201112/127830.html.

——.(2011c). Youeryuan jiaoshi zhuanye biaozhun (Shixing) ["Professional standards of kindergarten teachers (For trial implementation)"]. Available at: www.moe.gov.cn/public files/business/htmfiles/moe/s6127/201112/127838.html.

Peng, M. and Li, A. M. (2011). Zaizhi laoshi wunian jinxing zhuce kaohe shi jili hashi zengfu? ["Re-registration assessment of practicing teachers every five years: Is it incentive or additional burden?"], *Jiefang Ribao* ["Liberation Daily"], 19 October 2011.

PRCSC [People's Republic of China, State Council]. (1993). *Teachers Law of the People's Republic of China*. Beijing: author.

——. (1993). Zhongguo jiaoyu gaige he fazhan gangyao ["Outline of educational reform and development in China"]. Beijing: author.

——. (2001). Quanguo jiaoyu shiye dishige wunian jihua ["The Tenth Five-year Plan for the education enterprise of the nation"]. Beijing: author.

——. (2006). Zhonghua renmin gongheguo yiwu jiaoyufa ["Law of compulsory education of The People's Republic of China"]. Beijing: author.

Shen, J. L. and Sun, B. H. (2008). Jiaoshe pingjia neirong tixi zhi chongjian ["The reconstruction of the system of teacher evaluation content"], *Huadong shifan daxue xuebao (jiaoyu kexueban)* ["*East China Normal University Journal (Educational Science Edition)*"], 2, 38–43.

Tian, A. L. and Zhang, X. F. (2004). Dui xianxing zhongxiaoxue jiaoshi pingjia zhidu de diaocha yu fenxi ["Survey and analysis of the current evaluation system for secondary and primary school teachers"], *Jiaoyu lilun yu shijian* ["*Educational Theory and Practice*"], 3, 26–30.

Wang, X. L. and Lo, L. N. K. (2009). Qiwangzhong de jiaoshi zhuanyexing: zhengce wenben fenxi de shijiao ["Teacher professionalism in expectation: a perspective based on policy text analysis"], *Jiaoyu fazhan yanjiu* ["*Research in Educational Development*"], 2, 55–58.

Whitty, G. (2002). Re-forming teacher professionalism for new times. In G. Whitty (Ed.) *Making Sense of Educational Policy Studies in the Sociology and Politics of Education*. London: Paul Chapman, 64–78.

Yin, H. B. and Cao, T. S. (2008). Kecheng gaigezhong de jiaoshi shenfen ["Teacher identity in curriculum reform"], *Jiaoyu fazhan Yanjiu* ["*Research in Educational Development*"], 2, 35–40.

Yuan, G. R. (2011). Wuxiang gaige jifa jiaoyu shiye kexue fazhan huoli ["Five reforms to stimulate the scientific development of the education enterprise"]. *Xinhuawang* ["New China Net"]. Available at: www.edu.cn/buzhang_11341/20111229/t20111229_724675.shtml.

ZXXJS (Editorial office of *Secondary and Primary School Teacher Training*). (2011). Jiaoyubu shidian jiaoshi zige zhunru he tuichu jizhi ["Trial mechanisms of the Ministry of Education for entry qualifications and exit of teachers"], *Zhongxiaoxue jiaoshi peixun* ["*Secondary and Primary School Teacher Training*"], 12, 1.

4 The honourable road and its impact on teacher practice

An analysis of China's national honour system in cultivating professional development

Huan Song, *Xudong Zhu* and *Laura B. Liu*

Background

Aristotle, the ancient Greek philosopher, asserted in "Politics" that "justice is honorific. To reason about the telos of a practice – or to argue about it – is, at least in part, to reason or argue about which virtues it should honor and reward" (as cited in Sandel, 2009, p. 186). Aligned with this perspective, discussion of China's teacher honour system and the purpose of this award system entails identifying the professional teacher qualities worthy of being recognised and honoured.

A review of key honorary titles used to describe teachers across international educational systems demonstrates that teaching is recognised publically as a profession in many countries (Mackenzie, 2007). For instance, Carr-Saunders and Wilson (1933) highlighted in *The Professions* that the recognition of the teaching profession in the US dates back to the nineteenth century, when teachers were viewed by many on a parallel plane with pastors. Offering an alternative perspective, Ornstein (1981) concluded that teaching does not reflect the four key attributes of a profession (i.e., a defined body of knowledge; control over licensing standards; autonomy in making professional decisions; and high prestige and economic standing), and is only a quasi-profession.

Murphy (1990) expounded that the institution of a profession entails a legal process that includes formal education, status, and bureaucratic organisations. Research on teaching as a profession demonstrates the development of professional standards and professional licensure institutions as central to analysing the government's influence on the teaching profession (Collins, 1990; Jones and Moore, 1993). Chism (2006) asserted that the main motivation for setting up systems of teacher recognition is that "institutions hope to symbolically acknowledge their support for teaching, to recognize the accomplishments of excellent teachers, and to encourage other faculty to achieve similar levels of performance in teaching" (p. 589). In examining teacher honour selection standards and processes, previous studies have emphasised standards such as teaching strategies, concern for students, and mastery of subject matter (Adams, 1977; Chism, 2006; McNaught and Anwyl, 1993; Svinicki and Menges, 1996; Warren and Plumb, 1999). Others have focused on more implicit criteria that honour candidates adhere to (Donaldson, 1988; Goldsmid, Gruber, and Wilson, 1977). Further research has investigated evidence gathered in appraisal and selection processes (Chism, 2006) and the process of honour endowment on teachers (Dinham and Scott, 2003; Mackenzie, 2007).

In Confucian tradition, with propriety as foundational, respect for teachers and a high value for education is paramount. In cultures infused with this tradition, teachers have been idolised, as articulated in traditional Chinese phrases such as "heaven, earth, sovereign, parent, and teacher" (*tian di jun qin shi*, 天地君亲师). In seeking to maintain this tradition of societal respect for teachers and education amidst China's modern development, the Ministry of Education issued a national policy in 1955 to allow schools and educational organisations at different levels to identify and recommend prominent teachers. This policy ultimately aims to develop a strong professional teaching workforce, and initiated this work by recognising a group of "special-grade teachers" (*teji jiaoshi*, 特级教师) across the country. The positive influence of these *teji jiaoshi* on enhancing the quality of teaching in their local areas (Committee of National People's Congress, 1993) led the government to develop the policy further into the modern teacher honour system today.

The launch of this national policy in China was formally recognised in the Teacher's Law of 1993, and currently entails three levels of teacher commendation: (1) the national level, (2) local levels (provincial/municipal and municipal/district) and (3) the individual school level (see Appendix 1). From the beginning of their careers, teachers are expected to ascend a career development path from first receiving school-level honours, then provincial-level honours, and ultimately national honours. Englund's (1996) research highlights the inherently political nature to the teacher awards in that teachers are rewarded for adhering to policies to reach long-term educational objectives. Considering the extent to which this institutionalised system influences teachers in their professional lives, more studies are needed on China's teacher honour system, including what *teachers* think about the system and its role in maintaining the government's influence and even control over the teaching profession.

In response to the dearth of research on this topic, and the pressing need for greater understanding of the phenomenon of China's teacher honour system – including how this system impacts teachers in China and what teachers think about the system – this study was guided by the following three research questions:

1 What is China's teacher honour system, and what are the views of teachers, administrators, and government officials regarding China's teacher honour system?
2 How does China's teacher honour system impact teachers' professional lives, particularly their professional development?

3 How does the teacher honour system assert governmental influence over the teaching profession, while providing professional development opportunities?

Methodology

This qualitative study (Merriam, 2001) employed grounded theory techniques (Strauss and Corbin, 1998) to build a theoretical conception of China's teacher honour system, as experienced by those most impacted by and involved in it – the teachers and system administrators. A purposive sample of 11 recipients of honorary awards and five non-recipients were selected for the study. Sample selection was based on the recommendation from a key reference group com-missioned to research and improve the honour system by the government. Selection criteria involved finding participants who (i) were teaching at the primary, middle, or high school level; (ii) were key stakeholders as teachers, viceprincipals/principals, or administrative leaders; (iii) were award recipients, non-recipients, or administrative leaders in charge of teacher honour appraisal and awards; and (iv) represented recipients across the four levels in the system (school, municipal, provincial, and national). A total of 16 teacher honour recipients and non-recipients (Table 4.1) were selected in Beijing (northern China), C city of Anhui province (eastern China), and S city of Guangdong province (southern China).

Table 4.1 Participant profiles and participation details (interviews with teachers)

Sample	*16*			
Relationship to awards Recipients	Non-recipients			
	11	5		
Sex	Male	Female		
	6	10		
School level	Primary school Middle school	High school		
	8	4	4	
Experience	<5	5–15	15–25	<25
Years	4	5	5	2
Status	Teacher	Executive[a]	Vice-Principal/ Principal	
	9	5	2	
Highest Honour[b]	National	Provincial	Municipal	School
	2	3	4	2

Notes: [a] Including mid-level cadres of the Dean of Students and teaching and research team leader in the schools.

[b] In general, lower-level honours are prerequisites for higher-level honours; therefore, national-level teacher recipients have generally received provincial, municipal and school-level honours.

Focusing on China's institutionalised teacher honour system as a phenomenon to understand in more depth, this study involved generating and analysing "naturally occurring data to find the sequences ('how') in which participants' meanings ('what') are deployed and thereby establish the character of some phenomenon" (Silverman, 2006, p. 44). This work acknowledges researcher subjectivity, and does not seek to attain an "objective" view on the teacher honour system as a phenomenon (Banks, 1998). To account for this subjectivity, the researchers sought to attain a greater understanding of the honour system's influence from the teacher participants who held an "insider" status (Banks, 1998, p. 6). Ethical considerations were taken into account by using pseudonyms to protect participant anonymity and confidentiality (Merriam, 2001). Further ethical considerations included describing the study's purpose clearly to participants; representing the data as accurately and considerately as possible; and reflecting on how the study may impact participants (Merriam, 2001).

An interview guide was used to conduct semi-structured interviews inviting participants to talk about their (a) general attitudes toward the teacher honour system; (b) experiences of competing for the different honours; (c) views on the role and effectiveness of the system; (d) perceptions of how the honour system affected their professional development and work during and after receiving, or not receiving, an honour; (e) views toward the honour recipients (for non-recipients). Furthermore, four administrative leaders in the Ministry of Education and Beijing Educational Bureau who manage the teacher honour system were interviewed regarding governmental-level intentions and goals in institutionalising the teacher honour system throughout China. Additionally, official documents at different administrative levels related to teacher honour appraisal and selection processes were analysed to ascertain the ultimate aims this system was designed to achieve.

Grounded theory techniques (Strauss and Corbin, 1998) were utilised to analyse transcripts of the interviews and government documents. First, open coding analysis was conducted to classify words or sentences into groups representing a common concept or theme – thereby constructing a new code. Open codes that emerged through this process included: *professional honour*, *teaching expertise honour*, *standard*, *application requirements*, and "*face*", which is a term significant to Confucian culture and discussed further in the findings. In the second stage of our analysis, we carried out axial coding to sort and cluster the data into "discrete categories" based on their "properties and dimensions and then using description to elucidate those categories" (Strauss and Corbin, 1998, p. 19).

As a result of the axial coding process, four main thematic categories emerged from the data: (1) *the aims of the teacher honour system*; (2) *the criteria for the different teacher honours*; (3) *the review process for awarding teacher honours*; and (4) *the impact of the teacher honour system on teachers' professional lives and work.* Teacher professionalism was identified as a core concept under this fourth thematic category. Finally, theoretical coding was conducted to explore possible relationships among the thematic categories identified, particularly regarding the impact of the teacher honour system on Chinese teacher development and identity as professionals. This data analysis process remained true to a grounded theory approach in aiming to "build rather than test theory" (Strauss and Corbin, 1998, p. 13) by exploring the study participants' various perspectives on the phenomenon of the Chinese teacher honour system. This work sought to "identify, develop, and relate" key concepts identified by participants as the "building blocks" of the theoretical conclusions reached (p. 13).

Findings

Teacher honour as a system of academic and pedagogical awards

From the perspective of the interviewed teachers, the honorary titles can be divided into three categories: *teaching expertise* (*yewu*, 业务) *honour*, *political honour*, and *contest honour*. The selection criteria and appraisal processes for the three honours are distinct and each honorary title has a different impact on teacher professionalism.

The first honour is recognition of the teacher's long-term performance and expertise in relation to the excellence in their professional knowledge, capacities and attitude. Teachers who receive this honour at the school, municipal, or provincial level typically receive the title of *backbone teacher* (*gugan jiaoshi*, 骨干教师) or *subject leader* (*xueke daitouren*, 学科带头人). Compared with political or contest honours, the *teaching expertise honour* attaches more importance to long-term documented and quantifiable achievements in the profession. For example, the appraisal and selection conditions of City B's provincial *backbone teacher* include a rigid index requiring recipients of this award to conduct research and win awards for completing empirical research while also completing "municipal-level open classes, research classes or district-level open classes" (D-B-2010).[1] Each year, school-nominated candidates are ranked by a set of quantifiable criteria in the selection process. A female primary school teacher of 18 years' experience with a provincial *teaching expertise* honour confirmed that the *backbone* or *subject leader teacher* title is "endowed to teachers who over time have taken multiple open classes and published a number of research papers" (I-X-LI-20121010).

The second type of honour is the *political honour*. Teachers receive this recognition at the school, municipal (district), or provincial level, and are honoured with the title of *excellent teacher*. While the selection criteria for this honour include pedagogical components – including professional knowledge, skills, and attitude – study participants conclude that the *excellent teacher* recognition is not esteemed as highly as the *backbone teacher*. A male high school teacher of 22 years with the *excellent teacher* title reflected that the *excellent teacher* award is a "*political honour*", while "the highest-level *teaching expertise honour* is the C City *subject leader*" (I-C-QIN-20121004). Compared with *backbone teacher* awards, the appraisal and selection conditions for *excellent teacher* awards are broader and generally do not include a clearly defined set of criteria that are evidenced uniformly. For instance, Beijing's *excellent teacher* appraisal and selection standard includes "having profound academic skills, conscientiously updating knowledge, earnestly accomplishing educational teaching tasks . . . strong professional dedication, and noble teaching ethics" (D-B-2006). While these criteria require high levels of performance on the part of the *excellent teachers*, the evidence for attaining these criteria is not predetermined to the same extent as the *teaching expertise honour*. However, the *teaching expertise honour* and *political honour* are similar in that the appraisal and selection process narrowly limits the number of possible recipients.

The third type of honour is the *contest honour*. Teachers receive this recognition in a variety of contexts, such as the *teacher's basic skills contest*, which recognises a teacher's performance in organising educational and teaching activities, much like an athletic contest. Such contests are similar to the *teaching expertise honour*, in that a panel of judges utilises a clear set of criteria to measure or quantify teachers' professional knowledge, skills, and beliefs. A key distinction in the appraisal and selection process for this honour that sets it apart from the previous two honours is that contest administrators often provide professional development opportunities to prepare teacher "contestants" for the contest.

Teacher honour as professional recognition for individuals and collectives

Teacher participants discussed their participation in the teacher honour system as a process of building professional recognition, both as individual teachers and as professional collectives. For instance, a female primary school teacher of 14 years reflected that her municipal *teaching expertise honour* both confirms and encourages quality in her work as an individual teacher, yet her language suggests pride in her professional collective:

> It strikes me that this title's largest significance to a teacher is a confirmation to my work. Teachers care about it. When you have made a contribution, you are certainly encouraged through the appraisal and selection of this honorary title. This confirmation and encouragement is very important to me.
>
> (I-H-SONG-20121008)

The significance of the honour system's recognition is akin to the honour in other professions of receiving bonuses, additional certifications, or higher positions of management. However, in the teaching profession in China, monetary awards accompanying the honorary titles are low and not the primary source of motivation for professional growth. Rather, the individual and collective honour that comes with the awards is the impetus for continual improvement as a professional – thus, contributing to the professional status of the field overall. A male primary school teacher of eight years' experience and a municipal *contest honour* reflected that his award "would not cost one RMB if purchased from the market. It's just a piece of paper. Nevertheless, it's very precious for recognising teacher performance. You may gain this recognition just once or twice in your lifetime" (I-X-WANG-20121010). The honour is more than material gain.

Consistent with the Confucian concept of *face* (*mianzi*, 面子), the Chinese teacher honour system grants not just an award or piece of paper. This system bestows *dignity* upon an individual or group of practitioners. Conversely, a lack of awards may mean *losing face*, as suggested by a male high school principal with 28 years of teaching experience and a provincial honour: "When your ability is weaker than others, you will lose face . . . an invisible power [of face] is in place" (I-C-FAN-20121004). Building on this reflection, an "invisible power" of both *personal face* and *collective face* is in place, as teacher awards bring honour (while a lack of awards can bring dishonour) to the individual and to the collective subject team, school, or district of which the teacher is a part. This study found that *contest honours* brought recognition, or *face*, in greatest balance to the individual teacher *and* the collective subject team, school, and municipality to which the teacher belongs. A female primary school teacher of 19 years' experience with a municipal honour evidenced in her reflection that typically "the participating teacher is inwardly aggressive and unwilling to bring shame to the school. He/she will do his/her best" (I-X-CAI-20121010). A female primary school vice-principal with 22 years of teaching experience and a national honour similarly noted that in the "mutually beneficial" *contest honour* competitions, "if I win, I will thank my school and the colleagues who helped me" (I-X-GAO-20121010). The mutual benefit of this competition dilutes the personal recognition and expands the communal recognition merited by the teacher awards.

Thus, the type of teacher honour given shapes the significance of the professional recognition. The teacher participants expressed that they most valued the *teaching expertise honours*, followed by *contest honours*, and then *political honours*, due to differences in appraisal and selection standards. The *teaching expertise honours* and the *contest honours* have concrete appraisal criteria that may be evaluated. In contrast, the assessment criteria for the *political honours* are flexible and often shaped year to year by the award recipients. A principal participant illustrated the flexibility of the *political honour* – the *excellent teacher* title – in that one year it was given to a teacher who persisted in this teaching practice despite being ill with cancer. This teacher was selected as provincial-level *excellent teacher*. The principal observed that sometimes, "It's not important whether the candidate's teaching is good or not. The key point is that he still insisted on teaching when he was ill with cancer" (I-C-FAN-20121004).

However, in some cases the criteria for the *excellent teacher* recognition may be based more on political reasons, than on pure evaluation of practitioner ability. Evidencing this notion, a principal participant asserted that if a teacher "has already won a *backbone teacher* title, we will select a non-recipient instead of him/her as the candidate of the *political honour* for balance. So, sometimes, the teacher with the *excellent teacher* honorary title is not the best" (I-C-FAN-20121004). A teacher participant even stated that in contrast to the *backbone teacher*, receiving "the *teaching expertise honour*, there is basically no standard for the honour titles like *excellent teacher*" (I-C-QIN-20121004), making the award more vulnerable to be used for political reasons.

Teacher honour as professional development via internal and external motivation

In addition to bestowing teachers and their practitioner communities with professional recognition, China's teacher honour system provides an avenue for professional development that can benefit individual teachers and their schools, municipal and provincial areas. Teacher participants expressed that the *teaching expertise honour* and *contest honour* most directly promoted their professional development. *Teaching expertise honour* recipients received a predetermined set of professional development opportunities and resources as a benefit from the Educational Bureau. Moreover, honour recipients benefitted from the intrinsic motivation (Ryan & Deci, 2000) to develop their practices further, as a result of the professional recognition system. A female middle school teacher of 17 years' experience with a provincial *teaching expertise honour* asserted that award standards "such as publishing articles, prize-winning theses, and requirements for classroom teaching are useful. It can push you forward. This process encourages and pushes teachers forward" (I-Y-DONG-20121012). Teachers motivated to receive the *teaching expertise* honour will engage in rigorous professional development that involves conducting research and publishing articles with the aim of applying new learning to practice.

In some cases, the teacher honour system cultivates external motivation to avoid the negative reinforcement of not receiving recognition (Ryan & Deci, 2000). One teacher participant reflected on the *loss of face* in being a well-respected teacher who does not receive an honour: "If you are a *backbone teacher* and you are not selected . . . it suggests that you are not good enough. As a result, you should continue your efforts towards this goal. It's like a yoke" (I-X-CAI-20121010). This "yoke" provides a common social pressure found in Confucian cultures, and pushes teachers toward active professional development to improve their practices for recognition.

Preparation for the *contest honour* inherently involves professional development, as it entails conducting a well-planned and rehearsed *demonstration lesson* (*zhanshi ke*, 展示课). Before the contest, every team (subject area group, school, municipal or provincial area) represented by the candidate will organise a training program for the candidate to serve as a rigorous preparation process. The team helps the candidate to model strengths of practice as the "performer" in a show, with the supporting group serving as the scriptwriters and directors. Akin to recipients of the *teaching expertise honour*, recipients of a *contest honour* must demonstrate theoretical knowledge in explaining the theoretical basis for their pedagogical designs in the contest.

One teacher described preparing for the *contest honour* by performing a trial teaching situation followed by lesson discussion on how to improve the lesson to re-teach it for the municipal contest. This teacher shared that after two months of training beyond normal work hours, "we developed our theoretical knowledge or teaching expertise level rapidly because many experts were invited to help us to prepare lessons by hand. Actually, after that, I felt like I had been brainwashed" (I-X-SONG-20121010). At the same time, teacher participants consistently appreciated the process of preparing for the *contest honour* in improving individual and collective practice: "We feel that it's a symbol of a young teacher becoming a mature teacher, so we have deep impressions . . . after you complete this process, it is unforgettable" (I-H-SANG-20121008). Participants viewed the *contest honour* process as effecting deep change in their knowledge, skills, and hearts – thus, serving as a meaningful avenue for moving from one professional development stage to another.

Teacher honour as a challenging case of micro-politics

Along with the noble aims of the national teacher honour system come the challenges of managing inevitable micro-politics throughout the appraisal and selection process, particularly involved in the *political honours.* The first key challenge to address may be described as *symbolic politics.* Currently, the educational and administrative departments at the national and school levels are responsible for bestowing the teacher honours. An insight gleaned from this study is that the honour criteria become more *indistinct* the higher the level granting the award.

Evidencing this finding, a leader of the Ministry of Education reflected that when selecting recipients of national-level honours, "it is impossible to evaluate each candidate. It's hard to say who is better and who is worse. So, the standard is very vague. In fact, we don't care who the winner is, the key is that our country is doing it, indicating its appreciation and respect of teachers" (I-MOE-LONG-20120918). Thus, awarding teachers at a national level is more of a symbolic practice intended to appreciate teachers as a collective and professionalise the field as a whole. National honours acknowledge the efforts of all Chinese teachers, and the recipients serve as professional symbols representing the field as a collective. Developing detailed evaluation criteria to ensure selecting the "best" candidate is less important at the national level, as high-quality practitioners may reach a number of different standards. Thus, the door is open for more flexible – and subjective – evaluation.

A number of participants held the view that *symbolic politics* is a result of the inevitable difficulty experienced in attempting to distinguish among accomplished practitioners when performance reaches a certain level. The aims of honours granted at this level are not to rank professionals, but to signify symbolically that the national government esteems the teaching profession. When selecting the winner, the government considers the candidate's background in serving as a "symbol" or spokesperson for the profession in some way. A Ministry of Education participant shared that "when appraising *excellent teachers* . . . we generally emphasise teachers' ethics . . . In recent years, in appraisal and selection conditions, we favour the teachers in the western areas, rural areas, and border areas" (I-MOE-LONG-20120918). The Ministry of Education favours such locations in China because practitioners may not consider these areas as ideal places to work, due to limited financial benefits and poor working conditions. Teachers who work in these regions often are viewed as having a spirit of dedication and high sense of morality. The preference shown to these teachers in the honour appraisal and selection process is the government's expression of devotion to education and teachers across China.

A second key challenge involved in the micro-politics of the national teacher honour system may be described as *balance politics.* This dynamic often can be observed in the recommendations for the *political honour* shown to the *excellent teacher*. Due to the more flexible, sometimes ambiguous, appraisal and selection standards of the *political honours*, the educational and administrative departments across the levels (school, municipal, provincial, and national) use a distribution quota to ensure that recommendations are *balanced* in representing teachers across the collective. Recommendations at the school level involve distributing honours to teachers in turn to ensure *balance* in merited honour. One teacher expressed, "in general, if you are appraised and elected this year, you will not be appraised and elected next year . . . to give equal opportunity to more people" (I-XWANG-20121010). In this context, the *excellent teacher* title serves the role of building a strong morale among the school's professional community. This *political honour* benefits the professional development of collectives, more than individuals.

Another expression of the *balance politics* was observed as a vice-principal distinguished between expert and non-expert teachers. He shared that "teachers with teaching expertise, we will cultivate them to fight for *teaching expertise honours* and *contest honours.* As to some teachers who are fundamental [not expert teachers], we will create conditions for them to fight for *excellent teacher honours* and advanced worker awards" (I-X-GAO-20121010). Thus, the teachers are divided into two categories with two different roads for their professional development. One is for the outstanding performers to gain further teaching expertise and higher honour titles, and the other road is for the average performers to gain simply higher honour titles. The perspective of this vice-principal clearly frames the honours that involve theoretical study as being more rigorous than the purely pedagogical honour.

Discussion

Professionalising the field via rigour and relationship

The three types of teacher honours – *teaching expertise*, *contest*, and *political honours* – held different statuses in the participating teachers' minds. The former two have clearly defined evaluation criteria that entail *individual* recipients demonstrating professional academic knowledge *and* pedagogical skills. Moreover, these honours come with associated professional development opportunities. Thus, these honours are regarded by practitioners themselves as being more professionally rigorous and respected. *Political honours* recognise *excellent teachers* based on a broader and more flexible set of standards and often are controlled by *balance politics* to ensure all areas or practitioners have opportunity

Table 4.2 Academic and pedagogical honours for individuals and collectives

	Teaching expertise honours	*Political honours*	*Contest honours*
Appraisal and selection standards	Clearly defined index criteria	Less clear index criteria	Clearly defined index criteria
Appraisal and selection Process	Recommendation → Evaluation → Publicity → Follow-up professional development	Recommendation → Evaluation → Publicity	Recommendation → Professional preparation → Contest
Professional recognition	Individual	Collective	Individual and collective
Professional development	Follow-up professional development	N/A	Professional preparation
Micro-politics	Symbol politics	Balance politics and symbol politics	Symbol politics

for recognition – thereby building the morale and relationships of a professional *collective.*

Political honours do not require teachers to demonstrate academic knowledge as much as pedagogical practice or other practitioner-based criteria defined by recipients, and are more influenced by *symbolic* and *balance politics.* These awards are regarded by teachers as being less professionally rigorous, despite their intent to build the profession as a whole. As Menges (1996) and Chism (2006) noted, this symbolic value is what brings significance to the awards. Thus, *political honours* are awarded at the national level, while the highest *teaching expertise honour* is awarded at the provincial level in providing recognition for individual practitioners (Table 4.2).

Cultivating Confucian morality and professional standards

China's national teacher honour system aims to embody some of the key moral aspects of the teaching profession that Confucius encouraged. For instance, the appraisal and selection standards for honours at all levels are intended to build on the calling to selflessly devote oneself to "the motherland" by giving oneself to the profession and one's students. In the *teaching expertise honours* and *contest honours*, this moral calling ideally is a basis for a recipient's professional knowledge and skills. However, the *political honours* often require practitioner demonstration of this Confucian moral ideal, as with teachers who choose to teach in rural areas. In this case, the *political honour* highlights a teacher's *professional morality*, though not necessarily a teacher's *professional academic knowledge* and *pedagogical skills.* Some of the participants expressed that this "morality model" holds professional significance, but does not necessarily recognise the most proficient practitioner.

Though participants may have expressed less value for *political honours*, it is important to highlight that collective recognition was high primarily for recipients of the *political honours*. In a Confucian cultural context, providing recognition for one's group beyond oneself is highly commendable. Thus, the broader indices of the *political honours* provide the flexibility for China's teacher honour system to recognise aspects of teaching that bring honour to teachers as a *professional collective*. Nations where teachers experience a high degree of isolation in their work (Ross, Romer, and Horner, 2012) should consider how to develop policies that recognise individual teacher achievement while also honouring the professional collective of teachers. Some Western theoretical texts are seeking to revive the practice of honour in democratic societies today by reconciling notions of authority with notions of freedom (Cunningham, 2013, p. 80). Likewise, additional perspectives emphasise the need to cultivate "soft skills" (Cobo, 2013, p. 80) vital for building *both* innovative *and* collaborative communities of practitioners able to approach larger local and global dilemmas by learning from shared knowledge and challenges.

Along with the benefits demonstrated in China's teacher honour system, there is room for growth in the profession. Teacher practitioners should consider how to cultivate the knowledge, skills, and *dispositions* to support learners of all backgrounds (Hollins and Guzman, 2005). The concept of teacher disposition merges rigour and relationship by encompassing, for instance, teacher attitude toward one's learners as a professional quality to develop. Teacher disposition is increasingly well recognised as a vital trait of quality teachers to cultivate, as noted in formal international policies (Organisation for Economic Co-Operation and Development, 2005) and national teacher preparation program accreditation agencies (e.g., the US National Council for Accreditation for Colleges of Teacher Education), as well as professional development organisations run by practitioners (e.g., the US National Board for Professional Teaching Standards).

Accounting for collective culture mianzi (face)

As noted in the study, the collectivist cultural concept of *face* has countless ties to the teacher honour system. Hu (1944) discussed two key aspects of *face*: *lian* and *mianzi*. *Lian* can be defined as "the confidence of society in the integrity of ego's moral character, the loss of which makes it impossible for him [or her] to function properly within the community" (p. 45), while *mianzi* is "the type of prestige that is emphasised in this country: a reputation achievement through getting on in life, through success and ostentation. This is a prestige that is accumulated by means of personal effort or clever manner" (p. 45). Thus, individual conduct in collectivist cultures is driven by *mianzi* in addition to personal aspiration (Kim & Nam, 1998). Chinese teachers pursuing the *teaching expertise* and *contest honours* may be interested in gaining *mianzi* via recognition for individual professional performance. Conversely, teachers interested in achieving the *political honours* may be more interested in building *lian*. In this study, *mianzi* seemed more valued by the teachers.

Receiving a teacher honour increases or maintains one's *mianzi*, while not receiving or losing an honour may involve losing *mianzi*, particularly for accomplished practitioners expected to receive the awards (Ho, 1976; Kim and Nam, 1998). Thus, China's teacher honour system also creates an additional pressure for teachers. Likewise, in a Western cultural setting, Mackenzie (2007) found that "awards have had a positive impact on some recipients", while "others have experienced negative or mixed outcomes and there is evidence to suggest that some teachers feel disempowered by not receiving an award" (p. 202). Kim and Nam (1998) further observed "a positive correlation between one's social status in the organization and his/her sensitivity to face-saving" (p. 528). The higher a teacher climbs on the honour ladder, the more pressure the teacher may feel to continue achieving awards to maintain high *mianzi*.

Lightening this pressure, the professional cooperation often present in collectivist contexts (Earley, 1994; Triandis, Bontempo, Villareal, Asai, and Lucca, 1988) can "alleviate any residual negative effects of teachers' selfishness regarding appraisals. This makes teachers more willing to share resources, materials, and ideas, and leads to more joint work . . . [helping] teacher appraisal achieve its developmental purpose" (Zhang and Ng, 2011, p. 579). Such practices are akin to the "lesson study" experience for teacher learning found in institutions around the world (Paine and Ma, 1993; Pinar, Reynolds, Slattery, and Taubman, 1995). Yet, as a principal participant shared, divisions will continue to exist, as schools will encourage teachers to pursue honours of different types according to their different developmental paths.

In China's national honour system, *balance politics* will continue to operate in the collectivist cultural context to bring a sense of belonging and *collective face* to a group. Just as gaining face is gaining face for all members of a group, losing face also impacts the group members (Hu, 1944; Kim and Nam, 1998). This *collective face* can diminish the sense of competition among individuals competing in the honour system, yet *collective face* also can diminish the active influence of teacher awards on the intrinsic motivation of teacher individual development. The teachers interviewed even called the teacher awards a "yoke", indicating the awards can create external pressure that may inhibit the development of intrinsic motivation.

Professionalising the field via reflective and rigorous assessments

Professional teacher practitioners around the world today must collaborate in developing global teacher collectives to counter notions that teaching is only a "semi-profession on its way to achieving full professional status" (Ornstein, 1981, p. 196). Without a means for professional development and assessment that involves clearly defined criteria and measurements, this "semi-profession" status may be difficult to change. The field of education needs recognised measurements for professional knowledge to develop as a recognised professional field (Johnson, 1977), akin to the medical and law professions (Ornstein, 1981). Programs of teacher development and assessment across international settings are moving beyond the myth that:

> excellent teaching is impossible to define because it is ineffable, situation-specific, or individual; the belief that everyone knows good teaching when he or she sees it; or the lack of knowledge of the research literature on teaching (or lack of trust of these findings) on the part of those frame the awards.
>
> (Chism, 2006, p. 601)

Moreover, teachers can work beyond any limitations in group thinking within a collective by drawing upon and applying meaningful theory in their unique teaching contexts. Administrators and others in positions of authority can serve teachers by providing opportunities to gain professional recognition in their work (Larson, 1980).

The professional status of the teaching field in China can increase through both governmental leadership and professional independence (Lawn, 1996; Ozga and Lawn, 1988). While the Chinese government has the power to accredit teacher certification, Chinese teachers can lead in managing the details of their licensed professionalism (Ozga, 1995). The teacher honour system in China has the potential for serving as a professional ladder by which teachers not only gain recognition, but also a stronger sense of efficacy as professionals (Draper, 2013). The knowledge recognised by the government greatly influences the practices of teachers who may feel compelled to "show the teaching that the evaluators want to see", as noted by a female high school teacher of four years' experience with a provincial honour (I-S-LONG-20121017).

Teachers as a global professional collective must collaborate to ensure that their practices are based on strong theoretical ideals, and that their work does not fall prey to serving market-driven economies or government policies that are not informed and shaped by practitioners themselves (Hatcher, 1994). In China's teacher honour system the government plays a more involved role than in many other national settings, by endowing teachers with professional status as they attend to the values and interests articulated by the central government. Living up to the requirements of the government creates a new context for teachers to maintain *face*, or *mianzi*.

Supporting reflective self-assessment in professionalising the field

Research has shown that teachers need to be involved in determining and shaping teacher assessment and developing policy reforms in order for change to be sustainable. For instance, a study conducted by the Organisation for Economic Co-operation and Development (2005) concludes, "unless teachers are actively involved in policy formulation, and feel a sense of 'ownership' of reform, it is unlikely that substantial changes will be successfully implemented" (p. 15). Likewise, Draper (2013) asserted that cultivating effective teachers able to innovate in preparing students for the twenty-first century entails involving teachers in shaping the policy reform process.

Draper (2013) shared the concern that externally imposed "standards and competence frameworks may undermine experienced teachers who, while confident of their competence in the past, are less sure about their competence in the new environment" (p. 79). Falk and Darling-Hammond (2010) asserted parallel notions that effective teacher assessments involve a *practitioner*-led, reflective, performance-based documentary process to engage teachers in "problem-solving and dialogue that leads them continually to learn and improve their teaching" (p. 79). Thus, policies that evaluate and recognise quality professional practice must consider how to engage teachers in owning their work via personal reflection. Falk and Darling-Hammond concluded that documentation of teacher development and achievement is most effective when teachers play a leading role in the assessment of their own practice.

Such self-assessment often involves cultivating reflective practice next to a set of standards. As an example in the US, the National Board for Professional Teaching Standards (NBPTS) aims to provide recognition for teachers via a practitioner-led, reflective, performance-based assessment. NBPTS is a rigorous exam administered at the state level, with national professional organisations monitoring its effectiveness (Jones and Moore, 1993). This exam process involves engaging in reflective practitioner communities as teachers individually demonstrate their accomplishment via a performance-based assessment – much like China's *contest honour*. Akin to China's national honour system, NBPTS seeks to provide greater esteem and recognition for teachers as a professional collective.

Conclusion

China's teacher honour system is complex, composed of honours merited at national, provincial, municipal, and school-based levels to recognise academic and pedagogical professional development for individual teachers and professional collectives. This system balances government authority and teacher autonomy by providing recognition along with professional development opportunities serving as a means for career progression and simultaneously bringing greater professional status to the field of teaching. Such career trajectory paths are being forged in other regions of the world establishing and experimenting with reflective, practitioner-led, performance-based teacher assessments that do not simply rank practitioners, but that aim to provide honourable recognition and professional growth simultaneously.

A key aspect to understand about China's teacher honour system is its contextualisation in a Confucian culture in which individual and collective honour are key aims, and in which *mianzi*, or *face*, is important to preserve for many teachers. Benefits to this cultural context may include reduced teacher isolation, and more abundant professional support for teachers engaged in professional development – such as those preparing for the *contest honour*. Challenges that arise with this system include honours being merited based on subjective dynamics, such as *balance politics*, which open the door for less professional means for honour conferral, such as teachers with the "right connections", or *guanxi* (关系). This aspect of the system can be discouraging for teachers initially motivated intrinsically to put forth their best professional effort, particularly if they experience another's *guanxi* trumping their own genuine efforts. These aspects may find their expression in the current teacher honour system via honour quota distribution, ambiguity of award criteria, or pursuit of honours to gain or preserve *face*. At the same time, collective sharing of individual honour may strengthen professional morale by reducing peer competition and envy of honour recipients, while also maintaining the enthusiasm of non-candidates – as observed in previous studies (e.g. Dinham & Scott, 2003; Mackenzie, 2007). The practice of collectively sharing individual honour may play a connective, sustaining role.

National honour as a system cultivating professional rigour and relationships

A summary of the complex dynamics involved in China's teacher honour system is represented in Figure 4.1.

The three types of teacher honours – *teaching expertise honour*, *contest honour*, and *political honour* – are esteemed differently by teachers. The first two are considered more professionally *rigorous* with their emphasis on academic learning and individual effort – including built-in professional development opportunities. In contrast, the *political honour* is viewed as more *relational* with its pedagogical emphasis and more flexible criteria to serve *balance politics*. While the first two honours focus on engaging individual teachers in the professional development ladder, the *political honour* serves to recognise teachers' collective professional status and to demonstrate the government's value of the moral aspects of teaching.

Implications

This system seeks to balance broader government authority with local practitioner control over one's professional growth. While the Chinese teacher honour system is under government control, much of this authority is conferred to provincial, municipal, and school-based sites. As a professional collective, education practitioners and researchers in China must continue to develop a professional knowledge base so that top-down management via the national honour system does not become "a quick, cheap attempt at improving community confidence in teachers and schools by highlighting and rewarding a small number of quality teachers" (Mackenzie, 2007, p. 202). Teacher practitioners, researchers, and policy makers across international settings and cultural contexts have a shared aim of nurturing twenty-first-century learners in facing globally shared challenges of the future. Such an aim can only be achieved by including teachers as

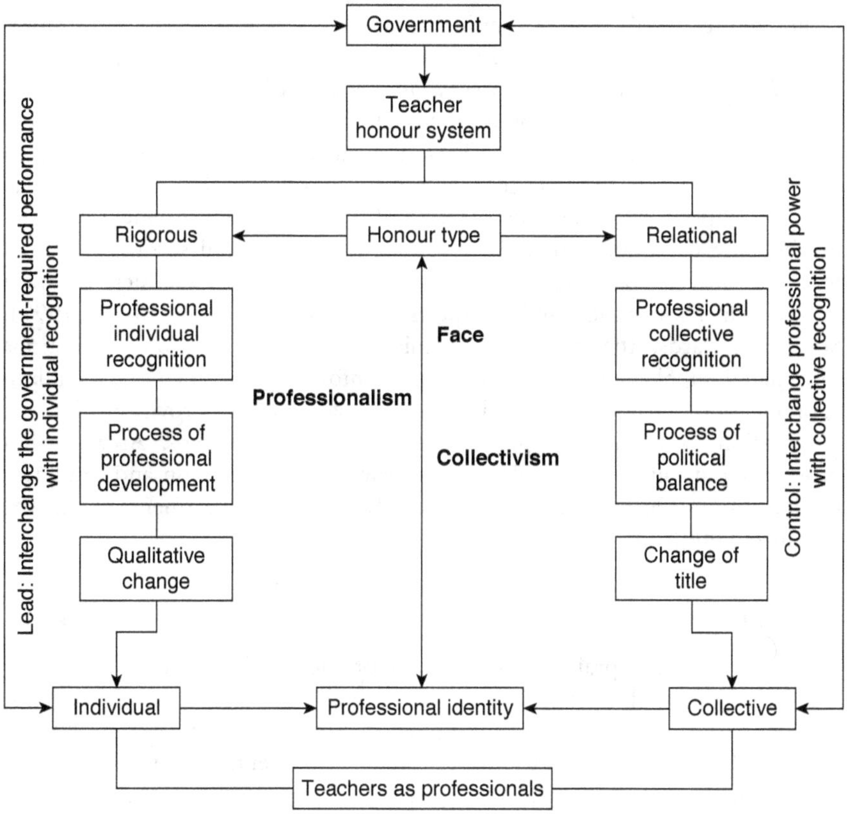

Figure 4.1 The impact of China's honour system on teacher professional recognition and development

efficacious practitioners in the shaping of policy for practice. As Svinicki and Menges (1996) asserted, "teaching is a difficult and honourable calling and deserves to be recognised as such. This is the time to bring teaching out of the closet, not to condemn those who do it poorly, but to honour those who add lustre to the calling" (p. 113). Individual and collective honours add to this calling.

Appendix 1. Chinese teacher honour system[2]

China has constructed a teacher honour system comprised of multiple layers, types, and organisations, ranging from the Central Government to local and school governments, from comprehensive to single-area, and from government endowment to enterprise participation.

Special-grade teacher honour

Although the special-grade teacher honour is set at provincial level, its institution is set by the Central Government and marked by the publication of *Provision of Special-Grade Teachers' Appraisement and Selection* in 1999 (MOE, 1999). This provision noted that the appraisal and selection of special-grade teachers is "encouraging the vast number teachers in elementary and secondary schools to devote themselves to the long-term educational profession, improve their social status . . . 'Special-grade teacher' is a title of professional advancement awarded by the state to honour especially excellent elementary and secondary school teachers. Special-grade teachers should exemplify teaching ethics, embrace modern education models, and be experts in the field of teaching" (MOE, 1999). Soon afterwards, the provinces, municipalities, and autonomous regions formulated supplementary provisions and enforcement regulation, including appraisal and selection standards, and created detailed provisions for the nomination, assessment, appraisal, and determination steps. Areas within provinces and municipalities also add on-the-spot investigation and candidate public announcement institution links (Education Department of Jiangxi Province, 2009).

National excellent teachers honour

The ratio of the appraisal and selection of the special-grade teacher titles was strictly limited to 1–1.15% of the overall numbers of teachers; thus, only approximately 30,000 teachers obtained these titles from 1978 to 2005 in China, which was unable to satisfy the developmental needs of the vast number of teachers. Therefore, beginning in the 1980s, China gradually established the terminal honour and award institution of China Excellent Teacher (along with the honour and award titles of China Excellent Educator, China Model Teacher, China Educational Institution Advanced Worker, and People's Teacher). In 1998, China published the "Teacher and Educator Award Provision" to stipulate honour and selection objectives, honour and selection conditions, award methods, and title revocations of the national titles, including "China Excellent Teacher". The above honour is awarded once every three years, and the ratio control of the recommendation quota of teachers in each province and municipality is limited to 2/10,000 (two in ten thousand) (MOE, 1998). The Central Government also set up more specific honourable titles, including "China Excellent Class Teachers in Elementary and Secondary Schools" for class teachers (*banzhuren*, 班主任), and "China Educational System Woman Model" for female teachers. Additionally, the Central Government specially honoured the teachers making important contributions during national emergencies, such as the temporary teacher honour titles of "Educational Institution Earthquake Relief Work Hero Team" after the 2008 Wenchuan earthquake.

Local and school teacher honour

The local governments and schools at all levels enacted honour titles similar to "China Excellent Teachers", creating teacher honour titles at all levels and of all types, including "Excellent Teacher", "Teacher Ethics Model", "Starlet at the Pulpit", etc. Additionally, referring to the "Teacher's Law" provision, some non-governmental organisations also set up honorary titles to recognise teachers.

Acknowledgements

We express our gratitude for the helpful perspectives and insights shared by all of the teachers, administrators, and policy makers who participated in this study. This work was supported by the MOE [Ministry of Education] Project of Key Research Institute of Humanities and Social Sciences at Universities (10JJD880003) and Teacher Training Based on Professional Learning Communities in the Context of the Curriculum Reform Project (2009 Annual MOE Youth Project Fund of National Educational Science Planning, EHA090450).

Notes

1. The documentation data is cited by "D – the first letter of city name – year". The interview data is cited by "I – the first letter of school name – the last name of interviewee – year and date".
2. The main resource of this appendix comes from the book which is based on a national survey of the Chinese teacher honour system, see Zhu and Song (2013).

References

Adams, C.C. (1977). *Faculty awards programs: Campus-based and systemwide.* Long Beach: California State University and Colleges, Center for Professional Development (ERIC Document Reproduction Service No. ED 136 725).

Banks, J.A. (1998). The lives and values of researchers: Implications for educating citizens in a multicultural society. *Educational Researcher, 27*(7), 4–17.

Carr-Saunders, A.M., and Wilson, P.A. (1933). *The professions.* London: Oxford University Press.

Chism, N.V.N. (2006). Teaching awards: What do they award. *The Journal of Higher Education, 77*(4), 589–617.

Cobo, C. (2013). Skills for innovation: Envisioning an education that prepares for a changing world. *The Curriculum Journal, 24*(1), 67–85.

Collins, R. (1990). Changing conceptions in the sociology of the professions. In R. Torstendahl and M. Burrage (Eds.), *The formation of profession: Knowledge, state and strategy* (pp. 11–23). London: Sage.

Committee of National People's Congress. (1993). *The People's Republic of China teacher's law.* Beijing: Author.

Cunningham, A. (2013). *Modern honor: A philosophical defense.* New York, NY: Routledge.

Dinham, S., and Scott, C. (2003). *Awards for teaching excellence: Intentions and realities.* Online Refered Article no. 24. Retrieved from http://www.austcolled.com.au

Donaldson, J.F. (1988). Exemplary instruction of adults. *Journal of Continuing Higher Education, 36*(2), 11–18.

Draper, J. (2013). Teacher self-efficacy: Internalized understandings of competence. In S. Phillipson, K. Ku, and S. Phillipson (Eds.), *Constructing education achievement: A sociocultural perspective* (pp. 70–83). New York, NY: Routledge.

Earley, P.C. (1994). Self or group? Cultural effects of training on self-efficacy and performance. *Administrative Science Quarterly, 39*(1), 89–117.

Education Department of Jiangxi Province (2009). *Selection requirements for distinguished teacher of Jiangxi province.* Retrieved from http://www.wljwt.com/WANGZHAN/ShowArticle. asp?ArticleID-1503

Englund, T. (1996). Are professional teachers a good thing? In I.F. Goodson and A. Hargreaves (Eds.), *Teachers' professional lives* (pp. 75–87). London: Falmer.

Falk, B., and Darling-Hammond, L. (2010). Documentation and democratic education. *Theory into Practice, 49*, 72–81.

Goldsmid, C.A., Gruber, J.E., and Wilson, E.K. (1977). Perceived attributes of superior teachers (PAST): An inquiry into the giving of teacher awards. *American Educational Research Journal, 14*(4), 423–440.

Hatcher, R. (1994). Market relationships and the management of teachers. *British Journal of Sociology of Education, 15*, 41–61.

Ho, D.Y. (1976). On the concept of face. *American Journal of Sociology, 81*(4), 867–884.

Hollins, E., and Guzman, M.T. (2005). Research on preparing teachers for diverse populations. In M. Cochran-Smith and K.M. Zeichner (Eds.), *Studying teacher education* (pp. 477–548). Washington, DC: American Educational Research Association.

Hu, H.C. (1944). The Chinese concepts of "face". *American Anthropologist, 46*(1), 45–64.

Johnson, T.J. (1977). The professions in the class structure. In R. Scase (Ed.), *Industrial society: Class, cleavage and control* (pp. 93–110). London: George Allen & Unwin.

Jones, L., and Moore, R. (1993). Education, competence and the control of expertise. *British Journal of the Sociology of Education, 14*(4), 385–397.

Kim, J.Y., and Nam, S.H. (1998). The concept and dynamics of face: Implications for organizational behavior in Asia. *Organization Science, 9*(4), 522–534.

Larson, M.S. (1980). Proletarianisation and education labor. *Theory and Society, 19*, 131–171.

Lawn, M. (1996). *Modern times? Work, professionalism and citizenship in teaching.* London: The Falmer Press.

Mackenzie, N. (2007). Teacher excellence awards: An apple for the teacher? *Australian Journal of Education, 51*(2), 190–204.

McNaught, C., and Anwyl, J. (1993). *Awards for teaching at Australian universities (Centre for the Study of Higher Education Research Working Papers, 93.1).* Victoria: University of Melbourne (ERIC Document Reproduction Service No. ED 368 291).

Menges, R.J. (1996). Awards to individuals. In M.D. Svinicki and R.J. Menges (Eds.), *Honoring exemplary teaching* (pp. 3–9). San Francisco, CA: Jossey-Bass.

Merriam, S. (2001). *Qualitative research and case study applications in education.* San Francisco, CA: Jossey-Bass.

Ministry of Education. (1998). *Reward regulations of teachers and educators.* Beijing: Author.

Ministry of Education. (1999). *Provision of special-grade teachers' appraisement and selection.* Beijing: Author.

Murphy, R. (1990). Proletarianization or bureaucratization: The fall of the professional? In R. Torstendahl and M. Burrage (Eds.), *The formation of profession* (pp. 71–96). London: Sage.

Organisation for Economic Co-operation and Development. (2005). *Teachers matter: Attracting, developing and retaining effective teachers.* Paris: Author.

Ornstein, A.C. (1981). The trend toward increased professionalism for teachers. *The Phi Delta Kappan, 63*(3), 196–198.

Ozga, J. (1995). Deskilling a profession: Professionalism, deprofessionalisation and the new managerialism. In H. Busher and R. Saran (Eds.), *Managing teachers as professionals in school* (pp. 21–37). London: Kogan Page.

Ozga, J., and Lawn, M. (1988). Schoolwork: Interpreting the labour process of teaching. *British Journal of Sociology of Education, 9*(3), 323–336.

Paine, L., and Ma, L. (1993). Teachers working together: A dialogue on organizational and cultural perspectives of Chinese teachers. *International Journal of Educational Research, 19*(8), 675–697.

Pinar, W.F., Reynolds, W.M., Slattery, P., and Taubman, P. (1995). *Understanding curriculum: An introduction to the study of historical and contemporary curriculum discourses.* New York, NY: P. Lang.

Ross, S.W., Romer, N., and Horner, R.H. (2012). Teacher well-being and the implementation of school-wide positive behavior interventions and supports. *Journal of Positive Behavior Interventions, 14*(2), 118–128.

Ryan, R.M., and Deci, E.L. (2000). Self-determination theory and the facilitation of intrinsic motivation, social development, and well-being. *American Psychologist, 55*(1), 66–78.

Sandel, M.J. (2009). *Justice: What's the right thing to do?*. New York, NY: Farrar, Straus and Giroux.

Silverman, D. (2006). *Interpreting qualitative data: Methods for analysing talk, text and interaction* (3rd ed.). London: Sage Publications.

Strauss, A., and Corbin, J. (1998). *Basics of qualitative research: Techniques and procedures for developing grounded theory* (2nd ed.). Thousand Oaks, CA: Sage Publications.

Svinicki, M.D., and Menges, R.J. (1996). Consistency within diversity: Guidelines for programs to honor exemplary teaching. In M.D. Svinicki and R.J. Menges (Eds.), *Honoring exemplary teaching* (pp. 109–113). San Francisco, CA: Jossey-Bass.

Triandis, H.C., Bontempo, R., Villareal, M.J., Asai, M., and Lucca, N. (1988). Individualism and collectivism: Cross-cultural perspectives on self-ingroup relationships. *Journal of Personality and Social Psychology, 54*, 323–338.

Warren, R., and Plumb, E. (1999). Survey of distinguished teacher award schemes in higher education. *Journal of Further and Higher Education, 23*(2), 245–255.

Zhang, X.F., and Ng, H.M. (2011). A case study of teacher appraisal in Shanghai, China: In relation to teacher professional development. *Asia Pacific Education Review*, *12*, 569–580.

Zhu, X., and Song, H. (2013). *Study on the Chinese teacher honour institution*. Beijing: Beijing Normal University Press.

5 Dilemmas of teacher development in the context of curriculum reform

Hongbiao Yin

Introduction

At the beginning of this millennium, Fullan (2000) astutely observed that a growing intensity in efforts at large-scale reform had been evident globally since the mid-1990s for which he coined the term "the return of large-scale reform". Almost a decade later, he revisited this issue to affirm that "large-scale reform comes of age" (Fullan, 2009). Quite a number of countries have initiated national or territory-wide educational reforms since 1997. For example, the *National Literacy and Numeracy Strategy* in England, the series of reform initiatives after the issue of *No Child Left Behind* in the United States, the emerging national curriculum in Australia, the national senior secondary education reform in the Netherlands, and the various educational reforms in Asian countries such as Japan, Singapore, South Korea, Thailand, Taiwan, Hong Kong and mainland China (Kennedy, 2007). In this global wave of large-scale reform, many of the same innovative ideas and practices were advocated by different countries, including decentralization, accountability, constructivism, curriculum integration, self-regulated and inquiry-based learning, and the cultivation of generic skills such as communication, cooperation and critical thinking (Yin et al., 2014).

The conceptualization and the analysis of the study reported in this chapter are based upon theories of dilemmas of teacher development and educational reform. Teacher development and the implementation of educational reform go hand in hand (Fullan and Hargreaves, 1992). Teacher development has been widely recognized as an important prerequisite of educational reform as well as one of the most important consequences, especially when the reform aims to bring fundamental transformation to the learning and teaching in classrooms (Borko et al., 2002; Darling-Hammond and McLaughlin, 2011; Hoque et al., 2011; van Driel et al., 2001). Just as Elmore and Bruney (1997) pointed out, professional development for teachers lies at the center of educational reform and instructional improvement, and is the main link connecting reform policies to school practice. Sustained and intensive professional development for teachers is related to student achievement gains, and collaborative approaches to professional learning can promote school change that extends beyond individual classrooms

(Darling-Hammond et al., 2009). However, the process of reform is full of uncertainties and ambiguities, and the effects of reform are often contradictions, leading to tensions or conflicts. As Flett and Wallace (2005) argued, these tensions, or dilemmas, are features that must be managed by those implementing reforms. Therefore, it has been repeatedly reported that teachers encounter many dilemmas during implementation of educational reform in schools (e.g., Fang, 2011; Lee and Yin, 2010; Walker and Qian, 2012; Windschitl, 2002). These dilemmas limit the possibilities for teacher development which in turn impede the implementation of educational reforms.

There is growing body of research into dilemmas in educational settings in developed nations reported in the international literature but comparatively few such reports about the dilemmas experienced by teachers during reform processes in nations such as China. This chapter therefore, attempts to depict the dilemmas of teacher development during the national curriculum reform of senior secondary education (SSE) in China. The sources of these dilemmas will be analyzed, and the influence on and implications for teacher development and curriculum implementation will be discussed.

The literature

Teacher development in educational reform

Teacher development and educational reform complement each other. As Zhu (2010) pointed out, teacher development cannot succeed isolated from education reform, or without policy support, because teacher change needs contexts and conditions. Meanwhile, education reform cannot succeed without teachers' involvement and their successful professional growth. When examining most curriculum change projects in the 1970s and 1980s, Scott (1994) commented that the separation between curriculum implementation and teacher development is a major reason for the failures which occurred. In contrast, when examining the success of Kentucky's educational reform, Borko et al. (2004) suggested that the success of this systemic reform effort was dependent upon "creating opportunities for teachers' continual learning and providing sufficient professional development resources to support these opportunities" (p. 971).

To make teacher development more effective for educational reform, scholars have summarized the characteristics of effective teacher development programs. For example, Garet and his colleagues found that three core features of professional development activities have significant and positive effects on teachers' self-reported increased knowledge and skills and changes in classroom practice. These core features are, focus on content knowledge, opportunities for active learning, and coherence with other learning opportunities. Moreover, the structural features that significantly affect teacher learning include the form of the activity (e.g., workshop vs. study group), collective participation of teachers from the same school, grade, or subject, and the duration of the activity (Garet et al., 2001). Penuel et al. (2007) highlighted the significance of teachers' perceptions about the coherence of their professional development experiences for teacher learning and curriculum implementation. They found that the incorporation of time for teachers to plan for implementation and provision of technical support for teachers are significant in promoting the implementation of a curriculum innovation. van Driel et al. (2001) suggested that developing teachers' practical knowledge should be put at the center of teacher development in the context of reform. Therefore, teacher development may consider adopting the following strategies: learning in networks, peer coaching, collaborative action research, and the use of cases. Desimone (2011) also summarized five core features of effective professional development, including content focus, active learning, coherence, duration, and collective participation. In a recent empirical study, Hoque et al. (2011) revealed that teachers' professional development activities have a significant impact on school improvement, and the maximum school improvement can be achieved if schools put more emphasis on teacher collaboration, in-service training and classroom observation.

Notwithstanding the above, after an examination of 13 lists of characteristics of "effective professional development," Guskey (2003) found that the lists vary widely, and the research supporting them is inconsistent and often contradictory. Hence, he suggested that researchers focus on criteria for effectiveness and the contextual factors of teacher development activities. His call for the context dependence of teacher development echoes Darling-Hammond and McLaughlin's (2011) emphasis on the situational character of effective teaching and learning practice. "The situation-specific nature of the kind of teaching and learning envisioned by reformers is the key challenge for teachers' professional development, and it is the chief obstacle to policy makers' effort to engender systemic reform" (p. 90). According to the views of these scholars, it is necessary for the policy makers and change facilitators to pay close attention to the contextual characteristics of teacher development in the context of educational reform, especially when the innovative ideas and practices advocated by the reform originate in other cultural or social contexts.

Dilemmas of teaching and teacher development

Dilemma is "a situation in which the participants are required to manage competing alternatives" (Flett and Wallace, 2005, p. 190). Dilemma situations contain elements of contradiction, conflict, paradox and inconsistency in the ways they are perceived, since an action to deal with one aspect may cause other aspects to become unsatisfactory or more problematic. In this sense, a dilemma means an argument between opposing tendencies within oneself in which neither side can come out the winner (Lampert, 1985). Hence, in the view of Cuban (1992), dilemmas can only be reconciled rather than resolved, making them more complicated than "problems" which are fairly routine and structured situations blocking the achievement of some desired goals.

Teachers are dilemma managers, balancing a variety of interests that need to be satisfied in classrooms (Lampert, 1985). Teachers always need to assume the role expectations of various people. As a result, the multiple identities of teachers and the contingencies of the classroom have the potential to create dilemmas for teachers. When teachers encounter these dilemmas, the process of reconciliation of these tensions and conflicts often draws on, though is not determined by, their sense of whom they are (Enyedy et al., 2006). The widespread existence of dilemmas in teaching puts forward challenges for teachers' professional development. Conceptualizing teacher development needs to include several interlocking elements: self, craft, relationships, values and ways of knowing (Lyons, 1990).

In recent years, research on dilemmas in teaching and teacher development tends to adopt a broader view on the nature of dilemmas, and calls for attention to the role of organizational or working conditions in understanding the sources of dilemmas in educational settings. For instance, Tillma and Kremer-Hayon (2002) noted several dilemmas that teacher educators face with respect to promoting self-regulated learning. These dilemmas connected to teacher educators' underlying conceptions of teaching and learning, as well as the demands of the setting in which they teach. Recently, Cabaroglu and Tillma (2011) differentiated two kinds of dilemmas that teacher educators encounter in their teaching. One is the internally driven dilemma which depends on one's views of teaching and usually deals with reconceptualizing teaching practice. The other is the externally driven dilemma caused by prevailing teaching conditions, which mainly deal with restructuring teaching conditions. When examining teacher professional development through collaborative action, Roblin and Margalef (2013) also named two kinds of dilemmas. One is intrapersonal dilemmas which have to do with conflicts in teachers' personal beliefs about curriculum, student learning, teaching strategies and assessment. The other is interpersonal dilemmas which have to do with the tensions resulting from teacher collaboration, and more specifically with the need to align individual goals, beliefs and teaching styles with those of the group.

On this point, Fransson and Grannäs (2013) went even further by arguing the importance of broader social context in understanding dilemmas in educational settings. In their views, dilemmas should not be seen as particular events, but rather as constitutive and ever-present in teachers' working lives. Therefore, they extended the understanding about dilemmas in educational settings by adding space as a relational category to the concept of dilemma, which "makes it possible to visualize how dilemmas emerge in a space between individuals and the context in which in which they find themselves" (Fransson and Grannäs, 2013, p. 7). The notion of "dilemmatic space" could be more fruitful to understand the nature and complexity of teachers' work, because it could lead to a re-positioning of the dilemma by moving it from the shoulders of the individual to an all embracing level.

Educational reform as the context of dilemma research

Consideration of context matters in research into almost all issues and topics in the field of educational research, and it is especially relevant to the research into dilemmas in educational reforms. Educational reforms always try to bring transformations to the local context where the reforms unfold, which inevitably causes some tensions or conflicts between the local context and the reform ideas and practices, especially when the reforms are imposed from outside. Just as Fransson and Grannäs (2013) stated:

> Different kinds of political and administrative policy decisions alter norms, values, tasks, guidelines, obligations and relations and (may) also change the very notion of dilemmas. Likewise, societal transformation changes the relations, positions and boundaries of the dilemmas, which in turn renders some aspects of dilemma more or less intense.
>
> (pp. 5–6)

Some conceptual frameworks have been put forward to understand the sources or formation of the dilemmas in educational reform. For example, Dimmock (1996) suggested that the values-institutional-resources framework is helpful for understanding the formation of dilemmas in school restructuring. In this framework, the sources of dilemmas in school restructuring are the asynchronous changes within or between three key domains of education and society: norms and values, institutional practices and structures, and resources. A dilemma may be caused by the asynchronous changes *within* the same domain (e.g., an existing norm may be rejected, while a new one forms) or *between* particular domains (e.g., a change in norms and values may not be matched by equivalent change in institutional structures, or in resource provision).

Instead of using "dilemma", Walker and Qian (2012) suggested the term "disconnection" to illustrate the inconsistencies and fractures in reform implementation. Specifically, disconnection refers to a lack of linkage between different reform components, purposes or intentions, and to a breakdown between what reforms propose and the processes that make them "work". They classified five types of reform disconnection: *instrumental disconnection* (the disconnection between what the reforms demand and the practical realities in schools); *intellectual disconnection* (the disconnection between purpose and content within and between different reforms); *political disconnection* (the disconnection between the reforms, the political structures, and the established order underpinning the life within school); *cultural disconnection* (the disconnection between what the reforms demand and the cultural realities of schools); and *communicative disconnection* (the deficiencies in how reforms and their outcomes are communicated and promoted within and outside the education community).

The framework suggested by Windschitl (2002) is more relevant to the professional practices of classroom teachers. When examining the difficulties of implementing constructivist instruction encountered by teachers, he framed four types of dilemmas which prevent theoretical ideals of constructivism from being realized in practice in school settings: *conceptual dilemmas* that are rooted in teachers' attempts to understand the theoretical underpinnings of constructivism;

pedagogical dilemmas that arise from the complex approaches to designing curriculum and fashioning learning experiences that constructivism demands; ***cultural dilemmas*** that emerge between teachers and students during the radical reorientation of classroom roles and expectations; ***political dilemmas*** that are associated with resistance form various stakeholders in school communities when norms and authorities are questioned.

It is evident that there are some overlapping areas among the three frameworks summarized above, though each has its own merits. These frameworks remind researchers of the multiplicity of sources of dilemmas in educational reforms, and call for researchers' attention to the dynamic interactions between the reform ideals and teachers' lived experiences in school settings. Moreover, when analyzing the dilemmas of teacher development in educational reform, researchers would be well advised to focus on the dilemmas directed related to their professional practices in classrooms. With this wealth of knowledge, this chapter tries to investigate the dilemmas that teachers encountered in the implementation of the national SSE curriculum reform.

The national curriculum reform of senior secondary education in China

The national curriculum reform is at the center of the agenda of basic education in China. The Chinese Ministry of Education (MOE) initiated the eighth round of national curriculum reform in June 2001. This nation-wide reform involves the entire basic education system which comprises six-year primary education and a six-year secondary education segments. The secondary education is divided into a three-year junior level and a three-year senior level. For the senior secondary education, the MOE issued the new curriculum guideline (experimental draft) and curriculum standards for 15 subjects (experimental draft) in 2003. The national SSE curriculum reform was implemented from September 2004 in four selected provinces (Guangdong, Shandong, Hainan and Ningxia) and has since gradually been rolled out across other provinces, including Jiangsu, Fujian, Liaoning, Anhui and Zhejiang. In June 2007, the first group of students to use the new SSE curriculum graduated from the four pilot provinces. By September 2011, all 31 provinces (autonomous regions and municipalities) in China have implemented the new SSE curriculum.

The MOE were attempting to bring about a systemic change to the SSE curriculum, emphasizing the following aspects (MOE, 2003):

- replacement of the existing subject-based curriculum structure with an integrative, three-level structure consisting of learning fields, subjects, and modules;
- decentralization of the educational system and encouraging school-based curriculum development;
- granting students the authority to choose courses, and adopting an elective course and credit system;

- adoption of new approaches to teaching and learning, such as cooperative learning, self-regulated learning, and inquiry-based learning;
- cultivation of students' generic skills, such as communication, problem-solving, team spirit and creative thinking; and
- the establishment of a formative student evaluation system and using growth portfolios to assess students' learning in schools.

With the SSE curriculum reform so clearly being a systemic, large-scale educational change, it can be considered as China's response to the global return of large-scale reform since the late 1990s (Yin, 2013). Not surprisingly, implementing such a large-scale curriculum reform is, for teachers, a very complex and difficult task, and it makes their existing knowledge and expertise insufficient for the requirements of reform. Cognizant of this fact, the MOE required all teachers using the new SSE curriculum had to participate in a general training to help them understand it. When dealing with personnel arrangements, the local educational authorities and schools had to follow the principle of "training before post; no training, no appointment". Various teacher development activities including lectures and seminars, short-term workshops, demonstration lessons, cross-district/province school visits and school-based teaching research were arranged by central and local government as well as the schools.

Although these activities had some positive influence on teachers' professional development and the implementation of SSE curriculum reform, researchers also found that there was still room for improvement in the content and forms of teacher training (Ma et al., 2009), and that the professional support that teachers obtained was far from adequate (Ma, 2009). While the reform was found to offer teachers an opportunity for re-professionalization, teacher development was revealed as having changed toward an assigned, limited professionalism (Lai, 2010). Lack of relevant research into teaching and teachers was seen as a serious bottleneck that impeded teachers' professional development and reform implementation (Zhong, 2006).

Following on from this, some dilemma situations have been revealed in a few studies on the implementation of curriculum reform in China. For example, Lee and Yin (2010) identified two major dilemmas encountered by teachers. One is the tension between the requirements of the new curriculum standards and the demands of the college entrance examination (CEE, *gaokao*), and the other is the gap between resource demands for realizing the reform and the actual "resource-stricken" situation of many ordinary schools. Fang (2011) also uncovered four reform dilemmas as follows: workload decrease vs. workload increase; diversity vs. uniformity; invisible vs. visible student participation; formal learning vs. informal workplace learning for teachers. Torn by the conflicts and dilemma situations in reform implementation, teachers had to make a great effort to negotiate the opposing imperatives in the reform, thereby they were described as "wearing new shoes to walk the old road" (Sargent et al., 2011).

In the light of the studies summarized above, the study reported in this chapter does not aim at merely depicting some concrete dilemma situations in the implementation of SSE curriculum reform. Rather, it attempts to explore the deep-seated reasons for the formation and existence of various dilemmas in reform implementation. Specifically, the contextual characteristics of the dilemmas that teachers encountered in the SSE curriculum reform will be more closely explored in order to enrich the understanding about the sources of dilemmas and their profound influence on teacher development in reform implementation.

Methodology

The present study is a part of a three-year qualitative research project (2005–2008) on the SSE curriculum in China. This project seeks to explore teachers' perceptions about, emotional and behavioral response to the implementation of SSE curriculum reform in Guangzhou, the provincial capital of Guangdong, one of the four selected pilot provinces implementing the SSE curriculum reform. Information about the whole of the first cycle of reform implementation was collected and examined.

There are a total of six key senior secondary schools in Guangzhou city which are well known for their teaching quality and, equally importantly, their results in the annual CEE. In addition, in September 2004 the Guangdong education department selected 54 schools with different academic backgrounds to be "exemplar schools" of the SSE curriculum reform in Guangdong province. These "exemplar schools", six of which were in Guangzhou city, were expected to be role models and providers of experience during the implementation of the reform. Teachers in schools entitled with "key" or "exemplar" in Guangzhou could have more opportunities for professional training and resource support from local educational administration sector. In order to study the implementation of the SSE curriculum reform in schools with different backgrounds, the present study selected four schools in Guangzhou which corresponded to the four areas in the matrix comprising key vs. non-key schools and "exemplar" vs. "non-exemplar" schools, and hence all four types of schools in Guangzhou were covered in the study. In each school, one school administrator with responsibility for teaching matters and several teachers from different genders, subjects, and teaching experiences were investigated. As a result, a total of four administrators and 25 teachers with different background in the four schools participated in the present study. Table 5.1 summarizes the background information about these schools and teachers.

Semi-structured interviews and document collection were used to collect the data. Each interview, conducted in a private space within each school, lasted at least one hour. It concentrated on teachers' perceptions and feelings toward the reform, and the tensions, conflicts and dilemmas they confronted during the reform. The main interview questions included:

- What is the impact of SSE curriculum reform on your work?
- Do you think the ideals of the SSE curriculum reform can be implemented in your classrooms? Why?

Table 5.1 Background information of the informants and summary of findings

School	*School background*		*Informants involved*		*Summary of findings*	
	Key	*Exemplar*	*School personnel*	*No. of teachers*	*Performance in reform implementation*	*Major types of dilemmas reported by informants*
S1	Yes	Yes	One teaching affairs director	Six	• Positive attitudes toward the reform in general • More commitment to the reform implementation among teachers • Praised by the local administration sector	• Cultural dilemmas • Professional dilemmas • Structural dilemmas
S2	Yes	No	One teaching affairs director	Five	• Negative attitudes toward the reform in general • More resistance or lip-service among teachers	• Cultural dilemmas • Professional dilemmas • Instrumental dilemmas
S3	No	Yes	One teaching affairs director	Seven	• School administrators showing more positive attitudes towards the reform than teachers • Praised by the local administration sector	• Cultural dilemmas • Professional dilemmas • Structural dilemmas
S4	No	No	One grade master teacher	Seven	• Informants showing more hesitation and reservation towards the reform • Slow, even progress in reform implementation	• Cultural dilemmas • Professional dilemmas • Structural dilemmas • Instrumental dilemmas

- Do you think the innovative approaches to teaching and learning can be implemented in your classrooms? Why?
- Can you obtain sufficient support from your colleagues, school leaders and other change facilitators? Why?
- What do you think of the effectiveness of teacher development in the SSE curriculum reform?

In addition, teachers' self reflection journals, the documents issued by the school and the researchers' field notes were included in the documents used for data analysis.

All interviews were transcribed and analyzed inductively. The overall analysis was an ongoing cyclical process in which categories and patterns emerged from the data and were later cross-checked (Miles and Huberman, 1994). During the data analysis process, NVivo 7 software was used to classify and cluster the data. Coding the transcriptions with NVivo enabled researchers to more effectively draw out the codes, concepts and categories step by step, to finally discover the patterns in the data.

Findings

The inductive process of data analysis generated a series of dilemma situations that resulted in dramatic tensions and conflicts for teacher development during the implementation of the SSE curriculum reform. According to the sources of these dilemma situations, these dilemmas can be categorized into four types, namely cultural dilemmas, structural dilemmas, professional dilemmas and instrumental dilemmas.

Cultural dilemmas

Cultural dilemmas refer to the dilemma situations caused by the conflicts between the new norms and values advocated by the reform and the existing educational, cultural traditions of the schools and the whole society. During the SSE curriculum reform, cultural dilemmas were one of the most frequently mentioned dilemma situations that impeded teacher development and the implementation of the new SSE curriculum. In the views of the informants, the SSE curriculum reform, led by a number of scholars with overseas study background, introduced many new educational ideals and practices from the West, such as constructivist instruction, inquiry learning and school-based curriculum development.

> In fact the new curriculum reform is led by a group of overseas returnees (*haigui*). They draw some ideals and models from the West and attempt to change China's education with these things.
>
> (S1-TM4)

> Teachers often ask where the reform came from? After several rounds of reading the new curriculum standards, many teachers think the reform was merely copied from the United States but with some small modifications
>
> (S2-TM3)

These "imported" reform ideals and practices conflicted dramatically with the pre-existing educational and cultural background in schools. The informants thought implementing such an exotic curriculum reform in schools was almost a mission impossible, because it was not suitable for the national conditions in China.

> The reform ideals could be new and innovative, but they have to be capable of resolving the problems in China. They can't merely import the western theories to guide our educational practice. It has to be relevant to the reality in China.
>
> (S1-TM3)

For teachers in this study, the long-standing "examination culture" was the most salient characteristic of China's education, requiring that all senior secondary schools had to be extremely cautious about their performance in public examinations, especially the CEE. This situation was intensified by the huge population pressures in contemporary China. All parents earnestly expected that the schools and teachers could successfully prepare their children for the annual CEE. Therefore, some teachers did not dare to fully embrace the new practices because they were worried that the implementation of the new curriculum would probably impair their students' performance in public examinations.

> In China, the pressure of competition and employment is always dominant because of the huge population. So many things advocated by the reform came from the foreign countries. Can it be possible to suit our national conditions? I doubt that!
>
> (S2-TM1)

> After all, we frontline teachers concern one thing – the examination performance of our students. Can they get 800 points in *gaokao*? How many students get 700? . . . Now I think there are some conflicts between the direction of the reform and our teachers' purpose to train more students with 700 or 800 in *gaokao*, and then many contradictions emerge.
>
> (S4-TM1)

Structural dilemmas

Structural dilemmas refer to the tensions and conflicts deriving from the ambiguities in various reform policies, or the asynchronous changes between the curriculum reform and other policies and administrative structures. The new curriculum guideline and curriculum standards issued by the MOE merely provided a grand blueprint for the reform. When they were put into practice, teachers soon found that there were a lot of ambiguities among the reform policies. For example, the reform required schools to adopt the credit system and divide each subject into different modules. The schools were empowered to independently assess whether their students get the credits after studying each module. However, teachers and schools were not provided with any clear criterion for the assessment. Many informants encountered serious confusions on these issues.

> I am quite confused about the criteria for the assessment, but no one can tell us . . . I guess the reformers are also in misty. They didn't give us any clear criterion. They only divided the subject into some modules, and required students to achieve a certain level, but they said nothing about the references of this level.
>
> (S4-TF2)

Teachers' adoption of inquiry learning also faced dilemmas caused by the various requirements of the reform. In the views of the informants, inquiry learning was more time consuming than the traditional pedagogy. To effectively adopt the inquiry learning methodology they needed more teaching hours. However, the reform stipulated that teachers had to finish one module in ten weeks; that is nine teaching weeks and the last week for module assessment. Teachers had to complete the teaching and assessment of two modules within one semester. These rigid requirements caused a lot of difficulties in classroom teaching, resulting in teachers' reservation on adopting the new pedagogies.

> The reform requires us to use inquiry learning. It needs more time to conduct inquiry learning. Nonetheless, I have only 32 teaching hours each semester consisting of about 17 weeks. In these 17 weeks, even if I can teach the content required by the curriculum standard, I have no time to conduct assess – it costs at least two weeks . . . Actually, there is no way for us to follow the requirements of the new curriculum.
>
> (S4-TM3)

More importantly, the asynchronous changes between the curriculum standards and the CEE schemes had teachers wallowing in a sea of uncertainties and ambiguities. All the informants hoped that the changes of the CEE schemes could match the requirements of the new curriculum, but unfortunately, the new CEE schemes in Guangdong seriously lagged behind the curriculum reform. Though the SSE curriculum reform was implemented in September 2004, the finalized CEE schemes in Guangdong were not issued until May 2006. This asynchronous change between the new curriculum and the CEE meant the teachers in Guangdong faced huge dilemmas during the implementation of the SSE curriculum reform, causing them to feel uncertain about the direction of their professional development and the curriculum implementation. The views of the informants reflected a structural problem in the organization and implementation of the SSE curriculum reform.

> The reform is brand new for our teachers, but at the same time, we have to cope with the baton of *gaokao*. The new scheme of *gaokao* has not been on the table until now. How could we be sure about the direction of the reform?
>
> (S3-TF1)

> It may be a structural problem. The designers of the new CEE schemes are not the developers of the new curriculum standards. There is a lack of communications between those two groups of people. As a result, we teachers encounter many confusions and difficulties when implementing the reform.
>
> (S2-TM4)

Professional dilemmas

Professional dilemmas denote the dilemma situations caused by the disconnection between the high requirements of the reform on teachers' expertise to deal with curriculum and pedagogical issues on the one hand and the insufficient or inappropriate professional support for teachers provided by the reform on the other. As previously stated, the SSE curriculum reform required teachers to adopt many new practices, such as constructivist instruction, inquiry learning, formative assessment and school-based curriculum development. These requirements placed high demands on teachers' professional competence. To effectively implement these new practices, teachers had to continuously develop their professional abilities to cope with the challenges of the reform. As the director of teaching affairs in one sample school said:

> Teachers feel a bit of a misfit during the reform. Though teachers in my school are still young, they all grow from the previous education system. In fact, their knowledge structure is not sufficient for the requirements of the new curriculum. If teachers don't continue to learn or improve our knowledge and ability, it is very difficult for them to cope with the teaching tasks today.
>
> (S2-AM)

To facilitate teacher development in the SSE curriculum reform, teachers needed at least two kinds of professional support. One was a set of coherent, well-organized textbooks and teaching materials, the other was an effective system of professional training programs. However, in the views of the informants, both of these were insufficient or inappropriate for the curriculum reform. They found that there were often gaps between the requirements of the curriculum standards and the new textbooks, and some new textbooks could not provide a coherent knowledge system within a subject or between subjects.

> Now there are different versions of new textbooks. However, not all versions can grasp the essence of the new curriculum standards. Gaps are often found among the textbooks of different subjects.
>
> (S1-AM)

> The new textbooks of compulsory modules are in a terrible mess! Take the example of new chemistry textbooks, there is little connection between chapter one and chapter two. Meanwhile, the content of some elective modules overlaps a lot with the compulsory ones.
>
> (S2-TF2)

The SSE curriculum reform included organization of various teacher development activities, such as lectures and seminars, short-term workshops and demonstration lessons as stated earlier. This was also the case in Guangzhou where the teaching research officers (*jiaoyanyuan*) in local education departments and university experts in curriculum studies or subject teaching usually assumed the role of teacher trainer. Though these activities provided some guides for teachers, they were often criticized as inappropriate, because university experts often paid little attention to the practice in schools, and the teaching research officers could not provide clear instructions for teachers due to their lack of experience of using the new curriculum. The insufficient professional support caused teacher uncertainty about their professional learning and growth.

> The teaching research activities provide little guidance. In these activities, they always demonstrate some experimental lessons. Some are good, but some are rubbish. However, the teacher trainer say "it is a good try" every time! So how can we know the direction? I guess they have no idea, either.
>
> (S4-TM2)

Instrumental dilemmas

Instrumental dilemmas denote the dilemmas rooted in the disconnection between the resource demanded by the reform and the realities of resource owned by the schools. As stated by the informants, the implementation of the SSE curriculum reform put heavy demands on school resources. To meet the expectation of the new curriculum, each school needed enough resources to set up laboratories, functional rooms, and computer centers, etc. However, only a small number of schools could meet these resource demands, even those in the capital city of an industrially developed province like Guangdong.

> The new curriculum requires an ample school environment and resource. My school can provide enough laboratories and set up four "inquiry laboratories" for students. It really cost a lot! Not all schools can afford.
>
> (S1-AM)

> Now even if school is over, many students still stay in classrooms, because they don't have computer at home. They have to use the computers in classrooms to finish their assignments. If this is the case for urban schools, what can it be for the suburban and rural schools?
>
> (S4-TF1)

Moreover, the informants thought that the new approaches to teaching and learning advocated by the reform, e.g., cooperative learning, inquiry learning, required an environment of small class sizes. However, in the senior secondary schools in Guangzhou, each class had more than 50 students. This reality caused lots of troubles for teachers to adopt these new teaching approaches. The instrumental dilemmas reinforced teachers' impression that the reform ideals were not suitable for the national conditions in China, and limited their willingness to try the new practices in their classrooms.

> How can it be possible to carry out the reform? Many reform practices won't work here! In the west countries, they usually have 25 students in each class. But for me, I teach eight classes and more than 400 students! In addition, the schools (in west countries) have enough classrooms for elective courses. Do we have enough resource here?
>
> (S3-TF2)

Discussion

The study reported in this chapter investigated the dilemmas that influenced teacher development and curriculum implementation during the national SSE curriculum reform in China. In addition to indicating that these dilemmas can be categorized into four types, i.e., cultural dilemmas, structural dilemmas, professional dilemmas and instrumental dilemmas, the results raised the following two issues worthy of further discussion.

The nature of dilemmas of teacher development in curriculum reform

As Lampert (1985) pointed out, teachers are dilemma managers and brokers of conflict solutions in classroom teaching. This claim is also applicable to the implementation of curriculum reform. The results of this study support Fransson and Grannäs' (2013) argument that dilemmas of teacher development in curriculum reform are constitutive and omnipresent, rather than some particular events. Ultimately, the engine of the various dilemmas in curriculum reform is the tension between the reform initiatives and the existing educational settings which is both the context where the reform initiatives unfold and the condition that the initiatives aim to change. Therefore, this study highlights the importance of contextual characteristics in understanding the nature of dilemmas that teachers encountered in curriculum reform.

As shown in this chapter, the dilemmas that teachers faced in curriculum reform can be classified into the four categories of cultural dilemmas, structural dilemmas, professional dilemmas and instrumental dilemmas according to their source. These findings indicated that the previous frameworks on dilemma formation are helpful for understanding the dilemmas that teachers encountered in curriculum reform, especially the values-institutional-resources framework (Dimmock, 1996) and the disconnection framework (Walker and Qian, 2012). Specifically, the cultural dilemmas can be traced to the asynchronous changes in norms and values between the reform ideals and the existing educational settings. These dilemmas echo the cultural disconnection and political disconnection in Walker and Qian's (2012) classification. The structural dilemmas are caused by the asynchronous changes, or even conflicts, among different reform policies, which echoes Walker and Qian's (2012) intellectual disconnection. The instrumental dilemmas, or the instrumental disconnection in Walker and Qian's (2012) terms, derive from the mismatch between what the reform initiatives demand and the practical realities of schools.

Although the classification suggested by this study recognizes the relevance of these two frameworks, it also highlights the influence of professional dilemmas on teacher development in curriculum reform. These dilemmas derive from the mismatch between what the reform required from teachers' expertise and the professional support provided by the reform. They directly relate to the professional practices of front-line teachers in curriculum reform. However, these professional dilemmas are absent in the values-institutional-resources framework and the reform disconnection framework. In this respect, the present study benefits a lot from Windschitl's (2002) wisdom. In the framework suggested by Windschitl (2002), the conceptual and pedagogical dilemmas denote the dilemmas that teachers faced when understanding the rationale of a certain innovation and the practical ways to implement the innovation in specific classroom situations. These dilemmas reflect the gap between what the reform demand of teachers' professional knowledge and skills and what teachers have in this regard. That is what the professional dilemmas refer to in the present study.

Implications for teacher development in curriculum reform

The connections between teacher development and educational reform have been widely recognized by researchers. At present, the educational reforms in many Asian countries including China put forward huge challenges on teachers' professional competence. Therefore, facilitating them to be independent professionals who can make proper judgments in complex situations and developing them to be responsible for their own professional growth are critical to the successful implementation of educational reforms.

The results of the present study indicated that under the context of educational reform, the once dominant training-and-coaching model, which emphasizes expanding an individual repertoire of well-defined classroom practice, was inadequate in terms of satisfying the requirements of present reform initiatives (Little, 1993), because both teachers and teacher trainers, in this case the teaching researcher officers and university experts, faced brand-new reform initiatives, and both groups were uncertain about the direction of reform implementation because of the ambiguities in reform policies. All of the four types of dilemmas made it very difficult for teacher development in curriculum reform to move forward. So how can the reformer, teacher trainers and change facilitators deal with these dilemmas in curriculum reform?

It is worth noting that one of the salient characteristics of the dilemmas in curriculum reform is that all of them were beyond the control of teachers or other stakeholders, including the reformers. This is why Cuban (1992) described that the dilemmas can only be reconciled rather than be resolved. To reconcile the dilemmas of teacher development in curriculum reform, one has to systematically handle these dilemmas from multiple angles.

It is suggested that change facilitators and teacher trainers need to carefully consider the fusion of pressure and support in curriculum reform. As Barber and Philips (2000) pointed out, only under conditions of high pressure and high support, can teachers make rapid progress and give a satisfactory performance in reform implementation. The results of the present study showed that teachers in curriculum reform need at least four kinds of support which are a favorable sociocultural climate, coherent reform policies, effective teacher development activities and sufficient resources. All change facilitators and teacher trainers should first examine whether the support provided by the reform to teachers is sufficient and effective.

The existence of various dilemmas in curriculum reform indicates that teacher change in curriculum reform may be a slow and complicated process. It is reasonable to find a mixture of old and new in teachers' behavior during the implementation of curriculum reform, the "wearing new shoes to walk the old road" (Sargent et al., 2011) referred to earlier. Though large-scale reforms target a systematic and fundamental change to the existing educational systems, front-line teachers "can only change in a small way" (Yan, 2012) because of the restrictions of various dilemmas. Therefore, change facilitators and teacher trainers need to adopt reasonable expectations on the pace and scope of teacher change in curriculum reform. Just as Cohen (1990) said, the past is the teachers' path to the future. Change facilitators and teacher trainers should help teachers find the connection between the reform ideals and their past experiences, and encourage teachers to take this connection as their starting point of change.

Flett and Wallace (2005) suggested three ways of resolving dilemmas: selecting one option only, dealing with both options simultaneously, or developing a workable compromise. The recognition of the connection between the reform ideals and teachers' past experiences means that teachers should develop a workable compromise between old and new, or between conflicting forces. Thus teacher development in curriculum reform must provide occasions for "teachers to reflect critically on their practice and to fashion new knowledge and beliefs about content, pedagogy, and learners" (Darling-Hammond and McLaughlin, 2011, p. 81). As suggested by Roblin and Margalef (2013), rather than hiding these contradictory forces, all key agents of curriculum reform, including change facilitators, teacher trainers and front-line teachers, should bring these dilemmas to the surface through critical reflection, and benefit from the opportunities provided by these dilemmas for teacher change and reform implementation.

References

Barber, M. and Philips, V. (2000). The fusion of pressure and support. *Journal of Educational Change*, 1(3), 277–281.

Borko, H., Elliot, R., and Uchiyama, K. (2002). Professional development: A key to Kentucky's educational reform effort. *Teaching and Teacher Education*, 18, 969–987.

Cabaroglu, N. and Tillema, H. (2011). Teacher educator dilemmas: A concept to study pedagogy. *Teachers and Teaching*, 17(5), 559–573.

Cohen, D. (1990). A revolution in one classroom: The case of Mrs. Oublier. *Educational Evaluation and Policy Analysis*, 12(3), 311–329.

Cuban, L. (1992). Managing dilemmas while building professional communities. *Educational Researcher*, 21(1), 4–11.

Darling-Hammond, L. and McLaughlin, M. W. (2011). Policies that support professional development in an era of reform. *Phi Delta Kappan*, 92(6), 81–92.

Darling-Hammond, L., Wei, R. C., Andree, A., Richardson, N., and Orphanos, S. (2009). *Professional Learning in the Learning Profession: A Status Report on Teacher Development in the United States and Abroad*. Dallas, TX: National Staff Development Council.

Desimone, L. (2011). A primer on effective professional development. *Phi Delta Kappan*, 92(6), 68–71.

Dimmock, C. (1996). Dilemmas for school leaders and administrators in restructuring. In K. Leithwood, J. Chapman, D. Corson, P. Hallinger and A. Hart (Eds), *International Handbook of Educational Leadership and Administration* (pp. 135–170). Dordrecht: Kluwer Academic.

Elmore, R. F. and Burney, D. (1997). *Investing in Teacher Learning: Staff Development and Instructional Improvement: Community School District 2, New York City*. New York: National Commission on Teaching and America's Future and Consortium for Policy Research in Education.

Enyedy, N., Goldberg, J., and Welsh, K. M. (2006). Complex dilemmas of identity and practice. *Science Education*, 90, 68–93.

Fang, Y. (2011). Pedagogy and curriculum reform in China – From the angle of one teachers' daily work. *Chinese Education and Society*, 44(6), 24–35.

Flett, J. D. and Wallace, J. (2005). Change dilemmas for curriculum leaders: Dealing with mandated change in schools. *Journal of Curriculum and Supervision*, 20(3), 188–213.

Fransson, G. and Grannäs, J. (2013). Dilemmatic spaces in educational context – towards a conceptual framework for dilemmas in teachers work. *Teachers and Teaching*, 19(1), 4–17.

Fullan, M. (2000). The return of large-scale reform. *Journal of Educational Change*, 1(1), 5–28.

Fullan, M. (2009). Large-scale reform comes of age. *Journal of Educational Change*, 10(2–3), 101–113.

Fullan, M. and Hargreaves, A. (1992). Teacher development and educational change. In M. Fullan and A. Hargreaves (Eds), *Teacher Development and Educational Change* (pp. 1–9). London: The Falmer Press.

Garet, M. S., Porter, A. C., Desimone, L., Birman, B. F., and Yoon, K. S. (2001). What makes professional development effective? Results from a national sample of teachers. *American Educational Research Journal*, 38(4), 915–945.

Guskey, T. R. (2003). What makes professional development effective? *Phi Delta Kappan*, 84(10), 748–750.

Hoque, K. E., Alam, G. M., and Abdullah, A. G. K. (2011). Impact of teachers' professional development on school improvement – an analysis at Bangladesh standpoint. *Asia Pacific Education Review*, 12, 337–348.

Kennedy, K. (2007). Curriculum reforms and instructional improvement in Asia. In T. Townsend (Ed.), *International Handbook of School Effectiveness and Improvement* (pp. 807–822). Dordrecht: Springer.

Lai, M. (2010). Teacher development under curriculum reform: A case study of a secondary school in mainland China. *International Review of Education*, 56, 613–631.

Lampert, M. (1985). How do teachers manage to teach? Perspectives on problems in practice. *Harvard Educational Review*, 55(2), 178–194.

Lee, J. C. K. and Yin, H. (2010). Curriculum policy implementation in China: Interactions between policy designs, places and people. *Curriculum and Teaching*, 25(2), 31–53.

Little, J. W. (1993). Teachers' professional development in a climate of educational reform. *Educational Evaluation and Policy Analysis*, 15(2), 129–151.

Lyons, N. (1990). Dilemmas of knowing: Epistemological dimensions of teachers' work and development. *Harvard Educational Review*, 60(2), 159–180.

Ma, Y. (2009). The implementation process, characteristics analysis and promotion strategy of the curriculum reform of basic education. *Curriculum, Teaching Material and Method*, 29(4), 3–9. (in Chinese)

Ma, Y., Yin, H., Tang, L., and Liu, L. (2009). Teacher receptivity to system-wide curriculum reform in the initiation stage: A Chinese perspective. *Asia Pacific Education Review*, 10(3), 423–432.

Miles, M. B. and Humberman, A. M. (1994). *Qualitative Data Analysis: An Expanded Sourcebook* (2nd ed.). Thousand Oaks, CA: Sage.

Ministry of Education (2003). *Programme on the Curriculum of General Senior Secondary School (Experimental) (putong gaozhong kecheng fangan (shiyan))*. Retrieved August 31, 2004, from http://www.moe.edu.cn/ (in Chinese)

Penuel, W. R., Fishman, B. J., Yamaguchi, R., and Gallagher, L. P. (2007). What makes professional development effective? Strategies that foster curriculum implementation. *American Educational Research Journal*, 44(4), 921–958.

Roblin, N. P. and Margalef, L. (2013). Learning from dilemmas: Teacher professional development through collaborative action and reflection. *Teachers and Teaching*, 19(1), 18–32.

Sargent, T., Chen, M., Wu, Y. J., and Chen, C. (2011). Wearing new shoes to walk the old road: The negotiation of opposing imperatives in high school new curriculum classes in China. *International Perspectives on Education and Society*, 15, 79–98.

Scott, F. B. (1994). Integrating curriculum implementation and staff development. *The Clearing House*, 67(3), 157–160.

Tillma, H. and Kremer-Hayon, L. (2002). "Practising what we preach" – teacher educators' dilemmas in promoting self-regulated learning: A cross case comparison. *Teaching and Teacher Education*, 18, 593–607.

van Driel, J. H., Beijaard, D., and Verloop, N. (2001). Professional development and reform in science education: The role of teachers' practical knowledge. *Journal of Research in Science Teaching*, 38(2), 137–158.

Walker, A. and Qian, H. (2012). Reform disconnection in China. *Peabody Journal of Education*, 87(2), 162–177.

Windschitl, M. (2002). Framing constructivism in practice as the negotiation of dilemmas: An analysis of the conceptual, pedagogical, cultural, and political challenges facing teachers. *Review of Educational Research*, 72(2), 131–175.

Yan, C. (2012). "We can change in a small way": A study of secondary English teachers' implementation of curriculum reform in China. *Journal of Educational Change*, 13(4), 431–447.

Yin, H. (2013). Implementing the national curriculum reform in China: A decade review. *Frontiers of Education in China*, 8(3), 331–359.

Yin, H., Lee, J. C. K., and Wang, W. (2014). Dilemmas of leading national curriculum reform in a global era: A Chinese perspective. *Educational Management Administration and Leadership*, 42(2), 293–311.

Zhong, Q. (2006). Curriculum reform in China: Challenges and reflections. *Frontiers of Education in China*, 3(3), 370–382.

Zhu, H. (2010). Curriculum reform and professional development: A case study on Chinese teacher educators. *Professional Development in Education*, 36(1–2), 373–391.

6 China's quest for world-class teachers

A rational model of national teacher education reform

Jun Li

The record-breaking performance of Shanghai students in all domains of the recent PISA results (Organisation for Economic Co-operation and Development, 2013) has again astonished the globe, though this achievement needs more prudent investigation. Worldwide attention has been paid to how Chinese learners are able to attain such a highly competitive edge over top students from the rest of the world. One of the key factors, as identified by Liu Jinghai, a well-known principal in Shanghai, rightly pointed out that teachers are the key to the success of Chinese students and education as well (Organisation for Economic Co-operation and Development, 2012).

China has tried to nurture world-class teachers for over a century, and the recent PISA results of Shanghai students confirmed the outcomes of such national endeavours. Although there has been a plethora of studies on Chinese teachers and teacher education reform, the impact of national policies on teacher education institutions (TEIs) still remains a mystery. How have TEIs reshaped their institutional missions and strategies to respond to the national reform? What institutional transformations have taken place? And what challenges are arising from this process? Adopting a case study approach, this study aims at using a rational perspective to investigate the institutional transformations resulting from teacher education initiatives in China.

The socio-historical and global context

The modern system of teacher education was established in China for political purposes to serve national survival and revival and to catch up with Western powers in the late nineteenth century. This post-colonial catch-up mentality has continued over a century, with four stages of development under various historical contexts: the first stage of establishment (1897–1911), the second stage of institutionalisation (1912–1949), the third stage of re-institutionalisation (1949–1993) and the most recent stage of pro-fessionalisation (1993–present) (J. Li, 2012).

A fundamental characteristic of the four stages of teacher education has been China's quest for a world-class teaching force that could serve its self-strengthening against Western imperialism and colonialism in the past and its modernisation in the new context of globalisation from the late 1970s. Since its door was opened to the world in 1978, China has had to face dual challenges to teacher education, arising from its post-colonial circumstances and ever-intensifying trends of globalisation. On the one hand, alternative pathways have been explored to raise the overall quality of the teaching force up to world-class standards and changes have been made to the system to meet global demands, i.e., a redefining of the multiple identities of teachers. On the other hand, the new model of teacher education has been built upon China's own traditions as a country that has a long history of education. In other words, China has been seeking a form of teacher professionalism that balances the global and the local (J. Li, 2012, 2013, 2015).

Key national initiatives

To search for world-class teachers who are highly qualified and first rate in teaching competency (The State Council, 2012), China has launched persistent national initiatives for the institutional changes of its teacher education system since the early 1990s (see Table 6.1).

Central to these policy mandates is the improvement of the overall quality of basic education through a variety of policy actions. These include a rational approach to improving the professionalism of the teaching workforce, and the reform of TEIs. The above 14 government policy documents articulate the rationale, policy problems, major policy goals and guidelines for nationwide teacher education reform since 1993.

Chinese policymakers have a strong belief in certain rational assumptions about human behaviour, and thus the following equation may be used to sum up these assumptions: TE→CT→QE/SA→QL→MD/EG→NAC. This simplified equation expresses the views of Chinese leaders that a better system for teacher education (TE) prepares more competent teachers (CT), better prepared teachers improve the quality of education and student achievement (QE/SA), higher educational quality and student achievement result in the higher quality of the labour force (QL), the higher quality of the labour force tremendously benefits the country's modernisation and economic growth (MD/EG) and eventually leads to China's national achievement and competitiveness (NAC). Based on these assumptions, teacher education is seen as the first and foremost domain for reform.

In addition to key national initiatives for teacher education, the Chinese government launched the expansion of higher education in the mid-1990s (Hayhoe, Li, Lin, and Zha, 2011), and the new curriculum reform for basic education in 1999. Both movements of reform have brought many challenges to TEIs. They pushed TEIs to focus on the unprecedented expansion in student enrolment within a few years, which placed high pressure on teaching staff and campus facilities. In the expansion process, new programs and departments were set up while TEIs were undergoing systematic restructuring; thus higher education expansion has had a notable impact on the system of teacher education. The New Curriculum System for Basic Education is viewed widely as the core of current reform and a key to promoting school excellence. As a result, it too creates high

Table 6.1 Policy initiatives for teacher education reform (1993–2012)

Policy documents	*Dates*
The Guidelines for the Reform and Development of Education in China by the CPCCC (Chinese People's Political Consultative Conference) & the State Council	13 February 1993
The Law of Teachers of the People's Republic of China by the Standing Commission of the National People's Congress	31 October 1993
The Ordinance of Teacher Qualification by the State Council	12 December 1995
The Ninth Five-Year Plan for China's Educational Development and the Development Outline by 2010 by the State Commission of Education (SCE)	10 April 1996
The Opinion on the Reform and Development of Teacher Education by the SCE	5 December 1996
The Action Plan for Educational Revitalisation Facing the Twenty-First Century by the Ministry of Education (MOE)	24 December 1998
The Opinion on Adjusting the Structure of TEIs by the MOE	16 March 1999
The CPCCC and State Council's Decision on the Deepening of Educational Reform and the Full Promotion of Quality Education by the CPCCC and the State Council	13 June 1999
The Decision on the Reform and Development of Basic Education by the State Council	29 May 2001
The Guidelines for Basic Education Curriculum Reform by the MOE	7 June 2001
The Tenth Five-Year National Plan for Education by the MOE	July 2001
The Opinion on the Reform and Development of Teacher Education during the Tenth Five-Year National Plan by the MOE	6 February 2002
The Rejuvenation Action Plan for Education 2003–2007 by the MOE	10 February 2004
Guidelines for Mid- and Long-Term Educational Reform and Development 2010–2020 by the State Council	5 May 2010
The National Training Project for Elementary and Secondary School Teachers (Guopei Jihua) by the MOE	11 June 2010
The Curricular Standards for Teacher Education by the MOE	8 October 2011
The Opinion on the Enhancement of the Teaching Workforce by the State Council	20 August 2012

pressure on the reform of teacher education, as it requires teachers, including prospective teachers and in-service teachers, to upgrade their professional skills and knowledge across a broad area. It has also challenged the national initiatives of teacher education in terms of setting higher standards and requirements for teachers. These national policies alternately reinforced each other in some areas and worked against each other in other areas.

Existing analyses

There are a number of existing analyses of teacher education reform in China which provide initial insights into various dimensions of its changes. Paine (1992) observed that China has introduced technical strategies to strengthen its teacher education system to attract better students, to enhance the curriculum and teaching, and to establish high standards by looking into two competing discourses, modernising and nationalising perspectives. Following Paine's accounts, Shen (1994) focused on teacher education reform in China under the national drive toward modernisation and a market-based economy. D.F. Li (1999) studied the recent reform by looking into the establishment of a nationwide network of teacher preparation and professional development centres, the launching of nationwide efforts at upgrading the qualifications of in-service teachers, the building of nationwide respect for teachers and consequent improvement in the treatment of teachers. Lin and Xun (2001) outlined new trends in teacher education development. Meanwhile, Ashmore and Cao (1997) acknowledged that the large number of unqualified teachers and low-level normal schools created obstacles for teacher education reform.

There are a number of other policy analyses that address China's reform of teacher education at the local level. Although the teacher education system was largely restored in the 1980s following the chaos of the Cultural Revolution, Ma (2000) pointed out that current TEIs are managed with little consideration by various governmental offices at different levels, and limited resources for teacher education are not efficiently allocated and utilised.

Some researchers are not satisfied with these analyses but instead reflect on their own experiments and point to new directions in the efforts of teacher education reform. In her experiment on combining teaching with research for the new curriculum reform for basic education, Ye (2000) concluded that the combination of theoretical research and practical research in school reform benefits the professional development of a new type of teacher in many ways. On the other hand, M. Li (2010) demonstrated how three different "logics" – of institutional strategies, economic demand and state political initiatives – have driven the developmental model of TEIs in China, with a detailed comparison of three leading universities for teachers. Foreign models of teacher education systems also provide China with valuable experiences (Hayhoe, 2002; Hayhoe and Li, 2010; J. Li, 2012; Zhu, 2001).

In addition, Dooley (2001) offered a case study conducted in Shanghai, vividly describing how "obedient students" are mechanically trained by teachers who received professional education from independent, closed and narrowly specified TEIs. Along similar lines, four problems of teacher education were identified by Leung and Xu (2000). These problems are the identity crisis, the mismatch between teacher supply and demand, the incongruence between teacher preparation and classroom realities, and the poor appeal of teaching as a career.

The above-mentioned studies provide valuable information about the background of teacher education reform in China and some core issues, but they have never focused on the key process, i.e., the micro-implementation of China's national quest for world-class teachers. Empirical studies on institutional change brought about by recent national initiatives are particularly lacking. This paper will try to address that gap. But first I will outline the rational framework that is being adopted and the methodological considerations that shape this effort.

The rational framework

Public policy is commonly accepted as a purposeful course of action advanced or authorised by higher institutional levels of the policy system in pursuit of influencing lower levels or units of the system (Fowler, 2013). From this point of view, it holds at least one basic assumption, i.e., public policy is a rational collective behaviour aiming to achieve proposed policy goals. Based on this assumption, the rational framework stands out as suitable to understand China's complex process of teacher education reform.

A cardinal assumption of the rational framework is that human behaviour is purposely rational and that a policy process is thought of "as purposive, goal-directed activity" by a rational unified player (Allison and Zelikow, 1999, p. 17). Further, a means–ends driven and goal-directed principle is practised by policy players and is evident throughout the policy process: "first the ends are isolated, then the means to achieve them are sought" (Lindblom, 1959, p. 81). To achieve the policy ends through chosen means, a policy process usually starts its linear journey with first identifying the substantial policy problems. Then, alternative strategies are considered, evaluated and compared. Optimal strategies that are likely to be most efficient are finally chosen to solve the identified policy problems. In addition, Jenkins (1978) assumed that policy emerges via a logical path. This assumption may help explain the policy action expressed in China's national initiatives and their impact on TEIs since the early 1990s.

The rational framework has been selected as it matches well the purpose of this study and the reality of the sociopolitical context of China. In addition, it can help, with its emphasis on logic, to order and simplify the complexity of the policy process, identify what is significant, and direct inquiry and research.

Methodological considerations

Since this study looks for in-depth descriptive interpretations of the sophisticated policy process of China's national reform of teacher education, it has adopted the theoretical sampling technique with a typical-case approach. The site of the case was limited to a medium-sized city in a mid-level-developed province in inland China. The gross regional product and per capita net income of households were used by this study to measure the socioeconomic development of the region. Similarly, the case was carefully limited to one institution which is typical of provincial normal universities in medium-developed provinces. Based on the above criteria, the province of Yangtze (a pseudonym) was selected as the site and Yangtze Normal University (YNU) as the case for this study.

YNU is situated in a busy inland metropolitan area in east China. Though YNU was a national comprehensive university in its early history, it was reconstructed as a key provincial teacher education institution in the early 1950s. By 2012, it had 16 schools on three urban campuses with a faculty–student ratio of 1 to 24. It offered around 70 undergraduate programs and had a total of 22,000 full-time students, with 36.6% receiving teacher education. YNU's College of Educational Science (CES) was formed in 2000, aiming to prepare educators, psychologists, educational administrators and researchers. With 70 faculty members, the CES has a total of 900 full-time undergraduate students in six programs of teacher education, plus 600 graduate students.

The theoretical sampling technique was also used for identifying individual interviewees. A total of 17 interviewees were successfully recruited from YNU's CES, with 11 leaders or administrators and six faculty members. In addition, documentation and archival records were collected as additional data sources for triangulation. Meanwhile, ethical codes and consent forms were used consistently throughout the study. The completed interview process involved a combination of three basic approaches for open-ended interviews, i.e., the informal conversational interview, the general interview guide, and the standardised open-ended interview (Pattern, 2002), as best fitted the situation. The field work was mainly finished in 2005 but efforts were made to follow on subsequent developments up to 2012. Data were triangulated with other data sources such as documents collected on-site, and verified by accounts of various participants. Data analysis with coding was made shortly after the transcripts were complete. The master codes included several key variables and their corresponding subunits of analysis, and the second level of codes was based on Bogdan and Biklen's 10 coding categories (1998, pp. 172–177).

Institutional transformations

Linear delivery of policy flow

It is common that Chinese TEIs are under the supervision of the MOE or the Provincial Bureau of Education (PBE). Generally, national policies are linearly channelled from the MOE/PBE to TEIs in two ways. Oftentimes, before a national policy of education is formally publicised, university leaders will be summoned for a special meeting to the MOE/PBE. After that, the university leaders will plan how to implement the policy on campus based on the policy document and its requirements. Sometimes a national policy is delivered via the official delivery system from the MOE to universities directly or via the PBE indirectly. In this process, the PBE serves as a conveyor or a buffer agency.

As a provincial key normal university, YNU usually receives national policies from the Yangtze PBE. Once national policies are officially passed down, YNU would hold special working meetings to implement them, especially major policies. For example, on 18 September 2004, YNU held the Third Working Meeting on Teaching, in order to implement the requirements of *The Rejuvenation*

Action Plan for Education 2003–2007 by the MOE (2004). The implementation goals and strategies were put into place soon after these working meetings. As shown in Figure 6.1, the policy flow at YNU for the implementation of the national policy was top-down and linear. This was taken as a rational, efficient and systematic way to deliver national initiatives to an individual institution.

Communication is a key process by which policy goals and strategies are mapped out for implementers and participants. Like many other TEIs, YNU routinely adopts policy delivery through regular official propaganda, *chuanda*, as a form of communication for the implementation of national policies, which literally means passing the message on and down. One of its major forms is holding special meetings or seminars such as officially organised political study sessions, *zhengzhi xuexi*. According to most participants the political study process has never been interrupted at YNU. When interviewees were asked about the specific communication means employed to implement the national reform of teacher education, two deans responded that it was the most popular channel through which the national policy was disseminated. Department chair Caifei[1] noted that it served as the major source for his faculty to learn about the national reform of teacher education. For dean Enwei, it is the mandatory form that everybody has to participate in.

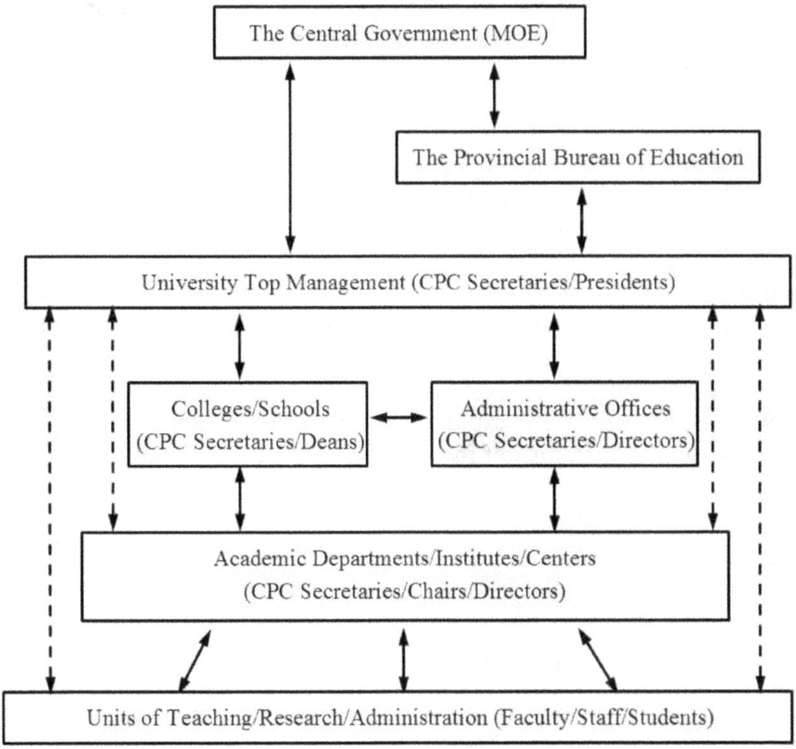

Figure 6.1 The policy flow

The new institutional mission

YNU's original mission before the 1990s was very typical and general, just like that of any other university in China, as stated below in one of YNU's official documents published in October 1983:

> Yangtze Normal University is a provincial key normal university with a long history, providing comparatively complete programs in science and liberal arts for training teachers. It aims to produce more qualified talents for socialist construction and contribute to the socialist country.

The university's top management and implementers met from 30 July to 2 August 2003, to plan for the future development of YNU. Debates took place on topics such as what type of university, fully comprehensive or focused on teacher education, should YNU become, and how to construct one or the other. In April 2005, the university's *Strategic Plan for the Eleventh Five-Year Plan and the Year of 2015* reshaped its mission as follows:

> We will strive to build up a comprehensive teaching and research university primarily featured with teacher education, to become a key base for producing high-level talents in research and technology innovation in the province and, to contribute to the revitalisation of Yangtze province through science and education.

The new mission clearly keeps its original statement that the university aims to be a provincial key teaching institution and a research base for teacher education and is evolving toward a *comprehensive* university featuring teacher education.

In addition, as professor Peishi and department chair Beihua have observed, YNU has taken substantial steps to establish its CES with a new vision by promoting teacher education and optimising resources for teacher education, improving the quality of the teacher workforce and promoting teacher professionalisation, building a prestigious college of teacher education in the province and becoming one of the bases for teacher education in the country. After the CES was established, as dean Hengtang suggested, teacher education programs at YNU retained their current numbers, but the teaching quality of the programs was considerably enhanced, and so was the status of teacher education at YNU.

Institutional focuses and strategies

To effectively implement the national initiatives of teacher education reform, YNU tried to strictly follow them, which urged TEIs to "build up a highly qualified teacher workforce" by redoubling their efforts toward the structural adjustment of teacher education programs, continuously enforcing the reform on training models and curricular systems, and improving training quality (MOE, 2002). The strategies YNU adopted encompassed a wide range of efforts.

Enhancing teaching for prospective teachers

In order to implement the national policies of teacher education reform and to enhance the quality of teaching at YNU, its leaders held three university-wide working meetings on teaching in 1996, 1999 and 2004, respectively. At the Third Meeting on Teaching, YNU's President warned that the quality and quantity of the faculty of YNU did not meet the needs of the university's development and the goals of the national reform. In the same year, *The Opinions on Deepening Teaching Reform, Speeding up Teaching Innovation, and Improving Teaching Quality in Yangtze Normal University* was formally published. In this document, the leaders reviewed and assessed the challenges YNU faced in improving teaching quality, and viewed the problematic teaching quality in the programs of various departments as the bottleneck restricting the development of YNU. They proposed various strategies for the implementation of the national reform in order to build a stronger and larger faculty for the university in the near term. These strategies included starting new degree programs, systematically transforming from the academic-year system, which the university had long used, to a new credit system, strengthening the teaching workforce and its management, upgrading teaching facilities and improving the learning environment.

Starting new degree programs

Since June 1994, YNU has offered new programs for undergraduates and graduates, in addition to its traditional ones. Since 2001 YNU has provided undergraduate students courses such as modern educational technologies to address new challenges in education from information technologies. In addition, many new graduate programs have been offered since 1998. These programs include Master's programs in aesthetics, modern Chinese literature, general theory of education, analytical chemistry, physical chemistry, applied mathematics, etc. Doctoral programs are offered as well, such as those in ancient Chinese history, ancient Chinese literature, ecology, organic chemistry, etc.

Since 1999, YNU has been accredited by the MOE to confer the Educational Master's Degree in Subject Teaching (MEd), which covers three graduate programs: administration of education, subject teaching of chemistry, and subject teaching of the Chinese language. The newly started Master's degree programs showed that YNU employed substantial strategies in implementing the national reform of teacher education to fulfil its goal of structural adjustment of teacher education programs. By 2012, around 600 students were enrolled in various postgraduate programs in the CES.

Strengthening the teaching workforce and management

YNU has tightened up the management process for ensuring its high quality of education, and adopted new quantifiable indicators to measure teachers' job performance. Some interviewees were proud of these measures because YNU was among the few pioneering universities that made this change in China. These measures, routinely undertaken at the end of each semester, evaluated teachers' job performance in classroom teaching and research by a list of quantifiable indicators. For example, the measures on teachers' classroom performance covered a wide range of indicators from teaching aims, to teaching attitudes and preparation, to teaching methods and teaching effectiveness. The assessment forms were filled out by students and administrators.

The university leaders reasoned that these quantifiable measures would serve the goal of strengthening the teaching workforce and its management. They were taken as rational steps to set high standards for the assurance of teaching quality. These strategies and actions, especially the recently enforced quantifiable measures for assessing teachers' job performance, however, were viewed by faculty participants in the study as instruments being used by the leaders to oppress them. They were pressured against their will to respond to these instrumental measures initiated by those in power, along the lines noted by Aronowitz and Giroux in their critical discussion of this issue (1993, p. 50). Professor Ningdong reported that the real purposes of these quantifiable measures were solely to determine if a faculty member could be promoted or not in the near future. For example, the university set 85% as the eligible score for the promotion to full professor. If a faculty member who was applying for the position of full professor only earned a score of 84%, his or her application would be rejected no matter how excellent the job performance was in other areas.

Enhancing teacher education as YNU's key feature

As a normal university, YNU took advantage of its characteristic teacher education programs to meet the requirements of the implementation of the national reform. After the credit system was adopted, a big change was offered to students in terms of taking teacher education courses. The ratio of teacher education courses required of undergraduate students jumped from 6% to 16% in the total required credits for a Bachelor's degree. At YNU, this was a key step in enhancing teacher education and teacher professionalism through the implementation of the national reform.

Like any other normal university in China, YNU provides mandatory core courses in teacher education in three areas: a general introduction to education, psychological studies and subject teaching pedagogy. The teaching contents are usually edited by senior scholars in the field of education. Now the university has upgraded the contents and requirements of teacher education courses. For example, the general introduction to education, a course intended for all undergraduate students in teacher education programs, used to consist of four major components adopted from Soviet educator Kairov's model: basic theories, pedagogy, moral education and school administration. Today those four components have been replaced with new ones such as the relationship of teachers and students, society and education, modern learning theories, etc. To the original trio mentioned above YNU added a fourth required core course: educational technologies. This was a significant gesture aimed at enhancing teacher education in response to the challenges from information technologies.

In addition to making available more choices of teacher education courses for prospective teachers, new in-service training programs were recently added for school teachers, principals and administrators of high schools, as noted by professor Mawei, a recently retired senior professor. Dean Hengtang pointed out the strand of new teacher education courses at YNU would never have come into being if it were not for the implementation of the national reform. Still, some faculty members viewed this strategy as insufficient to enhance student learning in teacher education, and most interviewees saw it as a political tactic the top management adopted for the narrow purpose of promoting the status of the CES, rather than fulfilling the lofty goal of improving the quality of teacher education as outlined in the national policy.

Restructuring academic departments for teacher education

Early in 1992, YNU was authorised by the PBE to establish the School of Adult Education, which was the first of its kind in Yangtze province. It was also the university's first attempt to reorganise academic departments for teacher education since the 1990s. In 2002, YNU underwent a radical reorganisation of its academic departments. In all, seven colleges were established to adapt to the new demands arising from the radically changing society.

As introduced earlier, the CES was founded in the year 2000, by merging the Department of Educational Technology, the Institute of Higher Education and the Department of Educational Science. The new CES was established to accommodate all the programs related to teacher education on campus, including the programs of subject-based teaching theories from each department of the campus. Most participants of this study, such as department chair Anping and professors Ningdong, Ouying and Peishi, saw the establishment of the CES as an optimisation of strengths (*qiangqiang lianhe*) intended to generate a new "super strength" to improve the quality of teacher education at YNU. The restructuring of academic departments for teacher education was adopted by YNU as a rational way of maximising academic strengths in order to implement the national reform.

Challenges in policy implementation

The national initiatives of teacher education reform have been in effect for more than a decade on the campus of YNU and have brought about remarkable institutional transformations, which cast two major types of challenge over the implementation of the national reform, i.e., the contextually less amenable and the institutionally remediable.

With the new mission, YNU's identity crisis has been contextually less amenable, in terms of the overriding influences of other nationwide policies, such as the expansion of higher education and the new curriculum reform for basic education. After the radical expansion of enrolment since the late 1990s, teacher education programs have been incapable of accommodating the large number of students or meeting the needs for socioeconomic development in Yangtze province. Therefore, YNU had to open new programs, e.g., non-teacher education programs. Professor Mawei was a retired senior professor of the history of education. He noted that the ambiguity of teacher education identity was to be traced to the radical expansion of student enrolment in higher education:

> We have to recruit students [for survival], so we could not limit student admission to teacher education. Like our college, teacher education students are only one-third, all the rest are non-teacher education students. Our identity is ambiguous now, the label we have is a normal university, but in fact we are no longer focusing just on teacher education.

While some interviewees deemed this change unavoidable, Professor Peishi was very critical about the trend. He held that the ambiguity in YNU's identity had led to conditions challenging the legitimacy and status of teacher education. That is, teacher education as the traditional focus and strength of YNU was being undermined. Department chair Beihua expressed his criticism in the following way:

> We are a normal university, right? Most of our students should be studying in teacher education programs for [our goals are to] prepare prospective teachers. But now our non-teacher education programs do not prepare teachers, and students in these programs are more than half of the total students registered.

Along with this challenge comes the observed decline of YNU's academic status. Department chair Caifei compared YNU with other prestigious universities in the province from four aspects, i.e., public funding, leadership and administration, academic strengths, and campus location, and worried that YNU may have lagged behind others in all four. Director Gangyang added that the decline in the quality of undergraduate teaching explained why YNU had lagged behind:

> The biggest contribution probably is the decline of undergraduate teaching quality. . . . It may be the radical expansion of recruitment, the low quality of the new students, the decline of investment in teacher workforce, etc. Thus, the whole social status [of YNU] is declining somewhat. The indicators of decline can be explained by some operational statistics, I think.

Although being institutionally possible, the effectiveness of the strategies YNU adopted for institutional transformations has given rise to widespread doubt. For instance, professor Peishi shared his concerns about how the above strategies were severely mitigated by the political tensions and adverse factors in the implementation process. In his view, there were many: the overemphasis on quantifiable measurements to evaluate teachers' work; the radical expansion of student enrolment since the late 1990s; the decline in quality of newly admitted students and the implementation of the national reform as more of a formality than a genuine change.

Policy implications for teacher education reform

Based on the above findings and discussions, key policy implications can be further raised from the YNU case of institutional transformations, with the examination of the two types of challenges.

The success of policy implementation relies on contextual factors

The success or failure of a public policy is commonly studied by examining the consistency between policy goals and outcomes (Van Meter and Van Horn, 1975, p. 459). In addition, in their view, the higher the goal consensus is, the larger the amount of change (outcomes of policy) will be, and vice versa. When this study tried to reveal how the institutional goals of YNU were developed, a surprising finding was that the institutional goals had at least deviated somewhat from the national reform of teacher education. Conversely, the mission of YNU became ambiguous in terms of its original identity for teacher education.

The ambiguity of the university mission had a negative impact on the implementation of the national reform. For example, most participants held negative perceptions on the change of their institutional identity. They were critical of the fact that teacher education had traditionally been the featured strength at YNU, but now it was neglected. Many interviewees observed that in recent years, the educational skills of graduates had not even been competitive with those from less prestigious normal universities. They also witnessed the drop in institutional social status and public image of YNU. To a certain extent, the ambiguous policy goals hindered the implementation of the national policy at YNU.

In addition, many participants complained that the leaders of YNU did not fully recognise the importance of teacher education reform. The implementation of the national reform therefore proceeded at a snail's pace at the institutional level. An example was that the university had planned for a new college of teacher education for several years but continued to await an official decision. As reported by many interviewees, the lack of policy recognition by key implementers greatly contributed to the unsatisfactory outcomes of the implementation of the national policy at YNU.

These have appeared to be reasons that can explain the dilemmas in YNU's institutional implementation of the national initiatives. But underneath the surface, the wider contextual factors, such as the national expansion of higher education and the new curriculum reform for basic education, played a significant and determinant role in limiting the scope of the changes expected from both policymakers and implementers in teacher education institutions, something which could not be simply and accurately anticipated or calculated from the rational framework.

Authentic evaluation ensures policy implementation

Evaluation is widely accepted as a rational and crucial step in the process of public policy. Browne and Wildavsky (1983) believed that "evaluation is a necessary component of program development and implementation", and that evaluation "can contribute to a continuing refinement in comprehension of the reasons why programs and policies do or do not work" (Browne and Wildavsky, 1983, pp. 182, 201).

Three major forms of evaluation of the implementation of the national reform were found at YNU: the university official evaluation system, the university regular or periodic evaluations on specific job performance, and the ad hoc evaluations conducted by the PBE. The first kind of evaluation was criticised by some participants as "a waste" because of its formality. The second one was blamed by some interviewees for putting additional job pressure on teachers. There was much criticism of the third one too, since it involved a lot of formalism and falsification. All of the three approaches to evaluation could be termed "pseudo-evaluations" (Dunn, 1981, p. 343), rather than "true evaluation" (Stufflebeam and Webster, 1981, p. 71). From the rational framework, the second implication for policy implementation is that evaluation is a controllable and amenable step which can be improved by involving independent, third-party participants to ensure effective measures.

Limitations of this study

Obviously the rational framework is not sufficient to answer why the intended outcomes were not strictly consistent with the policy goals and requirements as originally planned. In addition, the rational framework ignored political conflicts, e.g., conflict of interest between different stakeholders and is often criticised as "more an ideal than an actual description of how people act" (Baldridge, 1977; Baldridge, Curtis, Ecker and Riley, 1977, p. 16). Alternative frameworks, e.g., political, organisational, normative or critical perspectives, are needed for a more comprehensive examination of the dynamic, complex process of China's national initiatives and their impact on TEIs' institutional transformations. Multiple perspectives are therefore of great help to unearth "aspects and intricacies of policy that would be easily missed with a single lens look" (Malen and Knapp, 1997, p. 435).[2]

Additionally, this study adopted a single-case design and purposefully selected an information-rich case to look for an in-depth explanation of the institutional transformations of China's national reform on teacher education. A single-case design is vulnerable by nature, however, and might be a limited case, possibly not representative at all. In other words, it provides a weak basis for its findings to be transferred to other settings. To minimise the possibilities of misrepresentation, a multiple-case design is desirable for future research. As Herriott and Firestone (1983) argued, the multiple-case design enhances the ability to generalise findings while preserving in-depth description, and is often considered more compelling, and the overall study is therefore regarded as being more robust (Yin, 2009).

Lastly, TEIs are not limited to provincial normal universities in China, but cover a large range of higher education institutions such as key national normal universities, key provincial normal universities, and junior normal colleges. Although key provincial normal universities are the largest base for teacher education in China, and the findings of the typical case purposefully selected by this study can be applied to other settings, a multiple-case design consisting of all three types of TEIs would greatly extend the understanding of teacher education reform in China.

Conclusion

When the rational framework is applied, China's quest for world-class teachers through the reform of teacher education can be viewed as rational collective behaviour, in terms of policy initiation and formation as well as the implementation process and evaluation. In the case of YNU's institutional transformations, rational collective policy actions were evidently observed. Specifically, it was means–ends driven and followed goal-directed principles. There was a cause and effect link between the theories of action and the stated outcomes. Policy was delivered in efficient ways such as the regular official policy propaganda. The implementation was designed in stages in a linearly advanced policy flow employing the most effective communication form available. Efforts were made to optimise the goals and to adopt alternative strategies for substantial problem resolution. There was a persistent adherence to scientific evaluations. Additionally, the implementation of the national policy has been promising for the institutional transformations taking place at YNU. The experiences from YNU were rooted in the Chinese sociocultural context, but may be applicable to other societal settings with careful considerations of local contexts.

There are multiple challenges arising from YNU's institutional changes in the process of the policy implementation, as well as some dimensions that are unexplainable by a rational lens, such as the overriding effects brought about by the nationwide expansion of higher education and the new curriculum reform for basic education. Further studies are desirable to examine the phenomenon in a more balanced way with an alternative research design. Again, these lessons are also valuable for policymakers in other contexts to reflect.

Nevertheless, the findings of this study are quite transferable with a theoretical sampling strategy, as they are based on the typical case of a teacher education institution in China. Through the comprehensive investigation of how this typical TEI implemented China's national initiatives of teacher education since the 1990s, it can be concluded that China has systematically moved to a new stage of teacher professionalism and development with strenuous endeavours over recent decades. In this process, a Chinese model of teacher education reform is observable with rational thinking and logic, while priority of development is given to the excellent and steady provision of teachers by TEIs in meeting the challenges of teachers' new identities and roles in a radically changing social context. Along with its rising status, in terms of excellence in educational performance and students' academic achievement, as shown in PISA 2009 and 2012, China provides an alternative model of building a world-class teaching force and it is likely to contribute to the international community with multiple implications in the age of globalisation.

Notes

1. Pseudonyms have been used for all interviewees throughout this paper.
2. Please see: Li, J. (2015). *The Chinese Model of Policy Implementation: Multiple Perspectives on Teacher Education Reform.* Dordrecht: Springer.

References

Allison, G.T., and Zelikow, P.D. (1999). *Essence of decision: Explaining the Cuban missile crisis* (2nd ed.). New York, NY: Longman.

Aronowitz, S., and Giroux, H.A. (1993). *Education still under siege* (2nd ed.). Westport, CT: Bergin & Garvey.

Ashmore, R.A., and Cao, Z. (1997). *Teacher education in the People's Republic of China.* Bloomington, IN: Phi Delta Kappa Educational Foundation.

Baldridge, J.V. (1977). *Power and conflict in the university: Research in the sociology of complex organizations.* New York, NY: John Wiley & Sons.

Baldridge, J.V., Curtis, D.V., Ecker, G.P., and Riley, G.L. (1977). Alternative models of governance in higher education. In G.L. Riley and J.V. Baldridge (Eds.), *Governing academic organisations: New problems new perspectives* (pp. 2–25). Berkeley, CA: McCutchen.

Bogdan, R.C., and Biklen, S.K. (1998). *Qualitative research for education: An introduction to theory and methods* (3rd ed.). Boston, MA: Allyn & Bacon.

Browne, A., and Wildavsky, A. (1983). What should evaluation mean? In J.L. Pressman and A. Wildavsky (Eds.), *Implementation: How great expectations in Washington are dashed in Oakland; or, why it's amazing that federal programs work at all, this being a saga of the economic development administration as told by two sympathetic observers who seek to build morals on a foundation of ruined hopes* (2nd ed., pp. 181–205). Berkeley, CA: University of California Press.

Dooley, K. (2001). Re-envisioning teacher preparation: Lessons from China. *Journal of Education for Teaching, 27*(3), 241–251.

Dunn, W.N. (1981). *Public policy analysis: An introduction.* Englewood Cliffs, NJ: Prentice Hall.

Fowler, F.C. (2013). *Policy studies for educational leaders: An introduction* (4th ed.). Boston, MA: Pearson.

Hayhoe, R. (2002). Teacher education and the university: A comparative analysis with implications for Hong Kong. *Teaching Education, 13*(1), 5–23.

Hayhoe, R., and Li, J. (2010). The idea of a normal university in the 21st century. *Frontiers of Education in China, 5*(1), 74–103.

Hayhoe, R., Li, J., Lin, J., and Zha, Q. (2011). *Portraits of 21st century Chinese universities: In the move to mass higher education.* Dordrecht: Springer/Comparative Education Research Centre, University of Hong Kong.

Herriott, R.E., and Firestone, W.A. (1983). Multisite qualitative policy research: Optimising description and generalisability. *Educational Researcher, 12*(2), 14–19.

Jenkins, W.I. (1978). *Policy analysis: A political and organisational perspective.* London: M. Robertson.

Leung, J., and Xu, H. (2000). People's Republic of China. In P. Morris and J. Williamson (Eds.), *Teacher education in the Asia-Pacific region: A comparative study* (pp. 175–197). New York, NY: Falmer Press.

Li, D.F. (1999). Modernisation and teacher education in China. *Teaching and Teacher Education, 15*, 179–192.

Li, J. (2012). The Chinese model of teacher education: Retrospect and prospects over a century. *Frontiers of Education in China, 7*(3), 417–442.

Li, J. (2013, February 7). Jianshi jiaoshi jiaoyu de zhongguo moshi [An examination of the Chinese model of teacher education]. *Shehui Kexue Bao* [*Social Sciences Weekly*], no. 1349, 5. Retrieved from http://www.shekebao.com.cn/shekebao/2012skb/xs/userobject1ai5359.html

Li, J. (2015). *The Chinese model of policy implementation: Multiple perspectives on teacher education reform.* Dordrecht: Springer.

Li, M. (2010). From teacher-education university to comprehensive university: Case studies of East China Normal University, Southwest University and Yanbian University. *Frontiers of Education in China, 5*(4), 507–530.

Lin, Q., and Xun, Y. (2001). The institutional and policy development of teacher education in China. *Asia-Pacific Journal of Teacher Education* & *Development, 4*(2), 5–23.

Lindblom, C.E. (1959, Spring). The science of muddling through. *Public Administration Review, 19*(2), 79–88.

Ma, Q.R. (2000). Shanghai shifan jiaoyu gaige de xinqushi [The new trends of teacher education reform in Shanghai]. In B.Y. Lu (Ed.), *Yitihua: Shifan jiaoyu gaige de sikao yu shijian* [Amalgamation: Thought and practice of teacher education reform] (pp. 99–107). Shanghai: East China Normal University Press.

Malen, B., and Knapp, M. (1997). Rethinking the multiple perspectives approach to education policy analysis: Implications for policy-practice connections. *Journal of Education Policy, 12*(5), 419–445.

The Ministry of Education. (2002, February 6). *Guanyu shiwu qijian jiaoshi jiaoyu gaige yu fazhan de yijian* [The opinion on the reform and development of teacher education during the tenth five-year national plan]. Retrieved from http://www.moe.gov.cn/publicfiles/business/htmlfiles/moe/moe_290/200408/2546.html

The Ministry of Education. (2004, February 10). *2003–2007 Jiaoyu zhengxing xingdong jihua* [The rejuvenation action plan for education 2003–2007]. Retrieved from http://www.gov.cn/zwgk/2005-08/12/content_21704.htm

Organisation for Economic Co-operation and Development. (2012). *Strong performers and successful reformers in education.* Shanghai. Retrieved from http://www.pearsonfoundation.org/oecd/china. html

Organisation for Economic Co-operation and Development. (2013). *PISA 2012 results: What students know and can do – Student performance in Mathematics, Reading and Science* (vol. I). Retrieved July 23, 2013 from the OECD Web Page: http://www.oecd.org/pisa/keyfindings/pisa-2012-results-volume-i.htm

Paine, L. (1992). Teaching and modernisation in contemporary China. In R. Hayhoe (Ed.), *Education and modernisation: The Chinese experience* (pp. 183–209). New York, NY: Pergamon Press.

Patton, M.Q. (2002). *Qualitative research and evaluation methods* (3rd ed.). Thousand Oaks, CA: Sage.

Shen, A.P. (1994). Teacher education and national development in China. *Journal of Education, 176*(2), 57–71.

The State Council. (2012, August 20). *Guanyu jiaqiang jiaoshi duiwu jianshe de yijian* [The opinion on the enhancement of the teaching workforce]. Retrieved from http://www.gov.cn/zwgk/2012–09/07/content_2218778.htm

Stufflebeam, D.L., and Webster, W.J. (1981). An analysis of alternative approaches to evaluation. *Evaluation Studies Review Annual, 6*, 70–85.

Van Meter, D.S., and Van Horn, C.E. (1975). The policy implementation process: A conceptual framework. *Administration and Society, 6*(4), 445–488.

Ye, L. (2000). *Zai xuexiao gaige shijianzhong zaojiu xinxing jiaoshi: Mianxiang ershiyi shiji xinjichu jiaoyu tansuo xing yanjiu tigong de qishi yu jingyan* [Nurturing new teachers through the practice of school reform: Reflections and experiences from the Explorative Research on New Basic Education for the 21st century]. *Journal of the Chinese Society of Education, 4*, 58–62.

Yin, R.K. (2009). *Case study research: Design and methods* (4th ed.). Thousand Oaks, CA: Sage.

Zhu, X.D. (2001). Guowai jiaoshi jiaoyu moshi de zhuanxing yanjiu [Research on the transformation of the models of the teacher's education abroad]. *Studies in Foreign Education, 28*(5), 52–58.

Part III

What keeps teachers going

Identity, resilience and commitment

7 Professional identities and emotions of teachers in the context of curriculum reform

A Chinese perspective

John Chi-Kin Lee, Yvonne Xian-Han Huang, Edmond Hau-Fai Law and *Mu-Hua Wang*

Numerous studies in the field of teaching and teacher education have focused on teachers' professional identity in the past 20 years (Beijaard, Meijer, andand Verloop, 2004). Teachers' perceptions of their own professional identity affect the ways teachers teach and develop. Their perceptions also mediate and shape their attitudes and emotions toward educational and curriculum changes, which may have cognitive and emotional effects on them in return (Beijaard et al., 2004; Lee and Yin, 2011a). This study examines the professional identity of teachers based on teachers' narrative and emotional responses to curriculum reforms introduced by the central government in Mainland China. Furthermore, this study discusses factors that influenced and shaped teachers' professional identity realised in their interactions with others and within the educational context when reforms were implemented in their school.

Professional identity of teachers

The views on professional identity are diverse, and professional identity has different meanings (Knowles, 1992). Two perspectives on the concept of professional identity prevail (Tickle, 2000). In the first perspective, professional identity refers to the image of teachers that is widely accepted and well received in society based on the general concept of what a teacher should be and what role a teacher should play. In the second perspective, professional identity acquires a more personal dimension; it refers to what teachers themselves perceive as important in their prioritisation of their teaching experiences based on their frontline practices. The second perspective is shared by several scholars who argue that teachers' professional identities pertain to how teachers view themselves based on their interpretations of their continuing interactions within their context (Canrinus, Helms-Lorenz, Beijaard, Buitink, and Hofman, 2011, p. 594).

The formulation of teachers' professional identities is multidimensional or multifaceted in nature (Tsui, 2007). Several scholars argue that professional identity contains a set of disparate identity elements such as self-image, job motivation, core responsibilities, self-esteem, perceptions of teaching, subject, and subject pedagogy (Canrinus et al., 2011; van Veen and Sleegers, 2009).

Although these identity elements are disparate in nature, they are interwoven in interactions among personal, professional, situational, and social factors (Day and Kington, 2008, p. 11). Personal factors are elements found in teachers' lives outside the school and are linked to family and social roles. Knowles (1992) pointed out that teachers' professional identities are influenced by their early childhood experiences, previous teaching experiences, and significant people or early teacher role models. Reynolds (1996) emphasised that the expectation of others, the surrounding culture, and what the person is allowed to do unavoidably affect a teacher's professional identity. Situational and social factors refer to elements mainly found in a specific school; these factors include leadership, support, and feedback and may also include local or national policies that continue to shape the changing roles and responsibilities of teachers. Day and Kington (2008) reported that the influence of school-level factors such as team work, pupil behaviour, support from leadership, parental support, and in-school communication are closely related to teachers' professional identities. Three key factors, namely, school/departmental leadership, supportive colleagues, and family, positively contribute to a positive sense of agency, resilience, and commitment in many teachers. Frontline teachers consider problems of pupil behaviour and workload as negative factors that worsen their "vulnerability" (Figure 7.1).

Teachers' professional identities should be perceived as an ongoing process of interpretation and re-interpretation of teaching experiences on the part of the teachers (Kerby, 1991). It implies that teachers can play an active role in taking initiatives either in their professional practice or professional development, or it can be used strategically by policy-makers in planning and implementing changes in educational practices (Coldron and Smith, 1999). In the process of "being" a mathematics teacher, Schifter (1996, p. 2) likewise highlighted the plurality of a teacher's professional identity as "mathematical thinkers, as managers of classroom process, as monitors of their students' learning, as colleagues, and as members of the wider education community. 'Identities' in this sense – more a matter of what one does than who one thinks one is – are constructed in and realized through practices". Another factor that affects a teacher's identity is related to the impact of macro policies or curriculum change. Given that the perception of teachers on "what a teacher should be" is significantly influenced by the image of others, the requirements of macro policy or curriculum reform definitely exert a

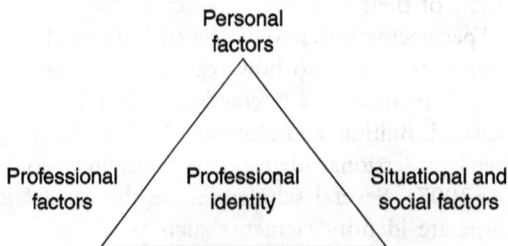

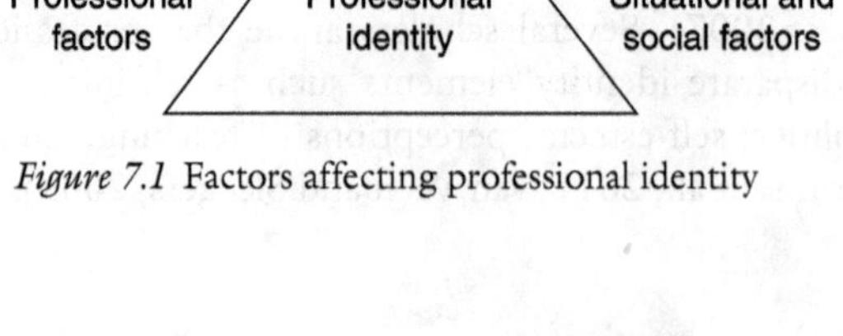

Figure 7.1 Factors affecting professional identity

fundamental impact on teachers' professional identities and their emotional reactions toward changes imposed by external agencies (Day, Kington, Stobart, and Sammons, 2006; Lasky, 2005).

Zembylas (2003) suggested that the process of transforming the professional identity of the teachers is inextricably linked to their emotions, with each emotion informing and redefining interpretations of the other because emotions are "the 'glue' of identity" and vice versa (Haviland and Kahlbaugh, 1993, p. 336). In the case of teachers in China, Bond (1993) asserted that emotional reactions in Chinese culture are of low frequency, intensity, and duration. The expression of emotion is cautiously controlled to maintain interpersonal harmony. Potter (1988) argued that Chinese culture usually emphasises overt behaviour rather than expression of inner feelings to ensure conformity or status hierarchies. Overt behaviour seems to facilitate harmonious relationships with others. The results of two empirical studies conducted by Lee and Yin (2011a, 2011b) support these conclusions. Their studies propose that the professional identity of teachers in China is closely but subtly related to their emotions and behaviour during their involvement in curriculum reform. Beijaard et al. (2004) further suggested more attention should be focused on the role of context in the formation of professional identity. Although several studies on the professional identity and emotions of teachers during educational reform in the West are available, such research in East Asia is lacking, especially in China. The present study adopts an eclectic approach in defining professional identities in the context of curriculum reform. How teachers react to the implementation of a policy imposed by central agencies reveals either conflict or accommodation between self-perceived professional identity and their identity image as embedded in these educational and curriculum policy changes.

The actions of the teachers during the reforms were diversified in daily practice and in specific school and classroom contexts when government officers or peers visited. These variations in actions of individual teachers in different contexts further reveal the potential conflict between their self-perceived professional images and therefore their perceived roles and responsibilities as demanded by the curriculum policy. The relationship between changing contexts and the changing professional identities of teachers then becomes critical to the formation of educational policies and the implementation strategies adopted by the policymakers. One should expect that greater negative emotional reaction among teachers during the reforms could lead to the lesser possibility of the implementation of policies in their original form.

The current paper intends to explore these critical issues, which have been neglected in the literature on the professional identities and emotions of Chinese teachers immersed in the context of curriculum reform.

Curriculum reform in China

Curriculum reform has been the focus of education in China since 2001. The eighth round of curriculum reform in the country is an unprecedented radical transformation that involves millions of schools, teachers, and students. Basic education in China is divided into three levels, namely, six-year primary education, three-year junior secondary education, and three-year senior secondary education. Curriculum reform for primary education in China was implemented in 38 cities and districts in 2001 and gradually extended to other districts. The Chinese Ministry of Education (MoE) announced in 2005 that the curriculum reform would be implemented throughout the country (http://www.moe.gov.cn/publicfiles/business/htmlfiles/moe/moe_2870/200907/49660.html).

When the reform was implemented, MoE issued the *Compendium of Curriculum Reform of Basic Education (Experimental Draft)* and corresponding subject–curriculum standards for primary and secondary schools. The compendium specifically defines the six goals of curriculum reform, namely (MoE, 2001):

- to replace centralised curriculum management with a three-tier system of national, local, and school curriculum management to make the curricula adaptable to local areas, schools, and students;
- to change the emphasis of the past curricula from simple knowledge transmission to learning;
- to change the discipline-centred curriculum structure and make the structure integrated and adaptable to the various needs of pupils in different regions;
- to revise the "difficult, complicated, prejudiced, and outdated" curriculum content and strengthen the relevance of the curricula to the students and society as well as to the development of science and technology;
- to change the emphasis of teaching and curriculum implementation from rote and drill to active learning and inquiry; and
- to place the emphasis of curriculum assessment on selection functions and to stress the function of assessment in promoting the development of students, teachers, and schools.

This round of curriculum reform is undoubtedly a large-scale educational change in which millions of teachers are involved. Most teachers encounter difficulties in meeting the requirements of this reform because of the fundamental changes in the curriculum, given that teachers are expected to function as school-based curriculum developers/leaders, active implementers of innovative teaching practices, and facilitators of student learning. The answers of frontline teachers to "what a teacher should be during curriculum reform" and how they make sense of their role in the implementation of the new curriculum influence their actions and participation. On the one hand, teachers may carry the weight of the expectations of the stakeholders, especially the policymakers and school administrators, in implementing the curriculum reform faithfully and successfully. On the other hand, teachers may not subscribe to the intentions or goals of the reform, and they might accommodate the required changes quite differently. Working within such a changing context at the policy, school and classroom levels, the professional identities and the emotional experiences of teachers may be shifted and shaped in a dynamic manner.

From an emotional perspective, teachers will react to curriculum changes more positively if congruence between the curriculum reform agenda and their own professional orientations exists, but teachers will display negative or mixed emotions if incongruence exists (van Veen and Sleegers, 2006).

Lee and Yin (2011b) explored the emotions and professional identity of secondary school teachers in Guangzhou, Guangdong Province, at the initial stage (2004–2007) of the Chinese curriculum reform. Connelly and Clandinin (1999) suggested that the identities of teachers might vary owing to changes in the educational landscape. Based on this view, the current study discusses the professional identities and emotions of primary school teachers approximately 10 years after the introduction of Chinese curriculum reform.

Research design

This study explores the professional identities and emotional experiences of frontline teachers in the context of curriculum reform implemented by central agencies in China. This study focuses on teachers' responses to curriculum reform and their various emotional experiences. It also explores the influence of contextual factors on the professional identities and emotions of teachers in Shenzhen, a coastal city and special economic zone in the southern part of China.

Shenzhen is one of the first cities in China that implemented curriculum reform. A qualitative approach is adopted in this research. In such an approach, both schools and teachers are considered units of analysis (Scholz and Tietje, 2002); however, this study merely focuses on teachers. Reputational case selection (Goetz and Locompte, 1984, cited in Miles and Huberman, 1994, p. 28) was employed to obtain comprehensive information for this research. Two primary schools in Nanshan and Futian districts were recommended and contacted by an educational expert who is very familiar with frontline schools in Shenzhen. A third school in Luohu was recommended by a principal of another primary school in the same district. The principal had worked in Luohu for over 20 years and has in-depth knowledge of curriculum reform in this district.

These schools are generally considered "reputational cases" (McMillan and Schumacher, 1997); they performed excellently in curriculum reform by displaying innovative practices and have experienced significant changes during the reform. These radical transformations must have influenced teachers' professional identity and emotions within the context.

The school in Futian district (S1) is a primary school established approximately 20 years ago. This school has received numerous awards for its excellent performance in ecological teaching. The principal of S1 is an instructional leader, and proposed and advocated the importance of catering for students' needs and individual differences in teaching and learning. The principal also actively supports the implementation of curriculum reform and promotes innovative practices. The second school (S2) is a newly built school located in Nanshan district, which is one of the demonstration districts for curriculum reform in China. This school has received numerous awards for its exploration of effective teaching with diverse teaching strategies. Every year, there is a competition for frontline teachers to share their curriculum and instructional designs. The school has held a competition called "Green Classroom", which encouraged teachers of S2 to take risks and conduct experiments on teaching. The third school (S3), which is in Luohu district, has a 23-year history. S3 has also received extensive recognition for its endeavours in curriculum reform. This school is renowned for effectively integrating information and communications technology with daily instructional practices. Thirteen primary school teachers of different genders, teaching subjects, and teaching experiences were selected and interviewed from each school. Table 7.1 provides a summary of the background information of the three schools as well as that of the 13 teacher interviewees who served as samples for this study. Qualitative data were collected from 2012. Each interview was conducted privately and lasted for approximately one hour. The perceptions of the teachers regarding the role they play in curriculum reform as well as their emotional experiences during this process were obtained. Two informants were summoned to a second round of interviews to clarify specific words or sentences in the first interview or to provide supplementary information to the researchers.

Semi-structured open-ended interviews were conducted with the teachers, and document collection was performed to gather information on the

Table 7.1 Background information of the informants

School	*Teacher*	*Gender*	*Subject*	*Teaching experience (years)*	*Other*
S1	A	F	Chinese	23	Subject panel of grade 5
	B	M	Math	20	Subject panel
	C	M	Music	1	
	D	F	Math	21	
	E	F	Art	8	
	F	F	Chinese	10	Subject panel of grade 2
S2	H	F	General education	14	
	I	F	Chinese	17	
	J	F	English	10	Previous subject panel
	K	M	Math	1	
S3	L	M	Chinese	2	
	M	F	Chinese	28	Subject panel
	N	F	English	24	

teachers' professional identity and emotions. The major interview questions are as follows:

- What measures have you implemented in your teaching to cater to the requirements of curriculum reform? Why did you change your teaching style (if teachers changed their teaching methods)?
- Were there any changes in your emotions during curriculum reform in the past 10 years? If there were any, what is the reason behind this/these change/s?
- What aspect in your teaching makes you the happiest (saddest)? Why?

The researchers asked further questions based on the teachers' responses. The teachers' reflection and emotional experiences were gradually revealed during the process. Interview data were transcribed and analysed.

Analysis of the interview transcriptions adhered to the four stages described by Marshall and Rossman (1995). These four stages include organising the data, generating categories and themes, testing any emergent hypothesis, and searching for possible alternative explanations. The analysis aims to identify central themes in the data by searching for recurrent emotions and feelings to allow the researchers to code, reduce, and connect different categories into central themes. The researchers were also involved in the cross-checking of these categories. The coding process was guided by the principles of comparative analysis (Strauss and Corbin, 1998), which involves the comparison of coded elements in terms of emergent categories. Lastly, the data comprising the entire data set were compared, leading to the identification of the four types of teachers in the context of the reform (see Appendix 1).

Day and Kington (2008) asserted that identity is composed of three sub-identities, namely, professional identity, situated or socially located identity within a specified school/department/classroom, and personal identity. This classification provides clarification to the analysis of impact factors in the professional identity of frontline teachers in the current study. Based on Day and Kington's theory and empirical data obtained from this study, the interactions of impact factors evolve as personal experiences, educational policies, and institutional contexts. The influence of these factors on teachers' professional identity during curriculum reform is discussed in detail below.

Findings

This section consists of two components: (1) teacher professional identities, which reflect teachers' emotional experiences and practices (actions), during curriculum reform; and (2) contextual factors that shape the professional identities and emotional experiences of teachers in the personal, district, school, and community (i.e., parents and student intake) aspect.

Analysis of actions and emotional experiences of teachers during the curriculum change

The diversity in the practical actions and emotional reactions of teachers during curriculum reform was revealed in terms of degree of involvement, emotional reaction, and self-reflection of the informants. While some teachers displayed expected performance only during external visits, others truly believed in the rhetoric of the curriculum and engaged themselves in the exercise. Their emotions varied and had different reflections of their own roles in the variable context of curriculum reform. Because of the small samples of teachers interviewed and the limitation of our study, the data did not warrant a robust classification of teachers into different types with the professional actions and associated emotional experiences (Table 7.2).

Teachers' negative emotions (painful and feeling helpless) and performed expected actions under external visits

Our study indicated that five teachers who have been passive during curriculum reform described themselves as conservatives. Teacher M of S3 said, "I don't have that ability. I am comfortable with traditional status." This type of teachers includes those who do not totally agree with the requirements and suggestions of curriculum reform but need to "perform" and exhibit practices that are in line with the reform. These teachers insist that their students can still benefit from traditional approaches to instruction. For example, Teacher B of S1 said, "Especially in primary school, students still need to learn by rote or receptive learning." Teacher M of S3 also has her own understanding of teaching Chinese. She insisted that "basic knowledge is very important for my students to construct a solid basis for Chinese language abilities". These teachers have evidently formulated their own interpretation of the teaching philosophy and effective teaching models based on their extensive teaching experiences. They have

Table 7.2 Distribution of four types of informants according to their practical and emotional reaction

Type	*School*	*Teachers*
Contradictory performers	S1	Teacher B, D, F
	S3	Teacher M, N
Active explorers	S1	Teacher E
	S2	Teacher H, I
Reform leaders	S1	Teacher A
	S2	Teacher J
Novice strugglers	S1	Teacher C
	S2	Teacher K
	S3	Teacher L

different competing views on how to effectively teach their students, although they generally agree with the direction of curriculum reform. As a consequence, these teachers apply new teaching strategies when school administrators inspect their classes during the opening day of the school year but opt to utilise traditional teaching models during regular schooldays. "Usually, I use traditional models, which are more effective and easy to conduct," Teacher N of S3 said.

The most typical emotional features of these teachers involve pain and helplessness. As Teacher B of S1 mentioned, "Teachers felt pain during curriculum reform. It is painful that you cannot use the teaching model you have used for many years." Indeed, innovative teaching strategies can improve the participation of students. However, whether student participation will lead to effective learning remains uncertain. These teachers are used to evaluating their instruction based on the academic achievements of their students in public examinations. However, they are confused as to how they should assess the learning outcomes of their students as advocated by the reform.

Teachers' experimental actions in line with curriculum reform led to dissatisfaction

Three teachers identified in our study were dissatisfied with traditional educational models and thus attempted to adopt more flexible methods to help their students learn more effectively. These teachers consider themselves as different from their other colleagues in terms of curriculum design and instruction. Teacher I of S2 is a Chinese teacher with 17 years of teaching experience. She stated, "I am a 'non-mainstream' teacher in our school." She established her own curriculum reform based on her "individual taste". In her first year of teaching, she paid careful attention to the stimulation of students' learning motivation and attempted to integrate student activities into her teaching. Although her instructional design was criticised for being disorderly and for causing disagreement among school administrators and her peers, she continued to apply her approach.

Three teachers in this type initiated their exploration journey as encouraged by curriculum reform. "Through outside learning and learning at our principal's direction, I began to realise that there is a better way to teach my students," Teacher H of S2 said. These teachers wish to learn more educational theories and technologies and attempt to conduct experiments with their students. Their self-esteem is built on new or different learning outcomes of students in the cognitive, psychomotor, and affective domain. These teachers initially felt satisfied at the initial stage of instructional change. However, they may eventually feel that instructional change, after various attempts, has become unsustainable. "Now, I feel incapable to teach. I cannot come up with new ideas as to how to change my current method of instruction," Teacher I said. Teacher H expressed the same concern. She pointed out that although her curriculum design has been regarded as excellent in the Nanshan district, she remains unsatisfied with it.

Teachers acting as reform leaders felt happy or exhausted

Two reform leaders were regarded as reform models in their schools because of their excellent performance during curriculum reform. They take responsibility in organising reform activities in their schools. They view themselves as responsible for leading the implementation of curriculum reform in their school. Teacher A of S1 is a Chinese language teacher with over 20 years of teaching experience. During curriculum reform, her experimental method of instruction was welcomed by many and was highly recognised in her school. Consequently, she became a model reform teacher in her school. The designation meant that she had to learn more educational theories and share these with her colleagues. She assisted her colleagues in conducting experimental teaching methods with strategies indicated in curriculum reform. She said, "in a sense, I am the main person shouldering the responsibility in our school". Teacher J of S2 is an English teacher with 10 years of teaching experience. Teacher J was assigned to teach English in S2 five years ago. She became renowned for her excellent integration of student-centred activities in her English teaching. She took on the responsibility of demonstrating teaching lessons for visitors and facilitating the fulfilment of instructional tasks under curriculum reform by her colleagues. Teacher J described her work as "being an English subject panel is similar to being a 'manual worker' in our school. I completed most tasks for English during curriculum reform in our school."

Reform teachers comprise the backbone of the implementation of curriculum reform in schools. Regarding the emotions of these teachers, Teacher A said that she was happy to take on the leadership role. She stated, "I am happy when I find that the outcomes of my endeavours in curriculum reform are successful." However, Teacher J felt exhausted at being the reform leader in S2. Teacher J said, "To tell you the truth, I am very tired of being a reform leader. My endeavours far exceeded those of my colleagues. This is the reason I quit from the position in the subject panel this year. I want to rest." The excitement Teacher J had for the reform waned because of the lack of support from her school.

Novice teachers struggling with their own professional image and practices with mixed emotions

Our study included three teachers who had less than two years of teaching experience. They have not formulated yet their own teaching belief or self-image. The advantage of having novice teachers in school is that these teachers are easy to convince to accept curriculum reform compared with veteran teachers. Teacher L of S3 said, "I am a novice teacher. I follow the direction of our school leaders. I do what they want me to do." The disadvantage, however, is that the effectiveness of the instruction model and curriculum design under curriculum reform depends on the professional abilities of the teachers. Thus, effective implementation of curriculum reform by novice teachers may be difficult to achieve. Novice teachers also experience difficulty in making stubborn students behave well in class.

They are not fully able to encourage students to participate in class activities with the principles of curriculum reform. Teacher K, a new math teacher for the first grade in S2, explained his dilemma: "I agree that the new approach to teaching can help motivate students. However, I worry about not being able to sustain proper classroom management because my students are very young." Novice teachers worry about uncontrolled incidents during their instruction; they are also anxious to establish their self-esteem as qualified teachers in their respective schools.

Complicated factors that shape teachers' professional identity in the context of curriculum reform

The findings showed that teachers were under practical and emotional tension between their professional beliefs and the expectations associated with their professional roles or identities as facilitators of curriculum reform. Empirical data show that several factors facilitate the promotion of innovative instructional teaching models and encourage teachers to conduct more explorations on curriculum reform. Data also indicate that certain factors discourage teachers to do the aforementioned. These factors can be categorised into three, namely, personal experiences inside/outside school, educational policy changes, and institutional contexts (i.e., districts and schools).

Personal experiences inside/outside school

Several researchers (e.g., Day and Kington, 2008) have emphasised that teacher identities are largely constructed based on aspects of their personal lives, including family and social roles, previous personal experiences, and unique characteristics. Teacher H of S2 is a supporter of curriculum reform and is self-critical. She seeks suggestions to improve her technique, although she has already won numerous awards for excellence in teaching in Nanshan district. The educational beliefs of Teacher H and the trend of curriculum reform jointly construct the professional identity of Teacher H, who actively participates in the implementation of curriculum reform. Teacher I of S2, who is similar to Teacher H, expressed, "When I was a student, my math teacher who was very stiff punished me because I drew pictures in his class. I hated math since then. I always remember how I felt, and I hope my students will never experience that in my class. Therefore, I pay more attention to the needs of my students and try to involve all of them in my class." The previous experience of Teacher I influenced her educational beliefs, which helped her formulate her interpretation of what a professional teacher is.

Personal factors can distract the attention of teachers on duty. While Teacher E of S1 subscribes to the direction and goals of curriculum reform, she describes her dilemma as follows: "I gave birth last year. I was active in curriculum reform before that, but now I need to take care of my baby who makes me tired all the time. I don't have enough energy to implement reform policies anymore." This example illustrates that family issues, such as taking on other social roles, may bring tension to a teacher. Teachers experience difficulty engaging in reform and adopting effective adjustments in their teaching practice.

Educational policy changes

As requested by MoE, a professional teacher should continue learning modern educational theories and should implement these to improve their instruction. Teachers can negotiate with other stakeholders to make decisions on student-centred instructional design. Teachers are expected to reflect on student learning outcomes and improve their teaching in the next cycle. These recommendations influence teachers' perceptions of the attributes of a professional teacher. Teacher A, who acted as a reform leader in S1, stated, "This round of curriculum reform made me realise what a good teacher truly is." Teacher H of S2 stated that stimulation of curriculum reform is the catalyst for her exploration of curriculum change.

Negative influence: tension between curriculum reform and examination culture

Frontline teachers cannot perceive the relevance of innovative concepts and professional practices because of the huge gap between aspiration and reality. Teachers experience difficulty in eliminating the tension between the requirements of curriculum reform and the examination culture. "Schools that claim to be model schools in curriculum reform always perform poorly in examinations. This could mean that this round of curriculum reform does not fit our educational system very well," said Teacher F, a teacher who only delivered the expected performance or practices in line with the curriculum reform. Teachers must construct their own interpretation of what a good teacher is by maintaining the balance between curriculum reform and examination culture. Five teachers have begun to question curriculum theories for lack of operational features or opportunities for professional development. Like Teacher F, Teacher D of S1 said, "We need professional workshops so that we may learn how to integrate new theories with realistic teaching. Contrary to our expectations, effective professional training is inadequate."

Negative influence: tension between curriculum intentions and practical realities

Teacher N of S3, like Teachers D and F, said that she began to question the new curriculum theories because the experts who have broad frontline teaching experience and are considered reform leaders in China are normally incapable of resolving many practical problems in curriculum reform. She said that students who underwent curriculum reform have a much poorer knowledge base than those who did not. Therefore, Teacher N felt frustrated, ceased applying the new theories, and went back to the traditional instruction model she used to practise. She said that as a good teacher, she should help her students become solid performers instead of ostentatious performers in academic learning. This finding reveals that the professional roles and identities of a teacher could change based on his/her own practical and emotional experiences during the process of curriculum reform.

Institutional contexts: districts and schools

POSITIVE SUPPORT FROM THE DISTRICT AND SCHOOL

School- and district-level factors are intensively connected to the formulation of teachers' professional identity. Several factors provide room and opportunity for teachers to obtain an in-depth knowledge of the curriculum, which indirectly affects the formulation of teachers' professional identity. Reform activities organised by the Educational Bureau at the district or school level are one of these factors. These activities, including teaching competitions and visits to other reform model schools, stimulate teachers to design or practise teaching in a flexible and innovative manner. The Educational Bureau of Nanshan district organises an annual teaching competition called "Excellent Class". S2 also organises a teaching competition called "Green Class" to adapt to the trend. All the teachers in S2 reported that their attempts at curriculum reform were greatly promoted directly or indirectly by these activities. The same scenario applies for Futian district. The Educational Bureau of Futian district has advocated "the reform of teaching strategies" in the past several years. Six of the teachers of S1 mentioned the effects of these activities with regard to teaching and instruction. School appointments play a critical role in the formation of teacher leaders. Both Teachers A and J have not considered becoming teacher leaders in curriculum reform. However, the school principals of S1 and S2 appointed them as members of the subject panel and expected them to perform as teacher leaders. Therefore, these two teachers began to learn more educational theories and attempted to conduct more experiments on curriculum reform. They represent their schools and are the main contributors to the construction of a professional learning community in schools.

NEGATIVE INFLUENCE OF STUDENT INTAKE AND PARENTAL EXPECTATIONS

Several factors, such as the abilities of students and perceptions of parents, may hamper teachers from exploring curriculum reform. Teacher F of S1 mentioned that she agrees with the core value of curriculum reform. However, she argued that the recommended instructional model and teaching strategies are only effective for students with high learning capacity. Given that students in S1 in Shenzhen are at the middle level, Teacher F insisted that traditional methods could be more effective for her students. Shenzhen is an immigrant city in the south of China. Consequently, the backgrounds of students in Shenzhen are diverse. This diversity poses challenging communication problems between teachers and parents. Thus, Teacher F implemented professional practices in line with the rhetoric of the curriculum reform only under special conditions such as external visits.

Teacher B of S1, like Teacher F, pointed out that contacting the parents of students is very important when conducting an experiment or adopting a new instruction style. Inefficient communication and parents' misunderstanding normally impede the implementation of curriculum reform by teachers. Continuous support and ample resources in schools are critical for teachers to continue addressing challenges and problems.

Discussion and conclusion

The responses of frontline teachers to external reforms which demanded changes in the professional responsibilities of the teachers and imposed changes in teachers' professional identities, elicited various emotional changes and reactions. These imposed changes caused by the external reform affected the emotions and affective feelings of the teachers, who reacted differently. Emotions derived from participation in the reforms varied drastically. Four teachers responded with positive and active participation, whereas others became alienated. The findings of this study provide an in-depth understanding of the complexity and diversity of teachers' professional identities during curriculum reform.

The continuous participation of teachers in the implementation of reform activities is often constrained by obstacles. These obstacles are personal, administrative, and cultural in nature. Some of the outcomes of this research are echoed in previous studies. With regard to personal dimension, Sugrue (1997) emphasised the impact of personality on the shape of professional identity. With regard to institutional and macro dimensions, several studies identified the influence of external demands on the transformation of professional identity (see Day and Kington, 2008; Lee and Yin, 2011b; Li, 2008; Smagorinsky, Cook, Jackson, Moore, and Fry, 2004). Similar to these studies, school leadership and the educational office of the district in the Chinese context were likewise established as key impact factors in this study. With S2 as an example, pressure to adhere to curriculum reform was mostly felt from the principal and educational office of the district; such pressure could be an indirect impact of the large-scale curriculum reform in China. Teachers' motivation to improve their curriculum and instruction (Teacher A in S1) or the resignation of a reform leader (Teacher J in S2) are, to a certain extent, influenced by institutional factors.

Beijaard et al. (2004) stressed that much attention should be provided to the role of context during the formulation or transformation of professional identity. In a sense, the present study is conducted based on the impact of the Chinese context on professional identity; its results may delineate the findings of Western studies. Although both Western studies and the present study found that school-level factors dramatically impact teachers' professional identity, the social context is different. Therefore, the following question remains: "Do the other specific features of Chinese culture affect the impact of school-level factors on teachers' professional identity?".

As a country influenced by Confucianism, the educational system in China is highly stable and hierarchical. Establishing an appropriate position in the system is crucial, and gaining acceptance or compliments from school managers and peers plays a key role in the process of constructing professional identity. The convergent characteristics of Chinese teachers cause them to behave in accordance with one another; they do not interpose their objection or express their real emotions publicly. This behaviour explains why Teachers M and N, who do not totally accept the suggestions of curriculum reform, opt to use recommended interactive teaching strategies during external evaluation. This finding supports the fact that novice teachers are likely to follow the directions of curriculum reform, although the greatest challenge for them is to manage the classroom effectively.

An individual feels comfortable in a group culture only if he or she is accepted by peers and constructs harmonious relationships with others. Teacher J of S2, a reform leader, pointed out that the threat to continuously being a reform leader in her school is the fact that she feels that her position in the subject panel is unacceptable to her peers who scarcely show support for curriculum reform. Teacher H of S2, who explored how to implement the ideas of curriculum reform, reported that she feels stagnated. She is not satisfied with her current method of teaching and hopes to improve it. However, she is unwilling to obviously express her anxiety because it could make her colleagues who are not well aware of the limitations of their own instruction, feel uncomfortable. Teacher H is anxious that she might be regarded as special, which may cause disharmonious relations with her colleagues and thus impede her further exploration of curriculum reform. This finding reflects, to some extent, the concept of identity being "managed" and the existence of both private and public image of identity. Satow and Wang (1994) analysed workplace culture in a similar manner and reported that "group approaches have been a dominating influence on Chinese social and working life . . . Harmonious relationships among team members and across and/or within organisational levels are emphasised and considered crucial to successful management" (p. 4). From this point of view, gaining the acceptance of peers and formulating harmonious relationships with others not only changes teachers' behaviour but also influences their professional identity. This finding can provide suggestions to future research on how to enhance school capacity or provide professional support for teachers through a top-down approach in the Chinese context.

While schools, like their counterparts in the Western context, need capacity building in coping with curriculum reform, the principal's instructional leadership and top-down support from the government are essential in the Chinese context. Ten teachers in S1 and S2 emphasised the profound influence of reform activities on their perceptions and behaviour at the school level including the instructional leadership of the principal and district level such as the support from the Educational Bureau. This finding indicates that school leadership could be useful to develop a comprehensive plan of actions comprising a set of coordinated actions (Marzano, Waters, and McNulty, 2005) and implement strategies that can sustain change and maintain the momentum of changes in institutionalisation within the infrastructure of the current school culture. In addition, change strategies should be developed collaboratively with participating teachers and stakeholders. Strategies should be feasible and should provide adequate support such as praise, promotion, and other awards. The emotional support provided by the school management team is evident in our study. Harris (2004) stated that educational change is emotionally highly charged. If front-line teachers feel puzzled and frustrated about the implementation of curriculum reform in the classroom, they will naturally lack confidence in the implementation of the reform. As mentioned previously, many teachers feel confused not only as to how to cope with the demands of curriculum reform but also about how to transform innovative curriculum theories into practical teaching practices. These confusing emotions and doubts negatively impact teachers' identities and perceptions of the role they should play as well as their understanding of curriculum reform. Harris (2004) suggested three emotional conditions for the sustainable development of teachers. The first condition, emotional fitness, promotes communication and allows teachers to evaluate their own strengths and weaknesses. The second condition, emotional literacy, emphasises the improvement of intrapersonal, interpersonal, and social processes within the school. The third condition, emotional alchemy, is the means through which teachers are willing to take risks in changing their teaching styles.

Five teachers encountered many challenges in transforming the suggestions of curriculum reform into daily instruction. These challenges cause dramatic tension and gaps, reflecting the need for future professional training to become operational and well directed. Training scholars and teacher educators must be taught to bridge theories and practices and pay attention to emotional issues. Such training can provide practical advice and examples to teachers in facilitating future curriculum reforms. In addition, teacher educators and scholars should be seen as instructional coaches who could help teachers reflect on and reconcile their private and public professional identities. Providing more attention to the emotional responses of teachers to curriculum reform may be useful in addressing teacher needs in professional development. The study conducted by Lee and Yin (2011a, p. 95) on the Chinese context suggested that "effective teacher development should focus on subject content knowledge, provide guidance for teachers' classroom practice, offer opportunities for active learning, and be coherent with teachers' other learning activities".

Four informants in this study mentioned the tension between the demands of external assessment and curriculum reform; thus, a diversified assessment system should be gradually developed. The unitary method of assessing student learning outcomes and teaching efficiency confuses or misleads the teachers during curriculum reform. Furthermore, the Chinese examination culture and high-stakes tests prevent teachers from modifying their teaching and instruction designs. Therefore, decreasing the negative washback effects of high-stakes tests and integrating multiple assessment types with daily instruction must be explored further.

This study, however, has several limitations. First, the cases selected in this research were obtained from excellently performing primary schools. Given that workplace culture and institutional management exert a profound impact on professional identity, schools of different levels with various cultures should be involved in future research. Second, as described previously, several studies on professional identity were conducted in Western countries; thus, the requirements for similar studies in other countries, such as in Asian countries, must consider the diversity of culture and context. The comparison of these different research results will lead to a comprehensive understanding of the conception and interaction processes of professional identity. Third, future studies with larger sample sizes and combined quantitative and qualitative approaches could ascertain whether different types of teacher actions and emotions exist. Lastly, Beijaard et al. (2004) emphasised that the creation of professional identity is an ongoing process. Future studies on this issue should therefore employ longitudinal research, which could help establish an in-depth understanding of teachers' professional identities over a long period.

Appendix 1. The refined coding system of professional identity and emotion for Chinese primary teachers

Theme	*Category*	*Interacting and influencing factors*		
		Personal experiences	*Educational policy changes*	*Institutional contexts*
Contradictory performers	Contradictory perceptions about curriculum reform		S1-F	S1-B
	No behavioural transformation in curriculum design and instruction		S1-D	S1-D
	Self-identified as conservatives Mixed emotions with more negative emotions		S3-N	S1-F
Active explorer	Welcome curriculum reform	S2-H	S2-H	S1-E
	Initial exploration	S2-I		S2-H
	Self-identified as "non-mainstream" teachers Mixed emotions with more positive motions	S1-E		S2-I

(Continued)

(Continued)

Theme	*Category*	*Interacting and influencing factors*		
		Personal experiences	*Educational policy changes*	*Institutional contexts*
Reform leader	Support curriculum reform		S1-A	S1-A
	Supportive to peers			S2-J
	Self-identified a colleague shouldering responsibility of implementing curriculum reform			
	Different emotions			
Novice struggler	Support curriculum reform		S1-C	S1-C
	Immature teaching behaviour		S2-K	S2-K
	Self-identified as followers		S3-L	
	Mixed emotions			

Acknowledgment

The research team would like to thank the Hong Kong Institute of Education for supporting this study. Sincere thanks are extended to Dr Qing Gu, the editors, and the reviewers for their valuable comments on improving this manuscript.

References

Beijaard, D., Meijer, P.C., and Verloop, N. (2004). Reconsidering research on teachers' professional identity. *Teaching and Teacher Education*, *20*, 107–128.

Bond, M.H. (1993). Emotions and their expression in Chinese culture. *Journal of Nonverbal Behavior*, *17*(4), 245–262.

Canrinus, E.T., Helms-Lorenz, M., Beijaard, D., Buitink, J., and Hofman, A. (2011). Profiling teachers' sense of professional identity. *Educational Studies*, *37*(5), 593–608.

Coldron, J., and Smith, R. (1999). Active location in teachers' construction of their professional identities. *Journal of Curriculum Studies*, *31*(6), 711–726.

Connelly, F.M., and Clandinin, D.J. (1999). *Shaping a professional identity: Stories of education practice*. London, ON: Althouse Press.

Day, C., and Kington, A. (2008). Identity, well-being and effectiveness: The emotional contexts of teaching. *Pedagogy, Culture and Society*, *16*(1), 7–23.

Day, C., Kington, A., Stobart, G., and Sammons, P. (2006). The personal and professional selves of teachers: Stable and unstable identities. *British Educational Research Journal*, *32*(4), 601–616.

Harris, B. (2004). Heading by heart. *School Leadership and Management*, *24*(4), 391–404.

Haviland, J.M., and Kahlbaugh, P. (1993). Emotions and identity. In M. Lewis and J.W. Haviland (Eds.), *Handbook of emotions* (pp. 327–339). New York, NY: The Guilford Press.

Kerby, A. (1991). *Narrative and the self*. Bloomington, IN: Indiana University Press.

Knowles, G.J. (1992). Models for understanding pre-service and beginning teachers' biographies: Illustrations from case studies. In I.F. Goodson (Ed.), *Studying teachers' lives* (pp. 99–152). London: Routledge.

Lasky, S. (2005). A sociocultural approach to understanding teacher identity, agency and professional vulnerability in a context of secondary school reform. *Teaching and Teacher Education*, *21*(8), 899–916.

Lee, C.K., and Yin, H.B. (2011b). Teachers' emotions and professional identity in curriculum reform: A Chinese perspective. *Journal of Educational Change*, *12*(1), 25–46.

Lee, J.C.K., and Yin, H.B. (2011a). Teachers' emotions in a mandated curriculum reform: A Chinese perspective. In C. Day and J.C.K. Lee (Eds.), *New understandings of teachers' work* (pp. 85–104). Dordrecht: Springer.

Li, L. (2008). Negotiating teachers' professional identity in a changing Chinese society. *Education and Society*, *26*(2), 69–84.

Marshall, C., and Rossman, G. (1995). *Designing qualitative research*. Thousand Oaks, CA: Sage.

Marzano, R.J., Waters, T., and McNulty, B.A. (2005). *School leadership that works: From research to results*. Alexandria, VA: Association for Supervision and Curriculum Development.

McMillan, J.H., and Schumacher, S.S. (1997). *Research in education: A conceptual introduction*. New York, NY: Longman.

Miles, M., and Huberman, A. (1994). *Qualitative data analysis*. London: Sage.

Ministry of Education, P.R.C. (2001). *The curriculum compendium of the basic education (experimental draft)* [in Chinese]. Beijing: People's Education Press.

Potter, S.L. (1988). The cultural construction of emotion in rural Chinese social life. *Ethos*, *16*(2), 181–208.

Reynolds, C. (1996). Cultural scripts for teachers: Identities and their relation to workplace landscapes. In M. Kompf, W.R. Bond, D. Dworet, and R.T. Boak (Eds.), *Changing research and practice: Teachers' professionalism, identities and knowledge* (pp. 69–77). London: The Falmer Press.

Satow, T., and Wang, Z. (1994). Cultural and organizational factors in human resource management in China and Japan. *Journal of Managerial Psychology*, *9*(4), 3–11.

Schifter, D. (Ed.). (1996). *What's happening in math class? Volume 2: Reconstructing professional identities*. New York, NY: Teachers College Press.

Scholz, R.W., and Tietje, O. (2002). *Embedded case study methods: Integrating quantitative and qualitative knowledge*. Thousand Oaks, CA: Sage.

Smagorinsky, P., Cook, L.S., Jackson, A.Y., Moore, C., and Fry, P.G. (2004). Tensions in learning to teach: Accommodation and the development of a teaching identity. *Journal of Teacher Education*, *55*, 8–24.

Strauss, A.L., and Corbin, J. (1998). *Basics of qualitative research: Techniques and procedures for developing grounded theory*. Thousand Oaks, CA: Sage.

Sugrue, C. (1997). Student teachers' lay theories and teaching identities: Their implications for professional development. *European Journal of Teacher Education*, *20*(3), 213–225.

Tickle, L. (2000). *Teacher induction: The way ahead.* Buckingham: Open University Press.

Tsui, B.M. (2007). Complexities of identity formation: A narrative inquiry of an EFL teacher. *TESOL Quarterly*, *41*(4), 657–680.

van Veen, K., and Sleegers, P. (2006). How does it feel? Teachers' emotions in a context of change. *Journal of Curriculum Studies*, *38*(1), 85–111.

van Veen, K., and Sleegers, P. (2009). Teachers' emotions in a context of reforms: To a deeper understanding of teachers and reforms. In P.A. Schutz and M. Zembylas (Eds.), *Advances in teacher emotion research: The impact on teachers' lives* (pp. 233–251). Dordrecht: Springer.

Zembylas, M. (2003). Emotions and teacher identity: A post-structural perspective. *Teachers and Teaching: Theory and Practice*, *9*(3), 213–238.

8 Sustaining resilience in times of change

Stories from Chinese teachers

Qing Gu and *Qiong Li*

Introduction

Over the past two decades it has been consistently reported that teaching is a physically and emotionally demanding job (Hargreaves, 1994; Kyriacou, 2000; Troman and Woods, 2001; Zembylas and Schutz, 2009). However, despite the internal and external pressures on teachers, research also consistently shows that many teachers across the world have managed to maintain their passion and commitment to helping children learn (Day and Gu, 2010; Organisation for Economic Co-operation and Development [OECD], 2005). We call these teachers resilient. The purpose of this paper is thus to answer a simple question: "What keeps them going?" Drawing upon findings of a questionnaire survey of 568 primary and secondary school teachers in Beijing and in-depth semi-structured interviews with a sub-sample of six teachers, this paper provides empirical evidence which contributes to understandings of resilience in Chinese teachers' work in times of reform and change.

There are two reasons that we choose to focus upon resilience in teachers. The first relates to their individual responses to the influence of context. The contexts of teaching are persistently populated by centrally monitored and controlled performativity agendas and initiatives (Day and Gu, 2010) which test teachers' capacity to teach to their best. It seems important, therefore, to discover how and why many teachers are able to sustain their commitment and integrity in such contexts. Our recent research work on teacher resilience suggests (Gu and Day, 2007, 2013) that resilience offers a useful lens which allows us to probe their internal and external worlds to explore which factors, individually and in combination, influence their capacity to sustain their passion, enthusiasm and strong sense of fulfilment.

The second reason relates to the needs of the system. Resilience in teachers is an important "quality retention" issue (Day and Gu, 2010; Gu, in press; Gu and Day, 2013), especially in a country like China where the teaching job provides a sense of stability and dropout rates are low (Liu and Onwuegbuzie, 2012). There is evidence in research which shows that pupils of highly committed teachers are more likely to perform better academically than their peers whose teachers are not able to sustain their commitment (Day, Sammons, Stobart, Kington, and

Gu, 2007). Thus, research into the qualities of the majority of teachers who have managed to maintain their "courage to teach" (Palmer, 2007) is likely to provide more productive insights for school leaders and policy makers whose job is to promote the learning of our students and enhance the improvement of standards.

The reform context and the dilemmas of Chinese teachers

Over the last two decades, the education system in China has experienced a wide range of government-led, deep structural, cultural and curriculum reforms, designed to bring about profound changes to how teaching and learning takes place in schools. Among these, selecting, developing and rewarding a highly qualified and knowledgeable teaching workforce has been a priority. In the 1990s, the promulgation of the Teacher Law marked an official recognition of teaching as a profession in society. Following this, central policies (Ministry of Education [MoE], 1993) focussed upon improving the conditions of teaching, raising teachers' social status and fostering the important role of teachers in the modernisation of the country. At the turn of the century, further efforts were put in place to overhaul teacher qualification certification with the intention to recruit suitably qualified personnel into the profession.

At the same time, the government remodelled the working conditions for teachers' continuing professional development (MoE, 1998, 1999). One of the most profound strategies for increasing teacher quality was to create grassroots teacher professional development mechanisms in schools. In the late 1990s, 10,000 highly skilled "backbone" teachers were trained across the country to create a critical mass of leaders who were expected to institutionalise the new models of teaching and learning as defined in a parallel national curriculum reform (MoE, 2001).

This "new" curriculum, in principle, was a positive and proactive response to the long-standing critiques of Chinese schooling. Essentially, it was "designed to broaden the intellectual horizon of students and to rectify their passive and mechanistic mode of learning" (Lo, Lai, and Chen, 2012, p. 24). Teachers are now expected to rethink and reconstruct their conventional beliefs about teaching and learning, transform their pedagogical principles and build a student-centred and creativity-oriented learning culture in their classrooms.

The reality is, however, quite different because the paramount place of examinations in the system remains practically untouched. Students' academic achievements continue to determine the paths of their future, the expectations of their parents, the reputation of their school and their teachers and, therefore, classroom pedagogies. In this sense, the bumpy journey of the Chinese curriculum reform affirms Elmore's (2004) observation that, "As performance-based accountability becomes test-based accountability these critical issues (i.e. those related to substantial investments in organisational capacity) recede, and a sensible policy becomes a nightmare" (p. 210). Evidence suggests that many teachers respond to these reforms with mixed emotions (Lee and Yin, 2011), that demands of additional workload add to their professional vulnerability (Gao, 2008) and a high level of stress (e.g. 42% in Meng and Liu's study, 2008), and that some would consider leaving teaching if opportunities arose (e.g. 40% in Liu and Onwuegbuzie's study, 2012). Thus, nurturing teachers' sense of resilience and commitment in such a reality of teaching is not an option, but a necessity.

The nature of teacher resilience

Over the past 20 years, a considerable body of research, mainly with children, but also with victims of trauma and conflict, has established that resilience is a relative, multidimensional and developmental construct, rather than an innate and immutable quality or characteristic (e.g. Luthar, Cicchetti, and Becker, 2000; Rutter, 1990). Although there are differences in how it is defined by scholars from different disciplines, there are also shared core considerations which suggest that resilience presupposes the presence of threat to the status quo and is thus a positive response to conditions of significant adversity (e.g. Gordon, Longo, and Trickett, 2000); that it is a dynamic process within a social system of interrelationships influenced by the interaction between the individual and the environment (Benard, 1995; Luthar et al., 2000); and that it can be promoted, nurtured and enhanced (Cefai, 2004).

Empirical work on resilience in adults, and teachers in particular, is still in its infancy. However, emerging evidence to date affirms that resilience in adults, like that in children, is not necessarily associated with personal attributes only (Luthar and Brown, 2007). Rather, it is "a social construction" (Ungar, 2004, p. 342) which can be influenced by multidimensional factors that are unique to each context (Ungar, 2004). Resilience is thus *context specific*. For teachers, resilient qualities are associated with the work of being a teacher which is shaped by not only "the more proximal individual school or classroom context", but also "the broader professional work context" (Beltman, Mansfield, and Price, 2011, p. 190). For example, the educational literature has been consistent in suggesting that in-school management support for teachers' learning and development, leadership trust and positive feedback from parents and pupils are key positive influences on their motivation and resilience (e.g. Brunetti, 2006; Day et al., 2007; Huberman, 1993; Leithwood, Day, Sammons, Harris, and Hopkins, 2006; Meister and Ahrens, 2011). Judgement and recognition by these "significant others" (Luthar and Brown, 2007) of their effectiveness in their major roles are found to have much to contribute to the development of teachers' individual and collective resilience (Beltman et al., 2011; Day and Gu, 2010, 2013).

Resilience is, also, *role specific* for teachers. In his research on teachers working in inner city high schools in the United States, Brunetti (2006) defined teacher resilience as "a quality that enables teachers to maintain their commitment to teaching and teaching practices despite challenging conditions and recurring setbacks" (p. 813). Moral purposes and ethical values are found to provide important intellectual, emotional and spiritual strengths which enable teachers to be resilient over the course of their careers (Day, 2004; Gu and Day, 2013; OECD, 2005; Palmer, 2007). Others have found that teachers' self-efficacy is one of the most important factors influencing their beliefs that they can help children learn and achieve effectively (Gu and Day, 2007; Hong, 2012; Morgan, Ludlow, Kitching, O'Leary, and Clarke, 2010).

The research reported in this paper takes account of these considerations. The conceptualisation of teacher resilience in this study is built upon Gu and Day's (2013) current work which takes Brunetti's definition further by demonstrating that teachers' resilient quality "is not primarily associated with the capacity to 'bounce back' or recover from highly traumatic experiences and events but, rather, the capacity to maintain equilibrium and a sense of commitment, agency and moral purpose in the everyday worlds in which teachers teach" (2013, p. 26).

The study

The study upon which the paper is based employed a qualitative and quantitative mixed research design (Creswell, 2003) to explore the nature of resilience as perceived by Chinese teachers themselves and the conditions required to enable them to sustain their sense of resilience and thus commitment and effectiveness over time.

Survey participants

The research began with a questionnaire survey amongst 600 primary and secondary school teachers in Beijing. They were randomly selected from 30 schools in three districts in Beijing taking into account factors such as age, gender and years of experience in teaching. All questionnaires were collected by researchers in participating schools. Teachers were assured about the confidentiality of the data and reportage and the rapport established through the face-to-face contact between teacher and researcher helped the rate of voluntary participation in the survey. A total of 568 questionnaires were returned representing a response rate of 85%. The respondents were predominantly female (84%), which largely reflects the composition of the teaching workforce in Beijing. Their years of experience in teaching ranged from a few months to 30 years. The largest groups were 8–15 years and 16–20 years, representing 33.2% and 27.3% of the survey sample respectively. The size of the three remaining groups was broadly similar, with 13.3% ($n = 73$) having up to three years in teaching, 12.6% ($n = 69$) 4–7 years, and 13.7% ($n = 75$)[1] 21–30 years.

Survey instrument

The design of the questionnaire was built upon three main areas of literature: (i) empirical work on teacher resilience, commitment and effectiveness (e.g. Gu and Day, 2007, 2013); (ii) research on school leadership and school improvement (e.g. Gu and Johansson, 2013; Gu, Sammons, and Mehta, 2008) including established measures for assessing trust and self-efficacy in schools

(Leithwood et al., 2006; Tschannen-Moran, 2004); and (iii) existing scales developed in the organisational health research which explore the impact of work conditions on employees' mental health and wellbeing (e.g. Griffiths, Cox, Karanika, Khan, and Tomas, 2006).

In accordance with the empirical evidence from these studies, teacher resilience was essentially conceptualised as a composite construct which is closely associated with *teachers' capacity to maintain their vocational commitment to help children learn and achieve in their everyday world of teaching*. The measurement of teacher resilience thus focused upon their perceived strength of moral purpose and ethics of care, ability to sustain their motivation and commitment as a teacher, job fulfilment, and sense of efficacy and effectiveness.

The 88-item questionnaire was divided into four sections. The 26 items in the first section were designed to measure teachers' perceived wellbeing and efficacy. Examples of items included: "I've been feeling optimistic about the future"; "I've been feeling interested in new things", and "I feel able to create a positive learning environment in my classroom." There were 26 items in the second section. Teachers were asked to rate the extent to which they were satisfied with leadership support (e.g. "support from line manager"; "feedback on my performance"), school culture (e.g. "consultation about changes in the school"; "opportunities for learning new skills") and school conditions (e.g. "clear school improvement goals"; "physical facilities for teaching"). The third section included 30 items designed to measure the levels of relational trust in schools (e.g. "Teachers in this school trust the principal"; "Students in this school can be counted on to do their work"). The six items in the last section were designed to provide overall measurements of teachers' emotional state (e.g. "I am happy in this school") and sense of resilience (e.g. "I have a sustained sense of motivation and commitment in teaching despite the circumstances"). A 6-point Likert scale was used in all of the measurements in this study. The questionnaire was translated into Chinese and piloted with a small group of Chinese teachers before it was finalised.

Survey analysis

Parametric and non-parametric tests of variance were used to examine the similarities and differences between teachers in different school contexts and with different years of experience in relation to their sense of resilience. Factor analysis was also used to explore the inter-correlations between variables relating to aspects of school conditions and identify underlying dimensions of teacher resilience. There was a high internal consistency of the items in almost all of the factorial scales identified (Cronbach's alpha ≥ 0.71; details in findings) which indicates a high degree of internal reliability of the questionnaire.

Interviews

Findings from the survey informed the design and focus of the face-to-face interviews. A sub-group of three primary and three secondary school teachers with different years of experience was selected to explore in greater depth the

Table 8.1 The interviewed teachers

Name	*Gender*	*Subject field*	*Years of experience in teaching*
Wei	Male	Mathematics	3
Li	Female	Mathematics	8
Feng	Female	Mathematics	10
Heng	Female	Mathematics	20
Wang	Female	Biology	20
Hou	Female	Mathematics	23

meaning of resilience, the role it played in sustaining their motivation and commitment in the profession over time and how and why their sense of resilience was developed (or diminished) over the course of their careers. Table 8.1 shows the name (pseudonym), gender, subject area and years of teaching for the six teachers who were interviewed. All interviews were conducted in Chinese and then fully transcribed, coded, categorised and transferred into an analytical matrix (Miles and Huberman, 1994) to enable cross-case analyses and identification of key influences and issues related to the nature and nurture of teacher resilience in schools.

Findings: exploring the meaning of teacher resilience

The accounts of teachers in this study suggest that the widely used definition of resilience as the capacity to "bounce back" from adverse circumstances is inadequate to describe resilience in teachers. The reasons relate to both the personal and workplace contexts of teaching.

Building resilience in the profession: influences of vocational commitment, efficacy and fulfilment

We performed an exploratory factor analysis on the 26-item measures of teachers' sense of wellbeing, efficacy and fulfilment at work. As expected we found five factors (with three relating to wellbeing (or the lack of it)), which we labelled: (i) being able to sustain motivation and commitment to help children learn and achieve (i.e. vocational commitment) ($\alpha = 0.94$), (ii) job fulfilment and professional optimism ($\alpha = 0.82$), (iii) sense of efficacy ($\alpha = 0.86$), (iv) sense of isolation and vulnerability ($\alpha = 0.71$), and (v) tiredness and feeling overworked ($\alpha = 0.69$), accounting for 65.5% of the variance (Table 8.2).

The first three scales were highly associated with each other, with loadings of ≥ 0.67 on each. They were also highly correlated with the overall measure which assesses whether teachers perceive themselves as being resilient in the profession, with loadings of 0.54, 0.56 and 0.52 on it respectively. What resilience means to

Table 8.2 Five factor solutions of the teacher resilience scale using exploratory factor analysis

Items	*f1*	*f2*	*f3*	*f4*	*f5*
Facilitate pupil learning in your class (A21)	0.84				
Create a positive learning environment in your classroom (A20)	0.83				
Generate enthusiasm for learning in your class (A18)	0.82				
Motivate students to learn (A17)	0.77				
Manage mandated changes (A19)	0.74				
Sustain your commitment to pupils (A25)	0.71				
Raising achievement on tests and examinations (A22)	0.70				
Sustain your motivation as a teacher (A23)	0.67				
Sustain your commitment to the teaching profession (A26)	0.65				
I've been feeling optimistic about the future (A1)		0.73			
I've been feeling interested in my job overall (A5)		0.69			
Sustain your job satisfaction as a teacher (A24)		0.62			
I've been feeling cheerful at work (A16)		0.61			
I've been feeling effective overall (A2)		0.53			
I've been interested in new things (A15)		0.41			
I've been feeling confident (A11)			0.78		
I've been feeling good about myself (A12)			0.76		
I've been thinking clearly (A10)			0.70		
I've been dealing with problems well (A7)			0.58		
I've been having a clear direction about what I want to achieve (A8)			0.48		
I've been feeling easily hurt (A14)				0.78	
I've been feeling isolated (A9)				0.77	
I've found it hard to make up my own mind about things (A13)				0.76	
I've become easily tired (A6)					0.82
I've been feeling overworked (A3)					0.78
I've been feeling easily annoyed or irritated (A4)					0.64
Eigenvalues	10.43	2.74	1.60	1.29	1.17
Percentage of variance explained	24.06	13.35	12.91	8.39	7.57

Note: Original magnitudes 0.40 or above are shown.

teachers in our research is explored through the lens of the message that each of the three scales conveys.

Vocational commitment: gaining emotional strength to teach

The survey results showed that two thirds of the respondents (67%, n = 368) sustained their "commitment to pupils", with almost one in five (19%, n = 106) in strong agreement. What is also interesting is that the "not significant" result of the chi-square test ($\chi^2 = 24.374$, df = 20, $p > 0.05$) suggests that such commitment to their students does not become weaker (or stronger) as the years of teaching go by. The large majority of the teachers in all professional life phases (57–78%) expressed strong or moderate agreement on their "sustained commitment to pupils".

There was overwhelming evidence in all the six interviews which shows how commitment to children's learning and achievement functions as a strong internal drive which enables teachers to remain meaningfully engaged in the profession over time. For them, those snapshot memories of children's success, albeit big or small, give them immense "pleasure" and "joy" and fuel them with sustained emotional strength to teach to their best.

> Looking back at the twenty years' journey in teaching, I must say that I always feel very happy and fulfilled. Sometimes the word "happiness" is not even strong enough to describe the emotions that I have experienced when I see my students learn and achieve. Their achievement has made me understand what being a teacher really means. Then, all the hard work becomes so worthwhile.
>
> (Heng, 20 years in teaching)

All six teachers told us that their vocational commitment embodied a strong ethics of care for their students and that the close connection between their students and themselves had been important to their feelings of being an effective teacher since their very first lesson.

What was also embodied in their vocational commitment was a strong desire for continuing professional learning and development. For example, when reflecting on her 23 years in teaching, Hou felt that the most rewarding periods of her career were those years when she was deeply involved in training, research and development, endeavouring to make a difference to the students' learning. Those were very difficult years because she had to constantly juggle between work and family commitments. Where possible, all her evenings and weekends were spent on research into teaching and learning. "But it was worth it, especially when you look back at it now," she felt, "because I helped the children learn and I also helped myself mature more quickly as a professional." Indeed, because of these very acts of learning, for her and the others in this research, teaching became not a string of repetitive chores and duties that they had to deal with, but rather "an open-ended series of new opportunities and possibilities"

(Hansen, 1995, p. 144) – in which they saw their confidence growing, their capacity to spark their students' interest in learning improving and, subsequently, their sense of moral, personal and intellectual fulfilment deepening. Morgan et al.'s (2010) work on what makes early career teachers "tick" also supports this observation.

Job fulfilment and professional optimism

Results of a one-way ANOVA test show that there was a statistically significant difference in the factor scores for teachers' perceived job fulfilment and professional optimism between those who reported a sustained sense of commitment to teaching and those who did not. Teachers who described themselves as being committed and resilient were more likely to experience a greater sense of fulfilment and optimism at work than those who did not ($F = 65.2$, df = 4, $p < 0.001$).

The meaning of the questionnaire items that were associated with job fulfilment (see Table 8.2) points to three broad areas: i) teachers' interest in the job (e.g. "I've been feeling interested in my job overall"); ii) their perceived effectiveness (e.g. "I've been feeling effective overall"); and iii) their ability to sustain their sense of satisfaction as a teacher over time (e.g. "I've sustained my job satisfaction as a teacher") – all of which speak to a strong sense of moral responsibility and commitment to have a positive influence on children's growth and achievement. If we employ "interest" in the sense in which Hansen (1995) applied it to teachers and teaching, then the connections between the three key components become even clearer:

> The teachers' testimony reveals a reciprocal relation between interest and success in the classroom. On the one hand, their active interest in the work provokes them to take students that much more seriously and to try new and better ways of working with them. On the other hand, the very act of developing these improved approaches deepens and animates their interest in teaching.
>
> (Hansen, 1995, p. 144)

It is perhaps, then, not surprising that teachers' job fulfilment and vocational commitment were found to be highly correlated ($r = 0.67$, $p < 0.001$) in our survey, reaffirming the "truism" that for many teachers in China and in other countries, helping children achieve is an inner drive of their commitment and seeing them thrive is, in and of itself, the primary source of their fulfilment.

Our interview data provided more insightful explanations of the meaning of job fulfilment to these teachers. As the following interview quote shows, teachers' job fulfilment is a satisfying state of mind which they attribute to the reward they derive from their students' success and also, the ways in which their capacities have developed to enable them to bring about such success. Moreover, students' appreciation of their effort connects their hearts and soul with the very people whom they care about and care for and adds an indispensible emotional dimension to their feelings of being fulfilled.

> I have stayed in teaching because after all, there are more rewarding and happy moments in my career than those unhappy ones. I love being a teacher and I like the simple and innocent relationships that I have with my students. It is always rewarding to see them go to university. We have worked hard together to achieve this. However, what touches my heart most is when they come back to visit me or wish me happy birthday after they have left school or even university. . . . They made me understand that teaching is a truly special profession.
>
> (Li, eight years in teaching)

We also found that resilient teachers were able to remain optimistic in this special profession. The meaning of the questionnaire items associated with this factor suggests that these teachers were interested in extending their own horizons ("I've been interested in new things") and that they tended to have a positive attitude about the future ("I've been feeling optimistic about the future"). This observation is broadly in line with the literature which defines optimism as a way to enlarge personal control (Seligman, 2006) and describes optimistic teachers as those who focus on the positive qualities of students, classrooms, schools and communities at work (Pajares, 2001). Our interview data add to this observation, by suggesting that a teacher's optimistic attitude encompasses not only an emphasis upon opportunities, but more importantly, a sense of agency to create and extend the opportunities for learning and development, so that they could continue to enjoy a sense of fulfilment in teaching. For example,

> There was a period in which my lessons were regularly observed by a district leader on research and teaching development. It was the same period when my husband was abroad and I was looking after our child on my own. It was a tough time. But I saw the recognition of the district leader as an excellent opportunity for professional development. I believed that working with him would help further improve and establish myself as a good teacher. . . . The outcome was somewhat unexpected. My students benefited the most! On reflection, those difficult times were also the happiest and most worthwhile moments in my career.
>
> (Hou)

Sense of being efficacious

In the limited research literature on teacher resilience, a sense of self-efficacy is identified as a significant individual protective factor (Beltman et al., 2011) or professional asset (Gu and Day, 2007) of resilient teachers. According to Hoy and Spero (2005, p. 343), teachers' sense of efficacy is their "judgements about their abilities to promote students' learning". These self-judgments and beliefs "affect the effort teachers invest in teaching, their level of aspiration, the goals they set" (p. 345).

In this research we also found that self-efficacy is highly associated with teachers' sense of being resilient ($r = 0.524$, $p < 0.001$). Results of the factor analysis (see Table 2) support the observation of earlier studies indicating that these Chinese teachers' self-efficacy encompassed their sense of confidence and effectiveness (e.g. "I've been feeling confident"), capacity to deal with challenges and problems (e.g. "I've been dealing with problems well"), and ability to think strategically and clearly (e.g. "I've been having a clear direction about what I want to achieve"). Moreover, those who perceived themselves as being resilient were more likely to agree that they were able to help their students achieve higher academic outcomes ($\chi^2 = 98.436$, df $= 12$, $p < 0.001$). What shines through in the reported experiences of all the teachers is their persistence and strong desire to learn and develop their capacity to teach, and through this, make a difference to their students' learning. For some (such as Feng), such learning and development were achieved through investment in upgrading their qualifications.

Building resilience in schools: conditions, professional life phases and workplace relationships

In this section, we will focus on three elements of context which influence teachers' capacities to be resilient: teaching conditions; teachers' professional life phases; and workplace relationships.

Teaching conditions

Because teaching is inherently emotionally and physically demanding, the testing of teachers' capacity to teach to their best in the unpredictable setting of the classroom is *constant* rather than occasional. Long working hours, excessive workload, disproportionate pressure and responsibility, and low salary and social status were described as the normal working conditions by teachers in this study:

> The pressure on teachers is enormous and this is related to the wide range of expectations that we have to shoulder. The most significant one is perhaps the responsibility to help children do well in examinations so that they can have a bright future when they leave school. The students expect you to help them succeed and so do the parents and the school. At the same time, the society is also watching you, but you do not receive much respect for what you do. . . . On top of that, we are now expected to complete a certain amount of online training each year which is a complete waste of time and energy.
>
> (Wang, 20 years of teaching)

For them, sustaining commitment to teach in such conditions requires "everyday resilience" (Day and Gu, 2013). One third of the survey respondents who struggled to do so cited these factors as the most common reasons for them to consider leaving teaching. However, the good news is that the remaining majority of the respondents (66%, n = 366) had not lost heart in teaching under similar policy and working conditions. Rather, they agreed strongly or moderately that they had "a sustained sense of motivation and commitment in teaching despite the circumstances".

Professional life phases

Over time teachers face challenges that are specific to their professional life phases.[2] Thus, what it means to be resilient may be different over the course of a teacher's career, but the intellectual, emotional and physical endeavour required to manage these challenges does not necessarily reduce or increase over time. The results of the survey analyses support this observation, indicating that years of experience did not make a significant difference to teachers' perceived sense of resilience (χ^2 = 11.122, df = 5, $p > 0.05$). The large majority of teachers (62–72%) in each of the six professional life phases reported strong or moderate agreement on their sustained motivation and commitment to teaching.

The account of Feng's experience offers further evidence. The start of her 10-year career in teaching was "painful" (Huberman, 1993). Unlike the other five teachers whom we interviewed, she had not had an opportunity to be mentored into the profession. Rather, the first two years of her teaching had been filled with feelings of isolation and struggles to learn to be an effective teacher. At the same time, she was also under tremendous pressure to upgrade her qualifications and this had meant that all her weekends were spent on attending courses for her first degree. It was not until five years into teaching that she had begun to feel more established and confident in the classroom. She then took on a new challenge to undertake a Master's degree in psychology. This was, at least in part, a proactive response to the wider government initiatives on upgrading teachers' qualifications in Chinese schools. During this period her performance became highly valued by the new principal in the school. As a result, she took on more responsibilities and the change in her professional identity in the classroom and the school was transformational. However, after eight years in teaching, she became a mother and this required her to reassess her priorities. Two years on, she was still experiencing tensions between wanting to be a devoted mother and a desire to fulfil her altruistic call to help her students to achieve.

What shows from Feng's experiences is that as teachers feel more confident, efficacious and stabilised in the classroom, they then enter a stimulating phase where they begin to take on additional responsibilities and experiment with new things at work. These responsibilities are often accompanied with greater expectations from themselves as well as their schools and as they grow older, greater family commitments and work–life tensions. Thus, the scenarios that challenge teachers in each milestone of their professional and personal lives may be different in nature (see also evidence from Mansfield, Beltman, Price, and McConney's

(2012) study), but the intensity of the physical, emotional and intellectual energy required to manage them can be very similar.

Workplace relationships

Teachers' worlds are made up of multi-layered relationships. Their resilience-building process is thus nested in a network of relations and is influenced, positively or negatively, by the quality of the relationships in which their work is embedded. A school environment which is characterised with trusting relationships between different stakeholders has been found to have a significant influence on teachers' capacity to sustain their commitment and effectiveness (Beltman et al., 2011; Bryk and Schneider, 2002; Gu and Day, 2013). Evidence from our research supports this observation.

Component factor analysis of the 56 questionnaire items in the second and third sections resulted in four constructs related to different aspects of school conditions and leadership support and four constructs related to trust in schools. Correlations between these factors and the overall measurement of teachers' sense of resilience showed that *relational trust between teacher and colleagues* had the highest association ($r = 0.528$, $p < 0.001$) with their perceived capacity to remain resilient, committed and effective in the classroom, followed by *teacher trust in parents and students* ($r = 0.467$, $p < 0.001$) and *teacher trust in the head* ($r = 0.439$, $p < 0.001$). These results were also supported by observations in the qualitative strand of the research.

RELATIONAL TRUST BETWEEN TEACHER AND COLLEAGUES

Our teachers mostly worked in two types of relationships with their colleagues: i) a mentor–trainee relationship when they first joined teaching and ii) collegialism developed with colleagues in teaching and research groups and lesson-planning groups. Both relationships were formally supported by schools. The salience of such institutionally structured and supported relationships in promoting an open and trusting relationship within the school community and fostering teachers' professional learning and development was highlighted by almost all the six interviewed teachers. For example, for Li, the support and guidance that she received from her mentor, an experienced senior teacher in her first school, significantly contributed to her increased self-efficacy and the "happy" beginning (Huberman, 1993) of her teaching career, which in turn made a difference to her positive professional identity and an increased sense of resilience as a teacher:

> I was allocated a *shifu* ("master") by the school. For a whole semester I was observing his lessons every day and then tried to apply what I learned from him to my teaching. He gave me a lot of tips on how to manage a class and how to effectively engage pupils in learning. As a result, I gained a deeper understanding of the art and methodology of teaching. . . .

> Now that I am eight years into teaching, I am still benefiting from the positive experience that I had in my first year. What I have learned has kept me going!

TEACHER TRUST IN PARENTS AND STUDENTS

The role of trusting relationships between schools and parents in promoting students' academic performance is no longer new knowledge. However, given the one-child per family control policy in China and the amount of attention that each child receives from their parents and grandparents, Chinese teachers usually do not need to seek parental support and assistance. Rather, they are under a rather different kind of challenge – which is often associated with excessive pressure from parents to help their child achieve. Stories of our interviewed teachers support this observation, suggesting that establishing a trusting relationship with the parents and "having them on your side" help pave the way for teachers' positive teaching experiences and students' positive learning opportunities. By extension, the reciprocity of these encounters was found to have very positive effects on teachers' capacity to sustain their commitment, resilience and effectiveness in the profession. For example,

> I had a terrible experience when I first started teaching. A parent disagreed with the ways in which I distributed his child's birthday cake to other children and made a formal complaint to the district education committee. The head then criticised me at the staff meeting. . . . What I learned from the incident was that I should have made an effort to establish a trusting relationship with the parents first. Once the parents have understood your way of working and trusted you, they will choose to talk to you directly if they have any queries, and in most cases, they will come and thank you. This means that you can now concentrate on your work as a teacher.
>
> (Feng)

Trusting teacher–student relationships are found to be essential for student learning (Bryk and Schneider, 2002). Our research shows that they are also crucial for maintaining teachers' job fulfilment and commitment in teaching. What we learned from the interviews was that trust between teacher and student involved more than a positive, open and caring emotional connection between the two parties. It also encompassed teachers' belief in students' endeavour to become competent learners. In the case of Heng, it was the closeness between her students and herself that kept her in teaching: "The children care about me and we love each other. I have found it impossible to leave them behind and do something else other than teaching." Such sense of reward and being cared for often gave them additional emotional, intellectual and vocational strengths, and thus enhanced resilience, to continue to make a difference to the lives of their students over time.

TEACHER TRUST IN THE HEAD

There is abundant evidence in the research which shows that trusting relationships between heads and their staff are a key feature of successful schools (e.g. Day et al., 2011). In their work on successful urban schools, Bryk and Schneider (2002) found that "teachers who perceive benevolent intentions on the part of their principal are more likely to feel efficacious in their jobs" (p. 29). In our research the six interviewed teachers also told us how trust in their heads' vision and heads' recognition and support of their work had motivated them to learn and develop and through this, make greater contributions to the achievement of their students and the success of their school. For example, in the case of Wei, his new head encouraged him to regularly reflect on his teaching and worked closely with him to review the weaknesses and strengths of his teaching. "He made sure that there were no lapses in my thinking. His attention felt like pressure sometimes. But I treasure it because I see it as an opportunity for my professional development." Over time Wei began to feel comfortable about sharing his thoughts, frustrations as well as achievements with the head. "His encouragement, advice and guidance were especially important to me when I felt low." Stories like Wei's were also found in Henry and Milstein's (2006) study, which led them to conclude that:

> Teachers, students, parents, support personnel are the fabric of the school. Leaders are weavers of the fabric of resiliency initiatives.
>
> (Henry and Milstein, 2006, p. 8)

Discussion and conclusion: beyond "bouncing back"

Drawing upon findings of the research, two key observations can be made.

First, in contrast to findings from the mainstream research which consider adverse conditions and recurring setbacks as prerequisites for resilience and which define resilience as individuals' capacities to "bounce back" in such challenging environmental circumstances (e.g. Oswald, Johnson, and Howard, 2003; Tait, 2008), the research reported in this paper supports an earlier observation by Gu and Day (2013) that being a resilient teacher means more than recovering quickly and efficiently from difficulties. This is because, at least in part, it fails to reveal and reflect the uncertain and unpredictable circumstances and scenarios which form the main feature of teachers' everyday professional lives and thus acknowledge the need for "everyday resilience" (Day and Gu, 2013). Such circumstances are an inherent part of the nature of teaching and present a constant intellectual and emotional challenge to those who strive to teach to their best.

Additionally, over a professional life span, teachers face distinctively key influences, tensions, professional and personal concerns (Day and Gu, 2010) in different phases of their careers. Thus, the ways in which teachers build and sustain their resilience are sophisticated and continuous. Their resilience may also fluctuate depending upon the effects of a combination of workplace-based and personal influences and also their cognitive and emotional capacities to manage these influences. For all six interviewed teachers, for example, undertaking pedagogy-focussed research and development projects and activities was a shared path in pursuit of their enhanced efficacy and effectiveness. However, their journeys were not always smooth and the results not always desirable. Long working hours, tensions between work and personal life and, at times, discouraging feedback from students and doubts from colleagues all imposed additional emotional strains on their capacities to cope. What their stories told us was that their sustained effort and perseverance in the face of such challenges often helped strengthen their sense of efficacy and resulted in a stronger sense of resilience and commitment. As one of the interviewee teachers commented, "if not careful, teaching could easily become a repetitive daily routine. The danger of that is that our lack of drive for learning and development will quickly rub off on our students" (Hou).

Our data suggest, therefore, a broader definition of teacher resilience than those who have examined it from a solely psychological perspective is needed; and that resilience in teachers is the capacity to manage the "unavoidable uncertainties" (Shulman, 2005, p. 1) inherent in the realities of teaching. This resilience is beyond "bouncing back" from adversity and setbacks. It is driven by their educational purposes and moral values and is thus closely associated with their vocational commitment to serve the learning and achievement of the children on an everyday basis and also, over the course of their professional lives.

Second, although the government policies in China require that there are formal structural and leadership supports for teachers' professional development in schools, what we have observed from the accounts of our teachers is that their drive and strong sense of agency enabled many of them to be activist professionals (Sachs, 2003), rather than victims of their social and educational contexts. However, to be able to act as activist professionals over time requires relational and organizational support. Our findings reaffirm observations of earlier studies that the nature and sustainability of resilience in teachers is not innate (e.g. Beltman et al., 2011; Gu and Day, 2007), but influenced by individual qualities in interaction with contextual influences in which teachers' work and lives are embedded. Thus, resilience-building processes in schools need to be consistent and ongoing and related to needs which themselves are likely to fluctuate in response to changes in policy, workplace and personal circumstances. Teachers' capacities to be resilient will be a consequence, at least in part, of a combination of the quality of interpersonal relationships and leadership support and their own cognitive and emotional abilities. In this "everyday" sense, resilience in teachers is the culmination of collective and collaborative endeavours driven by a common understanding of moral purpose. For resilient capacities to be sustained, they will need to be nurtured by the social and intellectual environments in which teachers work and live.

Our research would have benefited from a longitudinal design and a larger interview sample. Nonetheless, there is sufficient evidence from the study which enables us to argue that a central task for all concerned with enhancing quality and standards in schools is not only to have a better understanding of what influences teachers' capacities to sustain resilience over the course of a career, but also how resilience may be cultivated by policy and workplace in the contexts in which they live. What we have tried to establish through evidence provided in this paper is that in the context of persistent top-down neoliberal reforms in China's educational systems, what matters is sustaining the quality of teachers' commitment and capacity to learn and to teach to their best.

Notes

1. Missing data $n = 19$.
2. In the VITAE research teachers were found to have common characteristics and concerns according to their years of experience (Day et al., 2007). Six groupings were identified: *early years teachers* (professional life phase 0–3 and 4–7). These teachers' original motivation for entering teaching contributed to their high level of commitment. Support and promotion played a significant role in their perceived identities. *Mid-years teachers* (professional life phase 8–15). This is the key watershed of teachers' long-term perceived effectiveness. These teachers were at the crossroads of their professional lives, deciding whether to continue pursuing career advancement or to remain in the classroom fulfilling the original "call to teach". *Mid-late years teachers* (professional life phases 16–23, 24–30 and 31+). Excessive paperwork and heavy workload were key hindrances to their perceived effectiveness. However, a distinctive group of teachers in the final phase of their teaching continued to demonstrate a high level of motivation and commitment.

References

Beltman, S., Mansfield, C., and Price, A. (2011). Thriving not just surviving: A review of research on teacher resilience. *Educational Research Review*, *6*, 185–207.

Benard, B. (1995). *Fostering resilience in children.* ERIC/EECE Digest, EDO-PS-99.

Brunetti, G. (2006). Resilience under fire: Perspectives on the work of experienced, inner city high school teachers in the United States. *Teaching and Teacher Education*, *22*, 812–825.

Bryk, A.S., and Schneider, B.L. (2002). *Trust in schools: A core resource for improvement.* New York, NY: Russell Sage Foundation.

Cefai, C. (2004). Pupil resilience in the classroom: A teacher's framework. *Emotional and Behavioural Difficulties*, *9*(3), 149–170.

Creswell, J. (2003). *Research design: Qualitative, quantitative, and mixed methods approaches* (2nd ed.). Thousand Oaks, CA: Sage.

Day, C. (2004). *A passion for teaching.* London: Routledge Falmer.

Day, C., and Gu, Q. (2010). *The new lives of teachers.* Abingdon: Routledge.

Day, C., and Gu, Q. (2013). *Resilient teachers, resilient schools: Building and sustaining quality in testing times.* Abingdon: Routledge.

Day, C., Sammons, P., Leithwood, K., Hopkins, D., Gu, Q., Brown, E., and Ahtaridou, E. (2011). *School leadership and student outcomes: Building and sustaining success.* Maidenhead: Open University Press.

Day, C., Sammons, P., Stobart, G., Kington, A., and Gu, Q. (2007). *Teachers matter: Connecting lives, work and effectiveness.* Maidenhead: Open University Press.

Elmore, R. (2004). *School reform from the inside out: Policy, practice, and performance.* Cambridge, MA: Harvard Education Press.

Gao, X. (2008). Teachers' professional vulnerability and cultural tradition: A Chinese paradox. *Teaching and Teacher Education, 24,* 154–165.

Gordon, K.A., Longo, M., and Trickett, M. (2000). Fostering resilience in children. *The Ohio State University Bulletin,* 875–999. Retrieved from http://ohioline.osu.edu/b875

Griffiths, A., Cox, T., Karanika, M., Khan, S., and Tomas, J.M. (2006). Work design and management in the manufacturing sector: Development and validation of the Work Organisation Assessment Questionnaire. *Occupational and Environmental Medicine, 63,* 669–675.

Gu, Q. (in press). The role of resilience in teachers' career long commitment and effectiveness. *Teachers and Teaching: Theory and Practice.*

Gu, Q., and Day, C. (2007). Teachers' resilience: A necessary condition for effectiveness. *Teaching and Teacher Education, 23,* 1302–1316.

Gu, Q., and Day, C. (2013). Challenges to teacher resilience: Conditions count. *British Educational Research Journal, 39*(1), 22–44.

Gu, Q., and Johansson, O. (2013). Sustaining school performance: School contexts matter. *International Journal of Leadership in Education, 16*(3), 301–326.

Gu, Q., Sammons, P., and Mehta, P. (2008). Leadership characteristics and practices in schools with different effectiveness and improvement profiles. *School Leadership and Management, 28*(1), 43–63.

Hansen, D.T. (1995). *The call to teach.* New York, NY: Teachers College Press.

Hargreaves, A. (1994). *Changing teachers, changing times.* London: Cassell.

Henry, D.A., and Milstein, M. (2006, October). *Building leadership capacity through resiliency.* Paper presented at the Commonwealth Council for Educational Administration and Management, Lefkosia.

Hong, J.Y. (2012). Why do some beginning teachers leave the school, and others stay? Understanding teacher resilience through psychological lenses. *Teachers and Teaching: Theory and Practice, 18*(4), 417–440.

Hoy, A.W., and Spero, R.B. (2005). Changes in teacher efficacy during the early years of teaching: A comparison of four measures. *Teaching and Teacher Education, 21,* 343–356.

Huberman, M. (1993). *The lives of teachers.* London: Cassell.

Kyriacou, C. (2000). *Stress busting for teachers.* Cheltenham: Stanley Thornes Ltd.

Lee, J.C., and Yin, H.B. (2011). Teachers' emotions and professional identity in curriculum reform: A Chinese perspective. *Journal of Educational Change, 12,* 25–46.

Leithwood, K., Day, C., Sammons, P., Harris, A., and Hopkins, D. (2006). *Seven strong claims about successful school leadership.* Nottingham: National College for School Leadership.

Liu, S., and Onwuegbuzie, A.J. (2012). Chinese teachers' work stress and their turnover intention. *International Journal of Educational Research, 53,* 160–170.

Lo, L., Lai, M., and Chen, S. (2012). Performing to expectations: Teachers' dilemmas in East Asia and in Chinese societies. In C. Day (Ed.), *The Routledge international handbook of teacher and school development* (pp. 19–32). Abingdon: Routledge.

Luthar, S., and Brown, P. (2007). Maximizing resilience through diverse levels of inquiry: Prevailing paradigms, possibilities, and priorities for the future. *Development and Psychopathology, 19,* 931–955.

Luthar, S.S., Cicchetti, D., and Becker, B. (2000). The construct of resilience: A critical evaluation and guidelines for future work. *Child Development, 71*, 543–562.

Mansfield, C.F., Beltman, S., Price, A., and McConney, A. (2012). "Don't sweat the small stuff": Understanding teacher resilience at the chalkface. *Teaching and Teacher Education, 28*, 357–367.

Meister, D.G., and Ahrens, P. (2011). Resisting plateauing: Four veteran teachers' stories. *Teaching and Teacher Education, 27*, 770–778.

Meng, L., and Liu, S. (2008). Mathematics teacher stress in Chinese secondary schools. *Journal of Educational Enquiry, 8*(1), 73–96.

Miles, M.B., and Huberman, A.M. (1994). *Qualitative data analysis: An expanded sourcebook*. Thousand Oaks, CA: Sage.

Ministry of Education. (1993). Teacher law. [EB/OL]. Retrieved from http://www.gov.cn/banshi/2005-05/25/content_937.htm

Ministry of Education. (1998). Action plan to revitalize the education in the 21st century. Retrieved from http://www.moe.edu.cn/edoas/website18/37/info3337.htm

Ministry of Education. (1999). Regulation of secondary-primary teachers' continuing education. Retrieved from http://www.moe.edu.cn/publicfiles/business/htmlfiles/moe/moe_621/201005/88484.html

Ministry of Education. (2001). *Renew the concepts of training, and to transfer a new model into training activities*. Changchun: North-East China Normal University Publishing.

Morgan, M., Ludlow, L., Kitching, K., O'Leary, M., and Clarke, A. (2010). What makes teachers tick? *British Educational Research Journal, 36*(2), 191–208.

Organisation for Economic Co-operation and Development. (2005). *Teachers matter*. Paris: Author.

Oswald, M., Johnson, B., and Howard, S. (2003). Quantifying and evaluating resilience-promoting factors – Teachers' beliefs and perceived roles. *Research in Education, 70*, 50–64.

Pajares, F. (2001). Toward a positive psychology of academic motivation. *The Journal of Educational Research, 95*(1), 27–35.

Palmer, P.J. (2007). *The courage to teach: Exploring the inner landscape of a teacher's life* (10th anniversary edition). San Francisco, CA: Jossey-Bass.

Rutter, M. (1990). Psychosocial resilience and protective mechanisms. In J. Rolf, A.S. Masten, D. Cicchetti, K.H. Nuechterlein, and S. Weintraub (Eds.), *Risk and protective factors in the development of psychopathology* (pp. 181–214). New York, NY: Cambridge University Press.

Sachs, J. (2003). The activist professional. *Journal of Educational Change, 1*, 77–95.

Seligman, M. (2006). *Learned optimism: How to change your mind and your life* (2nd ed.). New York, NY: Pocket Books.

Shulman, L. (2005). The signature pedagogies of the professions of law, medicine, engineering, and the clergy. Delivered at the Math Science Partnerships Workshop. Retrieved from http://www. taylorprograms.com/images/Shulman_Signature_Pedagogies.pdf

Tait, M. (2008). Resilience as a contributor to novice teacher success, commitment, and retention. *Teacher Education Quarterly, 35*(4), 57–75.

Troman, G., and Woods, P. (2001). *Primary teachers' stress*. London: Routledge.

Tschannen-Moran, M. (2004). *Trust matters.* San Francisco, CA: Jossey-Bass.
Ungar, M. (2004). A constructionist discourse on resilience: Multiple contexts, multiple realities among at-risk children and youth. *Youth and Society*, *35*, 341–365.
Zembylas, M., and Schutz, P. (Eds.). (2009). *Teachers' emotions in the age of school reform and the demands for performativity.* Dordrecht: Springer.

9 How principals promote and understand teacher development under curriculum reform in China

Haiyan Qian and *Allan Walker*

In essence, on-going curriculum reform in China entails a shift from teacher- and text-centred to student-centred approaches to learning and teaching where students participate actively, authentically and creatively in their own learning (Sargent et al., 2011). The Chinese Ministry of Education launched the radical curriculum reform more than a decade ago to combat what it saw as the damaging effect of an almost exclusive focus on examination performance (Ministry of Education, 2001). The reform attempted an overhaul of the fundamental values, beliefs, and structures underpinning school curriculum (Cheng, 2010; Qian and Walker, 2011a).

Rhetorically, terms such as student participation and inquiry learning have been embraced in school development plans and teachers' professional writing in China (Ke, 2008). However, there appears little evidence that these "Western-inspired learner-centred reform measures" (Huang and Wiseman, 2011, p. 131) have taken root. In fact, reform implementation studies too often find that teachers are continuing to teach in traditional teacher-centred ways (Ke, 2011; Sargent et al., 2011).

If the reforms are to take root there is a need to transform teacher beliefs, commitment and capacity and align them more faithfully with reform requirements (Yin, 2012). Such transformation is directly linked to more effective teacher development which can help teachers understand and translate new curriculum principles into a set of workable classroom practices (Xu, 2009). In turn, this is unlikely to happen without renewed policy action to promote closer principal engagement with school-level teacher development programmes. Such logic has driven recent policy actions that attempt to link principals, curriculum change and teacher development.

In Shanghai, concerns about the lack of progress of school-level curriculum innovation prompted the Shanghai Education Commission to implement a policy which squarely locates principal leadership at the fulcrum of curriculum change. One of the recent policy initiatives was *Three-Year (2010–2012) Action Plan to Promote Principal Curriculum Leadership* (Shanghai Education Commission, 2010). Principals, as curriculum leaders, are called upon to "facilitate the professional growth of each individual teacher and teams of teachers; formulate and enforce the development plans for the whole school, different departments and subject panels and individual teachers; and boost teacher capacity for researching and implementing the curriculum" (Shanghai Education Commission, 2010, p. 4). In short, the policy instructs principals to be more hands-on and focused on teacher development.

This paper outlines and analyses the accounts of three principals in Shanghai as they introduced teacher development strategies to support curriculum change. The context for their accounts is the wider curriculum reform and specifically the recent call for "curriculum leadership". We had no intention to evaluate the effectiveness of the strategies. Given the lack of system data and our subsequent reliance on principals' interviews and school documents, the effectiveness question was beyond our scope. Instead, we sought preliminary answers to these questions: What teacher development strategies do principals adopt in response to school-based curriculum change? What trends in teacher development can be extracted from principals' narratives? Is there misalignment between teacher development strategies and curriculum reform? What implications can be drawn about principals' positions on curriculum reform, to teachers and to their own expected role?

The curriculum reform context

The major student learning challenge facing Chinese policy makers is the intractability of traditional exam-oriented education and how to promote holistic student development. To this end, a series of policy initiatives were released over the last 15 or so years. One of the highest profiles of these was the new curriculum reform launched in 2001 (Ministry of Education, 2001).

As an acknowledged pioneer in education reform, Shanghai is often granted the "privilege" of experimenting with reforms before their national endorsement (Cheng, 2010; Walker et al., 2011). The stage-2 curriculum reform introduced in Shanghai in 1998 was the forerunner to the landmark 2001 national curriculum policy (Hu and Li, 2005). The Shanghai reform demanded that both teachers and principals shift their norms of practice (Wong, 2012). That is, teachers needed to shift their primary role from conveyor of knowledge to facilitator of student learning, and principals needed to move beyond just monitoring school academic success to facilitating deeper learning through curriculum design. Through connecting curriculum reform, teachers, principals and school-level teacher development strategies, we map the context within which principals are increasingly accountable for teacher development.

Teachers

China has followed a nationally mandated curriculum since 1949 (Ma, 1996). Given the highly centralised nature of the Chinese education system, teachers generally adhere to common curriculum standards and use formally required textbooks (Fan et al., 2004). Teachers were considered "good" if they could successfully convey knowledge to students through completing the formal teaching plan (Ye, 2004). The 2001 and subsequent curriculum reforms challenged this notion and stipulated that schools adopt student-centred approaches to learning and teaching (Huang and Wiseman, 2011; Walker and Qian, 2012).

As such, the reforms expected teachers to develop new sets of capacities and skills. These expectations cannot be underestimated as they called for a major cognitive shift in how teaching is conceptualised and valued. This meant that teachers, to make the shift, needed to engage in a deliberate and on-going process of unlearning, learning and relearning to meet the curriculum reform requirements in their classrooms.

The complexity of the changes are borne out by recent evidence that the reforms have made little real difference in classrooms, and that the ways teachers teach remain influenced by cultural norms that favour teacher-centred practices (Ryan et al., 2009). For example, after analysing videos of demonstration lessons in Nanjing, Sargent et al. (2011) concluded that forms of student participation used remained highly constrained.

Principals

One of the major thrusts of the curriculum reform was the change from centralised curriculum management to a cascading structure of power sharing – from central government, to local government and to local schools (Huang and Wiseman, 2011). Schools were to develop curricula to match their context. For example, the new Shanghai curriculum structure is comprised of three components: the *basic*, *enriched* and *inquiry-based* curriculum. Schools are to design their own *enriched* and *inquiry-based* curricula which reflect their uniqueness, while reorganising *basic* curriculum offerings innovatively (Shanghai Education Commission, 2004).

The reforms granted principals greater latitude as school-based curriculum decision makers. This increased autonomy was accompanied by a matching escalation in principal accountability and responsibility to counter public perceptions that only academic results count (Ke, 2011; Walker and Qian, 2011). Principals are now expected to create an environment that shapes children's independent and critical thinking, nurture creative mindsets and provide learning opportunities beyond the confines of the classroom (Huang and Wiseman, 2011; Qian and Walker, 2011b).

For principals, this role shift is impractical without the support of teachers. Principals need to promote teacher capacity, commitment and potential in order to facilitate teacher change.

Principals leading teacher development under curriculum reform

Teacher professional development in China has traditionally engaged teachers actively in the construction and dissemination of pedagogical approaches through teaching and research activities (*jiaoyan huodong*) (Wong, 2012). The school-level teaching-research system was comprised of teaching-research groups (*jiaoyan zu*) and lesson preparation groups (*beike zu*) (Ni et al., 2011). Through these, teachers prepare lessons together, observe and analyse each other's teaching and discuss teaching issues with colleagues.

The teaching-research system generally had a positive effect when the major responsibility of principals and teachers was to enforce rather than develop curriculum and when the focus was on improving teaching rather than supporting learners. However, the new curriculum reform has brought very different expectations. To make curriculum change "happen" in schools, principals needed to move teachers away from a reliance on traditional knowledge transmission modes and stimulate their predispositions towards change. This shift was beyond simply familiarising teachers with a set of new textbooks or arming them with new ICT skills; it involved pushing teachers to actually redefine knowledge and processes of teaching and learning (Huang and Wiseman, 2011). Thus, principals could no longer rely singly on the traditional teaching research system. They needed to come up with some new strategies.

The next section explores how three school principals shaped their teacher development activities to build teacher understanding and capacity to meet the requirements of the curriculum reform.

Case studies

All the case schools are located in urban districts in Shanghai. Two are "all-through" schools that enrol students from Years 1 to 9 and one is a primary school (Years 1 to 5). They are all typical "ordinary" public schools. They are ordinary in two ways. First, Shanghai, like other constituencies in China, used to classify schools into "key" and "ordinary" and gave additional resources to "key" schools (Pepper, 1996). Despite the fact that these labels have been removed, the previously classified key schools remain privileged (Cheng, 2010) and as such attract higher parent and student interest than ordinary schools.

Second, public schools enrol students on a catchment basis (Cheng, 2010). However, privately run non-government (*minban*) schools are not bound by the same admission policy. Consequently, they are more selective and generally produce higher examination performance. Public schools are thus further disadvantaged in the market (Wu, 2005).

Without resource privileges or admission discretion, ordinary public schools often struggle to attract students and are therefore pressured to distinguish themselves through what they offer. To do this they rely heavily on staff talent and commitment. We purposefully selected ordinary schools for this study because of these reasons and because they best represent the majority of schools in Shanghai.

Data was collected through in-depth interviews with the principals and documents provided by the schools. The three in-depth interviews were conducted in August and December 2012; each lasted between two and four hours. The interviews were designed to solicit principals' views about their teacher development strategies, the reasons underlying the selection of the strategies, their interpretation of curriculum reform, and their assumptions about teachers' motives, needs and capacities.

Due to space limitations this paper does not seek an extended discussion of the research findings. A necessary compromise is to introduce the school backgrounds and then focus on the teacher development strategies that each principal deemed as most important and effective in their schools.

School A

The background

School A is located in downtown Shanghai. The school has 800 students (Years 1 to 9) and 90 teachers. Principal Ning is not a Shanghai native and used to work at a local teachers' college in another province. He moved to Shanghai 15 years ago and started as a middle school politics teacher. It did not take long before his leadership potential was recognised. School A was the third school in Shanghai that he had worked in either as principal or Party secretary.

Principal Ning believed that the school had progressed significantly since his arrival. One indicator of this was that five years ago many teachers sought to transfer to other schools. In contrast, teachers now want to stay – this demonstrates a stronger sense of belonging to the school. Ning attributed this to his efforts to enhance teachers' sense of happiness (*xingfu gan*). He holds that his leadership approach accentuates care for and understanding of teachers. To use his words:

> managing people is to manage their hearts (*guanxin*). You can never manage others' hearts if you do not care for them (*guanxin*). Caring for others requires that you use your own heart (*yongxin*) and using your heart means you show empathy to others and understand their needs, interests and motivations (*dongxin*).

Strategies

Ning believed that the turning point of teacher change in his school was participation in a national-level research project. The purpose of the project was to find out how neuroscience could inform new approaches to learning. School A was invited to join as a research partner to provide empirical data.

To kick-start the research Ning purchased and distributed neuroscience books so that teachers could better understand the approach. According to Ning, this was well received among teachers because "the literature provides a lot of practical tips about how to rear kids, while many of our teachers are young parents". The literature stressed the role of art in developing children's brains. Thus, after consultation with the research project investigators and other experts, Ning launched his new vision for the school – promoting art education and envisioning art as the key ingredient of the organic make-up of the school.

Art education was not new to the school but its position had faded over the years. The school had a long tradition of offering painting and calligraphy courses; in each year level one class enrolled talented art students. Thus it was not available for all the students. The school's strength in art had almost disappeared when Ning arrived because it could no longer attract talented students. By contrast, in Ning's new vision art was no longer the responsibility and privilege of the few art teachers. Instead, it was part of the professional life and responsibility of every teacher. Ning defined art education broadly in that the school environment should give teachers and students a holistic aesthetic experience which helped teachers to attend more intimately to student needs and school leaders be more supportive to teachers. Teachers would want to come to school and feel good about organisational membership.

Ning implemented a number of specific strategies. First, he redesigned the physical environment. Every corner of the school was decorated with student artwork according to a particular theme, such as calligraphy, painting, science or celebrity. He invested in a sound system to pipe music throughout the school and had a self-service coffee corner built so teachers had a space to interact with colleagues. Although these initiatives were expensive the payback was high in terms of teacher morale and closer professional relationships.

Second, Ning saw it as vital to tap teachers' need for development. He thus surveyed teachers to see what they wanted to learn about art and humanities. Based on their feedback, the school designed a three-year plan to cultivate teachers' artistic and humanistic competencies. For example, the school developed various activities to enrich teachers' spiritual life. There were yoga sessions for female teachers and calligraphy, ping pong, dancing and chorus activities for all. These seemed to give teachers something to look forward to when they came to the school.

Third, he encouraged teachers to participate in school action research projects. He was aware that not all teachers were motivated or intellectually prepared to conduct research so he established and championed a group of teachers as "research models" (*dianxing*). He encouraged Party members, backbone (*gugan*, competent) teachers, heads of teaching research groups (*jiaoyanzu*) and year groups (*nianji zu*) to be research pioneers and models for teachers. These models could then share their experiences and reflections with other teachers.

School B

The background

School B is also an "ordinary school" – it opened in the 1960s and has over 40 classes and 1000 students (Years 1 to 9). There are 120 teachers. Principal Gao spent most of his professional life at School B. He became head of curriculum more than 10 years ago, vice-principal in 2005 and principal in 2007. Gao has a deep attachment to the school.

The school spent quite a few years formalising a full range of structures and regulations, including clearly defined roles and responsibilities for different posts. When Gao became principal the focus shifted back to teaching and learning. Gao recognised that although organisational restructuring provided the necessary infrastructure for school change, it was classroom teaching that "set fire to the change engine". Gao held high expectations of teachers. He envisioned teachers as able "to contemplate and to collaborate" (*jingsi nengqun*) and championed a new slogan of "making every teacher a researcher".

Strategies

Gao's major concern for teachers was to enhance their capacity. However, he believed that teachers could not work effectively in an environment without positive interpersonal relationships. One strategy designed to promote teacher collaboration was to grant teachers freedom to select their own "teaching partners". Major subject teachers (for example, Chinese, mathematics and English) with closer relationships could form a team to take up the teaching load of one class. As the teams selected their own members, they generally worked in a more collaborative fashion to improve student learning.

Because of his concerns about teacher capacity, Gao ran a SWOT analysis to identify the state of play; a number of weaknesses were uncovered. These included a lack of teacher motivation for development and reluctance to engage in research or experimentation. Classroom teaching was seen as ineffective and there were too few competent mentor (*gugan*) teachers. To address these shortfalls he designed a development plan which adopted action research as a major tool to improve teaching and build "a research-oriented school". The plan included a number of concrete strategies.

First, he found financial and personnel resources to provide a better research environment. He funded school-based research to the tune of 100,000 *yuan* (US$15,000) each year. The school also formed a partnership with a curriculum centre at a major normal university in Shanghai. University faculty were invited to help optimise school curriculum through providing research support.

Second, he relied on teaching research groups (*jiaoyanzu*) to organise school-based action research to increase teaching effectiveness. The action research approach was similar to traditional lesson studies, that is, everyone in a research group prepared a lesson together and then one teacher taught the lesson. After observing the lesson, the team provided feedback. To expand its effectiveness the action research process added pre- and post-tests of student outcomes. These provided teachers with first-hand data about student learning and helped them to adjust teaching content and pedagogy.

Third, Gao used research as a pathway for the professional development of backbone (*gugan*) teachers. He selected a few young teachers as backbone candidates. Additional resources were assigned to these teachers on condition that they led research projects. A portfolio system was established for these teachers to document and evaluate their progress. Gao believed this strategy helped young teachers gain wider educative recognition.

School C

The background

School C was founded in the early 1980s. Due to the shrinking number of school-age children, the school was later merged with two neighbouring schools. However, when Principal Chen came to the school in 2003 it still faced declining enrolments. Over the past decade the school has gradually regained its reputation and no longer worries about attracting enough students. There are now about 500 students (Years 1 to 5) and 50 teachers. Chen's primary goal for the school was to win the trust and confidence of the neighbourhood community. She believed she had already achieved this goal.

Even though she was in her early 40s, Chen was considered a senior principal. She first became a principal when she was 29. This was because of her reputation as an outstanding teacher of Chinese. Although the principal's job kept her away from classroom teaching, Chen saw herself as "hip-deep in instruction and curriculum". Her stated philosophy was simple: "As a teacher, I need to perform my teaching task well (*jiaohaoshu*). Now I need to do a better job as a principal and to help teachers to teach well."

Strategies

Chen believed that the thorniest issue faced at School C was teacher fatigue. The average age of the teachers was 44. She believed that teachers lacked the motivation to keep pace with change as they were in the later stages of career development. Chen thus set out to cultivate an environment where teachers not only aspired to learn and develop, but had the necessary resources to make it happen.

First, she introduced financial rewards to motivate teachers. Those who were recognised as *gugan* or potential *gugan* teachers would join a studio (*gongzuoshi*) set up by the school. The members of the studio received a special bonus. Chen believed she could easily decide who should work in the studio. After nine years in the school she was confident in her ability to identify talent and gauge performance and no longer needed to observe complete lessons to do so.

Second, Chen believed that school-based action research enhanced teacher capacity. However, she also believed that engagement in too many research projects diverted teachers' attention from classroom teaching, that research was not teachers' primary job and that good research was beyond the ability of many teachers. Thus she only initiated one school-wide research project, which focused explicitly on instruction. The project attempted to promote teaching based on identified learning needs.

The school had a tradition of collaborative discussion within *jiaoyan zu*; this discussion was mainly about the interpretation of textbooks and virtually ignored individual student needs across different classes. The new highly focused project pushed teachers to adjust the common lesson plan to suit the cognitive levels and learning needs of their students, and to redesign their individual teaching plans. In this way, teachers no longer focused on textbooks only.

Third, Chen believed that harmonious interpersonal relationships were vital. She felt respected by teachers and had close relationships with them. She was careful not to threaten this even when dealing with the poor performers. She told the story of one poor-performing teacher who she believed had little prospect of improving (given her age). She would have liked to transfer the teacher to a less important subject but was worried if she did this she would be seen as an unjust leader. She therefore paired the teacher with a mentor in an attempt to promote improvement. When this improvement was not apparent after three years Chen decided to move the teacher. She believed teachers then adjudged her actions as fair and that school harmony was preserved.

Discussion

Analysis of the cases provides some insights into how principals proactively promoted teacher development in response to curriculum reform. However, they also exposed some breaches in their strategies. This section discusses the positive signs and perceivable gaps and explores principals' assumptions and interpretations of the curriculum reform, teachers, and their own roles in leading teacher development.

All the principals believed in the importance of teacher development and consciously provided a variety of learning opportunities. Teacher development practices included the use of teacher data, contextually relevant (and tailored) content, partnerships with consultants from outside the school, harnessing teacher collaboration and a dedication to action learning. These were positive signs. Specifically, the study identified a number of commonalities across teacher development strategies in the three schools.

- *Principals consciously used data to inform teacher development decisions.* They believed that an accurate understanding of the current status of teacher learning needs was essential for any teacher development plan to work. They intentionally sought teachers' views via different channels. For example, School A surveyed teachers' learning needs while School B conducted a thorough SWOT analysis.
- *Principals carefully selected and tailored teacher development strategies to their own contexts.* The principals made teacher development decisions based on their understanding of school antecedents, histories and resources. For example, Ning intentionally built upon the school's established strength in painting and calligraphy. Gao extended the collaborative structures already present in the school. Chen designed teacher development strategies to address teacher fatigue.

- *Principals emphasised the importance of a collaborative culture.* All the principals believed good relationships were important, even though the approaches differed. Ning's emphasis on relationships was constructed on a platform of "care". Gao emphasised formal policies and structures that encouraged teachers to find teaching partners. Chen took a more supportive stance towards incompetent teachers to avoid potential conflicts.
- *Action research was used to promote teacher development.* School-based research was regarded as the most effective strategy by all the principals. Action research was used to address reform related issues and to encourage teachers to reflect continuously on their practice. In all the schools, principals harnessed external resources to support the school action research projects.

Countering these positive signs, some gaps were identified. For example, teacher participation was conceptualised more in terms of structural implementation rather than the development of autonomous, motivated learners.

- *Principals did not demonstrate confidence in teachers' capacity or commitment.* The principals seemed to believe that teachers lacked motivation for developing the capacities necessary for successful curriculum innovation. For example, in School A, despite Ning's caring approach, he did not believe that teachers would voluntarily engage in action research. In School C, Chen held a strong belief that her teachers did not have the interest or patience to learn anything theoretical or profound.
- *Principals designed and implemented teacher development in a top-down manner.* There was little room for bottom-up initiatives. Principals acted as designers and architects of teacher development structures. While taking into account teacher needs, the schools lacked mechanisms that allowed teachers to decide what and how they would learn. Teachers could not opt out of development activities. Expectations of teachers were built around conformity rather than challenge. Thus, teacher autonomy was minimised and decision-making latitude restricted.
- *Few strategies fostered teacher creativity.* Strategies were generally oriented towards implementing curriculum reform, and focused mainly on content and classroom teaching. As such, they appeared a somewhat reductionist tendency devoid of opportunities for creative innovation. Strategies appeared designed just to help teachers simply deliver the new curriculum.
- *Few strategies built teacher capacities needed to develop, design and evaluate curriculum.* A trend across the three schools was towards research-based, data-driven teaching and reflection. When placed as the dominant strategy, reflection-in-action might be too restrictive a basis for teacher development and change (Day, 1999). In this sense, the development strategies may lack the power needed to help teachers become comprehensive change agents (able to develop, design and evaluate curriculum) as expected by the curriculum reform.

Pulling the positive signs and gaps together provides some insights into relationships between curriculum reform, school leadership and teacher development. We thus suggest some tentative answers to these questions: Do principals see curriculum reform entailing fundamental changes? Do they see a shift of role in teachers? Do they see themselves as change agents?

Do principals see curriculum reform entailing fundamental changes?

The principals talked very little about how they promoted teacher capacity to develop and design curriculum. When asked about school-based curriculum, principals tended to list the school strengths in areas such as art and sport. They answered the question with the statements such as "Our school offers calligraphy courses to all students" or "We offer swimming classes because I think swimming is a necessary skill for students." There was little concern about designing school curriculum to provide students with "integrated learning experiences" or foster students' ability to apply knowledge to "the modern society" (Huang and Wiseman, 2011, p. 130).

Principals demonstrated mixed feelings towards the curriculum reform. Although they were attracted by the prospect of the curriculum change, as frontline leaders they doubted that fundamental change would come easily or quickly. They were also concerned that some of the merits of traditional teaching practices had been lost within the new reforms. For example, Chen denied that the traditional teacher-centred approach neglected student needs. She believed that regardless of the pedagogies used, mature teachers would attend to both textbooks and learners. The beauty of the traditional system in China was that teachers had solid and well-ensconced basic skills. However, the new requirements, such as making PowerPoint slides or other learning packages, consumed a disproportionate amount of teacher time and risked attending to the superficial while neglecting the essential.

Thus principals took a highly pragmatic stance towards the curriculum reform – the change took time. As practitioners they could make only incremental, small-step changes. This underpinned the selection and priority of their teacher development strategies – they did not expect any massive change in teachers and they tended to focus on one improvement initiative for a substantial period of time.

Do principals see a shift of role in teachers?

Curriculum reform requirements expect teachers to travel beyond the confines of the classroom and assume the role of learning facilitator. They were also expected to shift the focus from knowledge transmission to promoting student participation and fostering students' positive inquiry, problem-solving and communication skills (Huang and Wiseman, 2011; Qian and Walker, 2011a; 2011b).

However, in the three principals' narratives, the primary and essential task of teachers was still defined in relation to classroom teaching. Most of the teacher development strategies focused on the enhancement of teaching capacity and arming them with the skills needed to deliver the new curriculum. While doing so, they held a deficit view of teachers (Gao, 2008). As a result, the improvement of teaching skills might not be accompanied by a meaningful shift in teacher beliefs and mind-sets. This, in turn, might impact the teachers' ability to adjust successfully to further changes.

Furthermore, while principals promoted strategies such as action research, they demonstrated a lack of confidence in teachers' capacity or commitment to participating in such activities. There appeared little acknowledgement that teachers as professionals actually wanted to learn and to grow (Walker et al., 2011). Continuous development was seen more as a teacher responsibility rather than an entitlement. Although there was no lack of care or close interpersonal relationships between principals and teachers, the lack of professional trust might result in low professional self-esteem.

Do principals see themselves as change agents?

The curriculum reform expected principals to be change agents. The discussion thus far indicates that they might not see themselves as such. They were very pragmatic rather than idealistic about the level and scope of change they could generate. This may well relate to principals' own capacity for change. If we examine principals' toolkits, their strategies rely mainly on teaching research groups to organise action research and promoting a collaborative school culture. These drew mainly from an inheritance or expansion of past practices. Principals did not appear to possess many new tools or ideas to promote teacher development in their changing contexts.

As a result, principals seemed more focused on driving first-order changes – to influence the quality of curriculum and instruction directly, rather than indirectly (Cuban, 1984, 1988). The task of generating second-order effects through increasing the change-making capacity of teachers to produce first-order effects on learning seemed noticeably absent (Hallinger, 2003; Lambert, 1998).

Implications can be drawn from these tentative conclusions for leader practice, leader development and policy making. In terms of principal practice, in addition to providing personal care there appears a case for principals to have more trust in teachers as professionals. With increased professional self-esteem and feelings of empowerment teachers may be more committed to their own development. In terms of leader development, there appears a need to expand principals' leadership repertoires for the long haul of school improvement. It needs to be recognised that knowledge based on past experiences might lose its validity "as a portent for future success" (Schley and Schratz, 2011, p. 277). Principals may benefit from development programmes that help them be more innovative and forward looking.

Finally, the policy officials – the makers of reform – could demonstrate a greater appreciation of the impact of teacher development. It seems that school-level teacher development is mainly evaluated in terms of the activities schools organise rather than the actual development of knowledge and expertise. Principals in turn tend to conceive teacher development in terms of inputs and not as the changes effected in teachers' thinking and practice. If the policy makers reworked evaluation policies, they might well provide more room for informal and spontaneous learning of teachers and so better position them within the requirements of the curriculum reforms.

Acknowledgements

The authors acknowledge the support of the Early Career Scheme (ECS) Grant (RGC Ref. No. e00441).

References

Cheng, K.M. (2010). Shanghai and Hong Kong: Two distinct examples of education reform in China. In *Organisation for Economic Co-operation and Development, Strong Performers and Successful Performers in Education: Lessons from PISA for the United States* (pp. 83–115). Retrieved from http://www.oecd.org/pisa/pisaproducts/46581016.pdf

Cuban, L. (1984). Transforming the frog into a prince: Effective schools research, policy, and practice at the district level. *Harvard Educational Review*, 54(2), 129–151.

Cuban, L. (1988). *The Managerial Imperative and the Practice of Leadership in Schools.* Albany, NY: SUNY Press.

Day, C. (1999). *Developing Teachers: The Challenges of Lifelong Learning.* London: Falmer.

Fan, L., Wong, N.Y., Cai, J., and Hu, J.Z. (2004). Textbook use within and beyond Chinese mathematics classroom: A study of 12 secondary schools in Kunming and Fuzhou of China. In L. Fan, N.Y. Wong, J. Cai, and S. Li (Eds.), *How Chinese Learn Mathematics: Perspectives from Insiders* (pp. 186–212). River Edge, NJ: World Scientific Press.

Gao, X. (2008). Teachers' professional vulnerability and cultural tradition: A Chinese paradox. *Teaching and Teacher Education*, 24, 154–165.

Hallinger, P. (2003). Leading educational change: Reflections on the practice of instructional and transformational leadership. *Cambridge Journal of Education*, 33(3), 329–352.

Hu, X.H., and Li, C.L. (2005). Stage-2 curriculum reform is showing its impact. *Shanghai Education*, 11, 10–11 [in Chinese].

Huang, T.D., and Wiseman, A.W. (2011). The landscape of principal leadership development in mainland China: An analysis of Chinese and English research. In T.D. Huang and A.W. Wiseman (Eds), *The Impact and Transformation of Education Policy in China* (pp. 125–152). Bingley: Emerald.

Ke, Z. (2008). An analysis of schools' implementation action of 'research-based learning'. *Research in Educational Development*, 24, 67–70 [in Chinese].

Ke, Z. (2011). How teachers' cultural cognition impacts on the implementation of curriculum: Using inquiry-learning policy as an example. *Global Education*, 40(3), 39–48 [in Chinese].

Lambert, L. (1998). *Building Leadership Capacity in Schools.* Alexandria, VA: Association for Supervision and Curriculum Development.

Ma, X. (1996). Curriculum change in school mathematics. In X. Liu (Ed.), *Mathematics and Science Curriculum Change in the People's Republic of China* (pp. 93–136). Lewiston, NY: The Edwin Mellen.

Ministry of Education. (2001). The curriculum reform guidelines for the nine-year compulsory education (trial version). Retrieved from http://edu.cn/20010926/3002911.shtml [in Chinese].

Ni, Y.J., Li, Q., Li, X.Q., and Zou, J. (2011). China's new millennium curriculum reform in mathematics and its impact on classroom teaching and learning. In T.D. Huang and A.W. Wiseman (Eds), *The Impact and Transformation of Education Policy in China* (pp. 99–124). Bingley: Emerald.

Pepper, S. (1996). *Radicalism and Education Reform in 20th Century China.* Cambridge: Cambridge University Press.

Qian, H.Y., and Walker, A. (2011a) Leadership for learning in China: The political and policy context. In T. Townsend and J. MacBeath (Eds), *The International Handbook of Leadership for Learning* (pp. 209–224). Dordrecht: Springer.

Qian, H.Y., and Walker, A. (2011b). The "gap" between policy intent and policy effect: An exploration of the interpretations of school principals in China. In T.D. Huang and A.W. Wiseman (Eds), *The Impact and Transformation of Education Policy in China* (pp. 79–98). Bingley: Emerald.

Ryan, J., Kang, C.Y., Mitchell, I., and Erickson, G. (2009). Cross cultural research collaboration in the context of China's basic education reform. *Asia Pacific Journal of Education*, 29(4), 427–441.

Sargent, T., Chen, M.Y., Wu, Y.J., and Chen, C.T. (2011). Wearing new shoes to walk the old road: The negotiation of opposing imperatives in high school new curriculum classes in China. In T.D. Huang and A.W. Wiseman (Eds), *The Impact and Transformation of Education Policy in China* (pp. 79–98). Bingley: Emerald.

Schley, W., and Schratz, M. (2011). Developing leaders, building networks, changing schools through system leadership. In T. Townsend and J. MacBeath (Eds), *International Handbook of Leadership for Learning* (pp. 267–295). Dordrecht: Springer.

Shanghai Education Commission. (2004). *Opinions on Promoting the Second Phase Curriculum Reform in Primary and Secondary Schools (and Kindergartens) in Shanghai* (No. 33). Retrieved from http://www.shmec.gov.cn/attach/xxgk/798.doc [in Chinese].

Shanghai Education Commission. (2010). *On the Notice of "A Three-year Action Plan to Promote Curriculum Leadership of Secondary and Primary School (and Kindergarten) Principals."* Retrieved from http://www.shmec.gov.cn/html/xxgk/201004/3022010002.php [in Chinese].

Walker, A., and Qian, H.Y. (2011). Successful school leadership in China. In C. Day (Ed.), *The Routledge International Handbook of Teacher and School Development* (pp. 446–457). London: Routledge.

Walker, A., and Qian, H.Y. (2012). Reform disconnection in China. *Peabody Journal of Education*. 87(2), 163–177.

Walker, A., Qian, H.Y., and Zhang, S. (2011). Secondary school principals in curriculum reform: Victims or accomplices? *Frontiers of Education in China*, 6(3), 388–403.

Wong, L.N. (2012). How has recent curriculum reform in China influenced school-based teacher learning? An ethnographic study of two subject departments in Shanghai, China. *Asia-Pacific Journal of Teacher Education*, 40(4), 347–361.

Wu, G.P. (2005). Policy analysis of public junior secondary schools in Shanghai. In Z. Yuan (Ed.), *Review of Education Policies* (pp. 104–118). Beijing: Educational Science Publishing House [in Chinese].

Xu, Y. (2009). School based teacher development through a school university collaborative project: A case study of a recent initiative in China. *Journal of Curriculum Studies*, 41(1), 49–66.

Ye, L. (2004). Let the classroom teaching be more vital. *Teachers' Friend*, 1, 49–53 [in Chinese].

Yin, H.B. (2012). Adaptation and validation of the teacher emotional labour strategy scale in China. *Educational Psychology*, 32(4), 451–465.

10 Teachers' beliefs and practices

A dynamic and complex relationship

Hongying Zheng

Research of teachers' beliefs

Exploring what teachers think, know and believe has been the focus of many educational research endeavours with the development of cognitivism since the 1970s. In the last 20 years, substantial evidence has indicated that teachers' beliefs are 'complex', 'dynamic', 'context-sensitive' and 'systematic', (Borg, 2006: 272; Feryok, 2010). Firstly, studies revealing teachers' beliefs to be complex focused on the exploration of the range and the modality of teachers' beliefs. Some studies have explored teachers' beliefs from a wide range of subjects, such as vocabulary instruction, reading comprehension, grammar, literacy instruction, and so on (Konopak and Williams, 1994; Borg, 1999; Johnson, 1992; Pajares, 1992; Meijer et al., 1999). Others have revealed that teachers hold beliefs with various degrees of convictions and they are not consensual (Thompson, 1992, Nespor, 1987). Secondly, two types of studies contribute to the revelation of the dynamic nature of teachers' beliefs. Some studies has focused on the exploration of teachers' cognitive development by conducting longitudinal studies (Richards and Lockhart, 1996; Freeman, 1992, 1993). While others comparing inexperienced and experienced teachers' beliefs, despite the lack of longitudinal perspectice, have indicated teachers' cognitive change over time (Johnson, 2003; Mok, 1994; Nunan, 1992; Tsui, 2003). Thirdly, studies extrapolating the internal and external situational factors have shown that teachers' beliefs are contextualised in that the context meiates and shapes teachers' beliefs (Borg, 2003, 2006). Evidence from a range of studies highlights that the inconsistency between teachers' professed beliefs and their practice may be due to the constraint of contextual factors (Crookes and Arakaki, 1999; Lim and Torr, 2007; Richards and Pennington, 1998).

As far as belief systems are concerned, there is considerable agreement that a belief system consists of substructures of beliefs, which are not necessarily logically structured (Richardson, 2003). The existence of conflicting, even contrasting beliefs makes it even more complex (Bryan, 2003). Some researchers have argued that the belief systems consist of primary and derivative beliefs, central and peripheral beliefs, beliefs with varying degrees of conviction (Green, 1971; Brownleeet al., 2002; Thompson, 1992). These statements indicate that teachers' beliefs may demonstrate qualitative differences, the interaction of which may lead to the emergence of new aspects of the relationship between beliefs and practice. The beliefs in a system never appear fully independent, which, consequently, argues for research to focus on teachers' beliefs as an interrelated system.

However, hardly any research has explored the qualitative differences between different elements of teachers' beliefs. Moreover, research so far has not investigated the substance of the interaction between different elements of teachers' beliefs in relation to their practice and contexts. As revealed by Borg (2006), of all the characteristics of beliefs, the least understood is the manner in which teachers' beliefs function as a system. He has thus suggested that further research needs to be carried out on 'how the different elements in teachers' cognitive systems interact and which of these elements, for example, are core and which are peripheral' (p. 272). Despite Feryok's (2010: 277) efforts in applying complex system theory to language teacher cognition, her attempts are only 'metaphorical re-analyses' of language teacher cognition data from her previously published case study. In this research context, my study is designed to approach the relationship between teachers' beliefs, practice and contexts through complexity theory that directly addresses the complex, dynamic, systematic and contextualised features.

Complexity theory in understanding teachers' belief systems

Complexity theory, originated in different disciplines, including biology, physics and mathematics, in the mid-twentieth century, breaks with the simple cause-and-effect research paradigm by adopting 'organic, non-linear and holistic approaches' of research (Cohen et al., 2007). The word 'complexity' does not mean the same in relation to the theory as it does in everyday language. It means 'edge of chaos' (Lewin, 1999), which refers to the point between mechanistic predictability and complete unpredictability (Bak, 1996). In other words, although systems are filled with turmoil and confusion, they still have the maximum potential to adapt, learn and develop. The word 'system' refers to a set of things so related as to form a unity or organic whole. Complex systems consist of different types of element or agent, which connect and interact in different and changing ways. These elements or agents may themselves be complex systems, which are coupled and tend to be non-linear. It thus emphasises the dynamic interaction between different components of systems, which aims to explain 'how the interacting parts of a complex system give rise to the system's collective behaviour and how such a system simultaneously interacts with its environment' (Larsen-Freeman and Cameron, 2008: 1). Moreover, it emphasises non-linearity, unpredictability, mutual-adaptation, co-evolution, dynamic interaction and self-organisation for organisational life. Since the mid-1990s, researchers have begun to apply complexity theory in examining cognitive development (Smith and Thelen, 1993; Thelen and Smith, 1994), second language development (de Bot et al., 2007; Larsen-Freeman, 1997, 2002;

Larsen-Freeman and Cameron, 2008; van Lier, 1998, 2004) and so on. These studies adopt complexity theory in emphasising the idea that a set of components in a complex system 'interact in particular ways to produce some overall state or form at a particular point in time' (Larsen-Freeman and Cameron, 2008: 26).

Hence, stressing holism, interconnectedness, and unpredictability, complexity theory provides a powerful challenge to conventional approaches to research on teacher beliefs, and, in a way, more accurately represents the diversity of teachers' mental lives, the meaning of which is constructed in the examination of interactions between and among the components of teachers' beliefs, practice and contexts.

The study

In 2001, Chinese government launched the National English Curriculum Standards for Nine-Year Compulsory Education and Senior High School Education (the NECS). The NECS aims to promote the concept of 'quality education for each and every student' (MOE, 2001: 2). For the first time in Chinese educational history, the NECS has promoted a paradigm shift from a traditional teacher-dominated, knowledge-based transmission mode of teaching to a more learner-centred, experience-based, problem-solving mode of teaching. However, shifts in educational orientation in the curriculum do not necessarily induce changes in teachers' beliefs and practice. The awareness of cognitive dissonance in practice may lead to changes in beliefs and/or practice. For an individual's belief system, a flexible system may be fostered by reflection on the cognitive dissonance in practice. Therefore, in order to promote language teachers' adaptation to the NECS, it is important to understand how the interactions between different components of language teachers' belief system contribute to the complex features of teachers' belief system.

Research questions

In the study, I regard EFL (English as a Foreign Language) teachers' beliefs as a complex system, within which the teachers' beliefs about EFL teaching and learning, classroom practice and contexts are sets of interacting components, while at the same time being complex systems themselves. In the context of curriculum reform in China, the changes in EFL teachers' belief systems involve complex interactive dynamics between these components in the teachers' belief system. Taking into consideration the diversity of EFL teachers' beliefs, and the filtering effect of teachers' beliefs in all aspects of EFL teaching, my study investigated the following two research questions:

1 What are the distinguishing features of the Chinese secondary school EFL teachers' beliefs in the context of curriculum reform?
2 How do the interactions between language teachers' beliefs and practices contribute to the complex features of the teachers' belief system?

Sampling

In order to explore the features of language teachers' belief system in great detail, I conducted a case study on six Chinese EFL teachers. The participant teachers were selected on the basis of the representativeness in relation to the research questions: (1) they were all experienced teachers, with more than three years' teaching experience; (2) they were teachers with relatively homogeneous current teaching situations, for example, they were all teaching state secondary school students aged from 13 to 15.

In order to maintain anonymity and confidentiality, I used pseudonyms for all the participant teachers and all data collected during the study were kept, and will remain, confidential. Moreover, the consent form was designed to ensure that no pressure was applied to the teachers as they had the freedom to decline involvement in the study. In order to conform to ethical guidelines, the participants were also informed of the general aims, the procedures, the benefits and potential harm of the study to the participant teachers.

Given the limitation of the space of the paper, I draw on the case of one teacher, who I have called Li, as an illustrative example. Li worked in a junior high school in Chengdu, Sichuan province in China. It is a state school under the administration of the Ministry of Education and EFL teachers in this school are required to follow the NECS as the general guidance for teaching, the fact of which makes Li no exception from the other five teachers in terms of contextual background. Li has worked in this school for 12 years since her graduation from a university that trains primary and secondary teachers. Her school head teacher recommended her to me as participant teacher in my study because of her industrious work and her success in helping students achieve high scores in exams. Moreover, she was chosen as an example because I had elicited rich data from her as she was eager to share her beliefs with me.

Data collection

Interviews, classroom observation and stimulated recall interviews were adopted as the ways to elicit data. Semi-structured interviews were conducted before classroom observations in order to elicit the teachers' professed beliefs about EFL teaching and learning. After the semi-structured interviews, I conducted classroom observations to ascertain the extent to which the teachers' classroom practice was affected by their beliefs. In order to achieve authenticity of the data, I conducted classroom observations on naturally occurring teaching for each teacher in their teaching of one unit, which usually covered eight to nine sessions. In order to explore how the teachers put their ideas into practice and how their professed beliefs related to their practice, I focused my observation on the following activities in each observed lesson: (1) the implementation of lesson planning for each lesson and for the whole unit; (2) vocabulary teaching; (3) grammar teaching; (4) listening comprehension tasks; (5) reading comprehension tasks; (6) speaking activities; (7) written exercises; (8) pair work and group work;

(9) error correction; (10) use of the target language. After each observation, I conducted stimulated recall interviews to elicit the teachers' beliefs underlying specific practices. These interviews involved the use of videotapes and sometimes field notes to aid the teachers' recall of the beliefs underpinning their practice in class.

Data analysis

Data analysis starts from the research questions. As complexity theory emphasises the 'interconnectedness' of complex systems, I explored the features of the teachers' beliefs not only from the perspective of the content of the beliefs, but also from that of the relationship between different beliefs. To be specific, I adopted template approaches by starting the analysis using pre-determined codes: beliefs about EFL; beliefs about EFL teaching; beliefs about EFL learning; beliefs about EFL learners; beliefs about EFL teachers. These initial codes served as a template for data analysis, from which basis I gathered relevant phrases, sentences or whole paragraphs under each code heading, forming five major categories of the teachers' beliefs. Then I further identified emerging themes and sub-themes within each category. The themes concerning the connections between the teachers' beliefs emerged when examining the features of the content of beliefs.

In exploring the relationship between the teachers' beliefs and practice, I adopted an open and 'inductive' approach to analysing the teachers' stimulated recall interviews by relating them to their practices. In the study, the initial data analysis revealed that 279 commentaries were used to rationalise 385 identified classroom practices by six teachers. I then drew up individual profiles for each of the teachers, in which I listed the beliefs thematised from commentaries articulated by each teacher, and alongside each item of belief, those practices that, according to the teacher, expressed or reflected particular beliefs. Each individual profile therefore displayed the links that the teacher made between their beliefs about EFL teaching and learning and related practice.

All the data analysed were kept in Chinese. In order to avoid transformation of the meanings expressed in the original transcripts through translation from Chinese to English, all analysis of the data was based on the original Chinese transcript. I only translated into English those quotations which I have inserted into the paper.

Findings: Li's complex belief system

As a teacher of 12 years' teaching experience, as well as language learner herself, Li held her own views about EFL teaching and learning based on her language learning and teaching experience. Moreover, against the background of the National Curriculum Reform, she was exposed to the influence of the NECS. In the process of accommodating the NECS, she also needed to adapt to the realities of each teaching situation in its own right. On the basis of the sociocultural understandings of teachers' beliefs and practice, complexity theory offers a framework by means of which beliefs cannot only be systematically investigated without isolating it from its social context, but also be given a role to play in adapting contexts (Thelen and Smith, 1994). In this case, Li's belief system was examined in the study in the here-and-now context, to which the experience of past language teaching and learning is fitted.

Li's complex beliefs

In the study, the teachers' beliefs were examined as being composed of the following five areas, including beliefs about EFL, beliefs about EFL teaching, beliefs about EFL learning, beliefs about EFL learners, and beliefs about the teaching roles. For example, in terms of beliefs about EFL – an epistemological issue about what English is about as a foreign language, Li believed that 'EFL is an instrument that helps students understand the world and pass exams as well'. Li expressed her belief about EFL teaching as involving 'a communicative process on both information and thoughts between teachers and learners'. Meanwhile, she emphasised that 'EFL learning is a process of habit formation, which requires repetition'. As to the teachers' role, Li believed that it would change according to different activities while teachers and learners were interlocutors'. She thus regarded the best way of teaching is to teach according to learners' differences, which 'are due to the learners' intelligence, learning habit and the degree of support from their family'.

Simply having beliefs about different areas may not fully explain the features of complexity of the teachers' belief system. The teachers might have held alternative beliefs about the same issue, with varying degrees of conviction. For example, Li explained her EFL teaching objectives by saying:

> My focus on developing learners' communicative skills has changed greatly with the implementation of the NECS. Teaching EFL is to teach the students ways to communicate with others. For example, when we learn something about 'invention', the purpose is not to teach the students several useful expressions or words, but to help them share their ideas about 'invention' with their peers. Only by communicating with others, can students internalise the language. However, I cannot deny that sometimes I also teach for exams as the students are required to get high scores in junior high entrance examinations.

This statement showed that Li assimilated the new concept about EFL teaching for communicative skills from the NECS into her beliefs, while the belief about teaching for exams co-existed with it. In the meantime, these two beliefs display different degrees of conviction. The above example revealed that Li's belief about teaching for communicative skills was stronger in degree of conviction than her beliefs about teaching for exams in this teaching context. Li's belief in the importance of teaching for exams outweighed her belief in the importance of teaching for communicative skills. Thus, the degree of conviction of the teachers' beliefs was not static, which varied according to different situations. In the study, Li's convictions about certain beliefs were stronger when they were grounded in previous teaching experiences than when they were based on theoretical justification. Once Li emphasised the importance of communicative language teaching by saying:

> Some teachers may stick to their previous way of teaching by focusing on grammar translation approach. However, I believe communicative language teaching approach can help learners learn real English. By doing so in recent two years, I realize that communicative language teaching can not only help my students communicate more fluently but also help them achieve high scores in exams.

The complexity of Li's beliefs also lay in the fact that different areas of her beliefs were interrelated with one another. In Li's case, her beliefs about EFL teaching and learning consisted of a coherent belief system. To be precise, Li's beliefs about EFL as a way of communication were related to her beliefs about how she conducted EFL teaching. Her emphasis on the approach of repetition was seen to be closely related to her beliefs about EFL learning as a process of habit formation. These connections were consistent and positive. However, there were also occasions when two inconsistent beliefs co-existed, such as the co-existence of contextualised and de-contextualised teaching. In the study, Li did not explicitly claim that she adopted de-contextualised teaching, which, however, was evident in some of her teaching practices. Such phenomena may be explained by the concept of 'token adoption', indicating that some new terms in the NECS such as 'contextualised teaching', 'CLT', 'learners as communicators', and so on were only picked up by her without real understanding. These beliefs were professed explicitly by Li in the study, but were not directly related to her practice. Whether these professed beliefs were the beliefs underpinning the teachers' practice needs to be examined by relating to their classroom practice.

Dynamic and non-linear relationship between Li's beliefs and practice

Most previous study of the relationship between teachers' beliefs and practice focused on the exploration of consistency and inconsistency. As most instances of inconsistency in beliefs identified in the literature are arguably partly due to the fact that researchers have not distinguished between the teachers' professed beliefs and their implicit beliefs underpinning practice, my study explored teachers' beliefs by juxtaposing their professed beliefs and their beliefs in practice so as to elicit the interactive complexity existing between the two. In order to obtain the data of the teachers' beliefs in practice, I focused on their retrospective commentaries upon the immediate context (i.e., the context in which the teachers' actions took place). As the exploration of the teachers' retrospective comments extrapolated the meanings the teachers attributed to their practices, the possible patterns of the links between beliefs and practice emerged. Such an exploration reveals the dynamic aspect of the system, which implies that the relationship between the teachers' beliefs and practice changes all the time as the teachers' belief system is not isolated but connected to a dynamic context of educational reform.

In the study, in most cases, more than one belief underpinned a practice. These beliefs dynamically interacted with each other in particular teaching contexts. They might either be compatible with, or contradictory to, each other, exerting different influences on the teachers' practice according to different classroom circumstances. In the case of Li, the study identified 86 individual classroom practices in Li's observed lessons and 47 commentaries underpinning these practices, which indicated the complexity of Li's belief system in relation to the features of diversity and interaction of her beliefs in practice.

Firstly, the teachers' practice seemed to be in fact determined by a combination of a range of compatible beliefs. Here the term 'compatible beliefs' indicates that different beliefs are consistent and co-exist in underpinning certain practice without causing conflict. For example, under the influence of the beliefs that 'prior knowledge helps learners to understand new knowledge', 'the introduction of prior knowledge can arouse learners' interest and stimulate them to participate in learning actively', and 'contextualised introduction can leave learners deep impression', Li introduced new words in class by referring to learners' prior knowledge. That is, the way in which the learners undertook the learning process and the learners' needs were the major concerns for Li in this specific context and they were compatible with promoting the contextualised vocabulary introduction. Therefore, whether the beliefs can work in harmony to underpin a certain action or not depends mostly on the extent to which they are compatible with the teachers' core beliefs about EFL teaching objectives and the ways to achieve these teaching objectives. In this case, Li's beliefs about EFL teaching objectives worked as a core belief in underpinning her practice.

Secondly, the consistency between the teachers' professed beliefs and practice may be superficial. That is, the teachers may adopt an officially promoted teaching concept, in name only, not in essence, which is called the practice of 'token adoption' (2001: 45). In the case of Li, such practice was mostly revealed in relation to her implementation of new concepts in the NECS. For example, although Li claimed that she adopted TBLT in her teaching, her practice revealed a variety of activities, which deviated from real TBLT in that they failed to achieve the purpose of learning to communicate. That is, Li regarded the mere adoption of tasks as the practice of TBLT. Li explained in one episode that 'the main purpose of using these tasks in teaching was to promote learners' interest in learning', which differs from the original aim of TBLT: to create a real purpose for language use and provide a natural context for language study and to promote constant learning and improvement (Willis, 1996). The reasons behind the issue may partly be her misinterpretation of TBLT, and partly her pedagogical knowledge and so on.

In relation to complexity theory, the practice of 'token adoption' exemplifies the non-linear feature of the development of the teachers' belief system at the time of change. The introduction of the new concepts of the NECS did not cause the teachers' beliefs and practice to change in ways that were expected. That is, if the teachers misinterpreted certain new concepts in the NECS as being in tune with the beliefs they already had, they did not necessarily change their practice. Thus, the interactions between their existing beliefs, the new concepts of the NECS, their interpretation of the NECS, and the teaching reality produced tensions which might have led to the practice of 'token adoption'.

Thirdly, the study provides strong evidence for the fact that not all the beliefs can operate without conflict and tension. The tensions between beliefs were a distinct feature of the teachers' belief system, and reflected non-linearity in the development of their belief system at a time of the curriculum reform. For example, in the study, Li revealed tensions mostly related to her existing beliefs and the new concepts promoted in the NECS, such as the tensions between teacher-centredness and learner-centredness, between promoting learners' overall language competence and teaching for passing exams, between behaviourist approach and CLT, and so on. In commenting on an episode when she interrupted learners to correct their errors, Li explained:

> I planned to focus on meaning and ignore the errors in conducting this task because I believed that by focusing on meaning, learners can experience a real language situation with an information gap. It can help them to be more engaged in the follow-up listening task. The learners made mistakes in applying this sentence pattern, which is the focus of this lesson the learners must master within the time frame of this session. If I do not correct these errors immediately, the students will make the same mistakes in exams.

Contrary to her belief about the importance of ignoring the errors to focus on meaning, Li's belief in practice was to conduct immediate error correction. In this case, when encountering the conflicts between beliefs, Li showed greater concern about immediate learning outcomes at the cost of the learners' affective and cognitive needs. Therefore, the belief about promoting immediate learning outcome by correcting errors immediately after the students made them were the ones that mirrored in Li's practice. In the study, this belief was called the core belief. These core beliefs were stable and exerted a more powerful influence on practice than other peripheral beliefs. In the above example of Li, she abandoned peripheral beliefs that were in conflict with her core beliefs.

Moreover, the teachers were also found to adopt an eclectic way of teaching when they were aware of the tensions in teaching. That is, when encountering unfavourable contextual factors, the teachers did not necessarily choose totally to reject their teaching plans. They might adopt an eclectic way to ease the tensions in teaching. The following episode illustrates how Li adopted the eclectic approach in teaching vocabulary.

Li: For some good apples, they are sweet and . . . what?
Ss: Crispy.
Li: Crispy. Read after me: crispy.
Li: And for some cookies, if they are fresh enough, they are crispy. OK, are you clear?
Ss: Yes (hesitation).
Li: OK, read these words together.
Ss: Sweet, sweet, crispy, crispy.
Li: Now answer this question in a sentence: what does the apple taste? S1.
S1: The apple tastes sweet and crispy.
. . .

When commenting on this episode, she recalled her thinking at the time as follows:

> I really wanted to present more examples for the students to understand but those words such as 'cookies', 'biscuits' which taste crispy are also new words to them. I thought of using English explanation of 'easily broken' but they only learned its meaning of 'being damaged'. Therefore, it is difficult to offer appropriate examples or explanations. I know vocabulary is better to be learned experientially but it needs constant exposure to authentic language, which is not accessible to learners with the limited time in the foreign language learning environment. So we had to ask students to preview words before class, and then we explained them contextually in class for better understanding and memorisation.

In this episode, Li introduced the new word by using examples and she also relied greatly on learners' previews and de-contextualised drills. Referring back to her professed beliefs, Li labelled her EFL teaching as 'a combination of the traditional way of teaching and the modern way of teaching'. This indicated that Li was aware of these tensions. Thus she believed that an eclectic approach was the best way to ease the tensions. In this case, the consciousness of the tensions in teaching might lead to cognitive change, prompting new practice. These examples from Li reveal the dynamic interaction between beliefs. To be exact, when all related beliefs serve or are not at odds with core beliefs, they are compatible in terms of underpinning the teachers' action and vice versa. When contradiction happened, certain beliefs which were in line with the teachers' core beliefs took priority in influencing practice.

Moreover, contextual factors such as limited exposure to authentic language, time constraints and teachers' pedagogical knowledge cannot be ignored in examining the relationship between the teachers' beliefs and practice. In the study, there were occasions when Li practised contextualised teaching while there were also occasions when she taught vocabulary in a de-contextualised situation. The shift from contextualised to de-contextualised teaching was conditioned by different teaching purposes and her interpretations of the ways in which these teaching purposes could be achieved. Therefore, the relationship between beliefs and practice was not absolute but conditioned by different teaching situations.

Discussion: complex and dynamic belief system

Teachers' belief systems are complex. The complex feature of the teachers' beliefs has to do 'not with what is believed but with how it is believed' (Green, 1971: 47). My study did not only reveal what the teachers believed, but also how they believed what they believed. To be specific, the study revealed that no single belief was totally independent of all other beliefs. Individual beliefs took their place in belief systems, never in isolation. Some of them were positively related, while others contradicted each other. Among positively related beliefs, certain beliefs about EFL teaching objectives played a core role in determining the teachers' practice that showed consistency with their beliefs. On the other hand, those conflicting beliefs might cause tensions. When confronting these tensions, the teachers usually gave different priority to certain beliefs in guiding their practice on the basis of core beliefs. Unlike other studies that examined the consistent or inconsistent relationship between teachers' beliefs and practice (i.e. Phipps, 2009), my study provided evidence to argue against the general comment on such relationship as the teachers' practice had always been determined by certain beliefs. The inconsistency may only exist between teachers' practice and certain aspect of teachers' beliefs, such as their professed beliefs. In this case, my study revealed that it was the interaction between core and peripheral beliefs that determined the relationship between the teachers' beliefs and practice, which, in a way, presented more accurately the relationship between teachers' beliefs and practice than previous studies. In this case, any attempt to change teachers' beliefs and practice should take teachers' core beliefs into consideration and the mechanism of interaction between the teachers' beliefs and practice.

Moreover, the examination of the interactions between different components of the systems provided a perspective from which to view teachers' belief systems in a dynamic way. When examining the relationship between the teachers' beliefs and practice, the practice of 'token adoption' emerged which represents a dynamic feature of the teachers' complex belief system. As revealed in the study, some consistent relationship between the teachers' beliefs and practice may be superficial in that the teachers only adopted the name of certain practice without implementing them in the real practice. As the beliefs underpinning the practice of 'token adoption' were implicit, both teachers and researchers might have been blind to such practice, and to the actual beliefs underpinning such practice. The exploration of the discrepancy between what the teachers claim to be their beliefs and what they really do in the classroom can help to make the issue explicit; in this case, the process would give the teachers the opportunity to reflect on their implementation of the NECS. In the context of English language teacher development in China, if we manage to make more implicit beliefs explicit, the tensions between their existing beliefs, the concepts of the NECS, the teachers' interpretation of the NECS, and the teaching reality may be exposed so that more effort can be made by both the teachers and the related agents to prevent the practice of 'token adoption'.

As a way to ease the tensions in the teachers' belief system, an eclectic approach was revealed in examining the teachers' practice. Such practice has been referred to as 'eclecticism' by some researchers (e.g. Grittner, 1977; Gu, 2007; Prabhu, 1987). Echoing some research findings regarding the features of Chinese teachers' practice (e.g. Gu, 2007: 86; Zheng and Davison, 2008), my study indicated that Chinese teachers tended to regard the eclectic approach as 'an effective option in the face of change'. The co-existence of different approaches to teaching adopted by the teachers indicated that such eclectic practice was a typical feature of their practice. From the complexity perspective, I regard the practice of 'eclecticism' as part of the dynamic process of development of teachers' beliefs and practice. It is an approach that does not rigidly follow a single paradigm of teaching, but instead draws upon multiple teaching approaches to meet different teaching objectives and expectations in different teaching contexts. In the study, Li's practice reflected the variety of her belief systems, which was bound to vary both in response to different teaching situations and as a consequence of interactions between beliefs. In this case, the teachers' eclectic practice can be regarded as a sign of diversity, that is, diversity of beliefs, diversity of practice, and diversity of the ways in which beliefs, practice and contexts interact to contribute to this non-linear interactive result.

Conclusion

People may argue that the non-linearity and diversity of belief systems leads to chaos. Complexity theory does reveal the chaotic nature of complex systems. However, it is important to note that chaos is not complete disorder, but is rather behaviour that arises unpredictably in a complex system. The value of complexity theory lies in the fact that it offers a theoretical framework to, on the one hand, break away from a reductionist view, and on the other hand, draw patterns from diversity and non-linearity. It is true that some patterns emerged in the study such as the practice of 'token adoption', the eclectic way of teaching and so on. Early reductionist representations of the relationship between beliefs and practice presented a linear view of being either consistent or inconsistent. By adopting complexity theory, I have been able to theorise the network of interactions between beliefs and practice in a way which more accurately represents the diversity of teachers' belief systems. Future research on the relationship between teachers' beliefs and practice should abandon the search for dualistic evidence of consistencies or inconsistencies between beliefs and practice, rather the research focus should be diverted to the exploration of the interactive features of teachers' beliefs and how such interactions impact their practice. In this way, the study contributes to the research agenda in that it provides a framework for examining teacher beliefs as a whole.

What needs to be acknowledged is that the study is restricted by an exclusive reliance on the teachers' and the researchers' perspectives of the teachers' belief systems. If values and beliefs about language teaching and learning had been examined from the perspectives of students, colleagues, school leaders, administrators, more tensions would have emerged from the data. Moreover, the two perspectives adopted in this study limited the research focus to the pedagogical aspects of the teachers' belief systems. To give a more complete account of teachers' belief systems, a more thorough exploration of the cultural and social perspective of the systems is needed. In this case, an ethnographic study is suggested to provide a description of the culture and social structure of a social group.

Some evidence in the research shows that this kind of in-depth case study plays a role in producing change in beliefs and practice. However, as my study is more of a descriptive nature, such analysis of the changes in teachers' beliefs and practice is limited. Nevertheless, in order to explore ways to change beliefs, an interventionist study would need to be conducted with reference to some of my findings. As revealed in the study, core beliefs played a more important role than peripheral beliefs in underpinning practice. Changes in teachers' beliefs and practice may thus become more possible if new concepts are introduced as core beliefs in certain teaching situations. As teachers' belief systems are complex and different components in the systems are not related in a simple cause-effect way, such attempts to change beliefs involves taking account of other related components, such as school policies, administrative roles and so on.

References

Bak, P. (1996). *How Nature Works: The Science of Self-organized Criticality*. New York: Copernicus.

Borg, S. (1999). Teachers' theories in grammar teaching. *ELT Journal*, 53(3), 157–167.

Borg, S. (2003). Teacher cognition in language teaching: A review of research on what language teachers think, know, believe, and do. *Language Teaching*, 36(2), 81–109.

Borg, S. (2006). *Teacher Cognition and Language Education*. London: Continuum.

Brownlee, Joanne M., Boulton-Lewis, Gillian M., and Purdie, Nola M. (2002). Core beliefs about knowing and peripheral beliefs about learning: developing an holistic conceptualisation of epistemological beliefs. *Australian Journal of Educational and Developmental Psychology*, 2, 1–16.

Bryan, L. A. (2003). The nestedness of beliefs: Examining a prospective elementary teacher's belief system about science teaching and learning. *Journal of Research in Science Teaching*, 40(9), 835–868.

Cohen, L., Manion, L., and Morrison, K. (2007). *Research Methods in Education* (6th edn). London and New York: Routledge.

Crookes, G., and Arakaki, L. (1999). Teaching idea sources and work conditions in an ESL program. *TESOL Journal*, 8(1), 15–19.

de Bot, K. (2008). Introduction: Second language development as a dynamic process. *The Modern Language Journal*, 92(2), 166–178.

de Bot, K., Lowie, W., and Verspoor, M. (2007). A dynamic systems theory approach to second language acquisition. *Bilingualism: Language and Cognition*, 10(1), 7–21.

Feryok, A. (2010). Language teacher cognitions: Complex dynamic systems? *System*, 38(2), 272–279.

Freeman, D. (1992). Emerging discourse and change in classroom practice. In J. Flowerdew, M.Brock and S.Hsia (Eds), *Perspectivees on Second Language Teacher Education*. Hong Kong: City Polytechnic of Hong Kong.

Freeman, D. (1993). Renaming experience/reconstructing practice: Developing new understandings of teaching. *Teaching and Teacher Education*, 9(5/6), 485–497.

Green, T. (1971). *The Activity of Teaching*. New York: McGraw-Hill.

Grittner, F. (1977). *Teaching Foreign Languages*. New York: Harper and Row.

Gu, Q. (2007). *Teacher Development: Knowledge and Context*. London: Continuum.

Johnson, K. E. (1992). The relationship between teachers' beliefs and practices during literacy instruction for non-native speakers of English. *Journal of Reading Behavior*, 24(1), 83–108.

Johnson, K.E. (2003). *Designing Language Teaching Tasks*. Basingstoke: Palgrave Macmillan.

Konopak, B.C. and Wukkuansm N.L. (1994). Elementary teachers' beliefs and decisions about vocabulary learning and instruction. *Yearbook of the National Reading Conference*, 43, 485–95.

Larsen-Freeman, D. (1997). Chaos/complexity science and second language acquisition. *Applied Linguistics*, 18(2), 141–165.

Larsen-Freeman, D. (2002). Language acquisition and language use from a chaos/complexity theory perspective. In C. Kramsch (Ed.), *Language Acquisition and Language Socialization* (pp. 33–46). London: Continuum.

Larsen-Freeman, D., and Cameron, L. (2008). *Complex Systems and Applied Linguistics*. Oxford: Oxford University Press.

Lewin, R. (1999). *Complexity: Life at the Edge of Chaos*. Chicago, IL: The University of Chicago Press.

Lim, C., and Torr, J. (2007). Singaporean early childhood teachers' beliefs about literacy development in a multilingual context. *Asia-Pacific Journal of Teacher Education*, 35(4), 409–434.

MacDonald, M., Badger, R., and White, G. (2001). Changing values: What use are theories of language learning and teaching? *Teaching and Teacher Education*, 17(8), 949–963.

Meijer, P.C., Verloop, N., and Beijaard, D. (1999). Exploring language teachers' practical knowledge about teaching reading comprehension. *Teaching and Teacher Education*, 15(1): 59–84.

MOE (Ministry of Education). (2001). *National English Curriculum Standards for Nine-Year Compulsory Education and Senior High School Education*. Beijing: People's Education Press.

Mok, W. E. (1994). Reflecting on reflections: A case study of experienced and inexperienced ESL teachers. *System*, 22(1), 93–111.

Nespor, J. (1987). The role of beliefs in the practice of teaching. *Journal of Curriculum Studies*, 19(4), 317–328.

Nunan, D. (1992). The teacher as decision-maker. In J. Flowerdew, M. Brock and S. Hsia (Eds), *Perspectives on Second Language Teacher Education* (pp. 135–165). Hong Kong: City Polytechnic.

Pajares, M. F. (1992). Teachers' beliefs and educational research: Cleaning up a messy construct. *Review of Educational Research*, 62(3, 307–332.

Peacock, M. (2001). Pre-service ESL teachers' beliefs about second language learning: a longitudinal study. *System*, 29(2), 177–195.

Phipps, S. (2009). The relationship between teacher education, teacher cognition and classroom practice in language teaching: A case study of MA students' beliefs about grammar teaching. Unpublished doctoral dissertation, The University of Leeds, Leeds.

Prabhu, N. S. (1987). *Second Language Pedagogy*. Oxford: Oxford University Press.

Richards, J. C., and Lockhart, C. (1996). *Reflective Teaching in Second Language Classrooms*. Cambridge: Cambridge University Press.

Richards, J. C., and Pennington, M. (1998). The first year of teaching. In J. C. Richards (Ed.), *Beyond Training* (pp. 173–190). Cambridge: Cambridge University Press.

Richardson, V. (2003). Preservice teachers' beliefs. In J. Rath and A. C. McAninch (Eds), *Advances in Teacher Education* (pp. 1–22). Greenwich, CT: Information Age.

Schulz, R. A. (2001). Cultural differences in student and teacher perceptions concerning the role of grammar teaching and corrective feedback: USA-Colombia. *Modern Language Journal*, 85(2), 244–258.

Smith, L., and Thelen, E. (Eds). (1993). *A Dynamic Systems Approach to Development: Applications*. Cambridge, MA: The MIT Press.

Thelen, E., and Smith, L. (1994). *A Dynamic Systems Approach to the Development of Cognition and Action*. Cambridge, MA: The MIT Press.

Thompson, A. G. (1992). Teachers' beliefs and conceptions: A synthesis of the research. In D. Grouws (Ed.), *Handbook of Research on Mathematics Teaching and Learning* (pp. 127–146). New York: Macmillan Publishing Company.

Tsui, A. B. M. (2003). *Understanding Expertise in Teaching: Case Studies of Second Language Teachers*. Cambridge: Cambridge University Press.

Tudor, I. (2001). *The Dynamics of the Language Classroom*. Cambridge: Cambridge University Press.

van Lier, L. (1998). *The Classroom and the Language Learner*. London: Longman.

van Lier, L. (2004). *The Ecology and Semiotics of Language Learning: A Sociocultural Perspective*. Boston, MA: Kluwer.

Willis, J. (1996). *A Framework for Task-based Learning*. London: Longman.Zheng, X., and Davison, C. (2008). *Changing Pedagogy*. London: Continuum.

Index

Locators shown in *italics* refer to tables, figures and appendices.

ability, student: impact on teacher identity 137–8
accountability: conceptual confusions over teacher 57–8
acquiescence, teacher: significance for teaching and reform 58
action research: use to promote teacher development 174
analysis, data: of research on EFL teacher beliefs and practice 184
assessment, self-: need for to professionalise teaching 76–7
assessments, school: tensions between reform aims and systems of 10–11
assessments, teacher: professionalisation of teaching via 75–6; *see also* self-assessment
authority, government: teacher honour system as enforcement of 77
autonomy: honour system as enforcement of teacher 77; vulnerability of teacher 15–16
awards, teacher: characteristics of honour system 67–8, 72–3, 79–81; history and drivers for instigation of 64; implications of 78–9, *79*; research on impact and teacher opinion of 64–72, *65*; role of in accounting for 'face' 74–5; role of in cultivating morality and standards 73–4, *73*; *see also particular implications e.g.* authority, government; autonomy; connections, individual; professionalism, teacher; rigour, teaching

balance politics: teacher honour system as 72
beliefs, educational: challenges to 11–12; *see also outcomes e.g.* development and education, teacher
beliefs, teacher: complexity theory in understanding 181–2: existing research on 180–1; research study of EFL 182–91

capacity, teacher: lack of confidence of principals in 174; lack of use by principals to enhance curricula 174
case studies: education institution transformation 109–19, *111*; role of school principals in teacher development 168–77
change education: and context of teacher dilemmas over 88–90; and dilemmas facing teachers 146–7; history of in China 4–6; impact and teacher dilemmas over 46–9; international overview 85; recent history 41; tension between aims of and assessment systems 10–11; tension between teacher professional development and 12–13; *see also* policies, reform; *see also factors affected by e.g.* duties, teacher; professionalism, teacher; *see also focus of e.g.* curricula; development and education, teacher
change, institution: analyses of teacher development 108–9; case study of educational 109–19, *111*
coding: of primary teacher emotions and identities *141–2*

collaboration: use to promote teacher development 174
colleagues: impact of relationship with on teacher resilience 158–9
collection, data: on EFL teacher beliefs and practice 183–4
commitment, personal: as factor underlying teacher resilience 150–3, *151*
commitment, teacher: lack of confidence of principals in 174
complexity theory: use in understanding teacher beliefs 181–2
conditions, working: impact of variations in on teacher education 13; impact on teacher resilience 155–6
conflicts, teacher: over reform of SEE curricula 90–9, *93*; *see also* dilemmas, teacher
Confucianism: influence on teacher education and development 26–7; interaction with other ideologies of China's teacher education 33–4; purpose of cultivating morality and standards of 73–4, *73*
connections, individual: threat to respect for teacher honour system 78
contest honour: characteristics of teacher award of 67, 68, 70
context: and expectations of principals for curricula reform 166–8; impact on curricula reform 135–8: influence on teacher dilemmas 88–90: of education reform 146–7; of teacher development and education 105–6; significance for policy implementation 117–18
continuing professional development, teacher: analyses of reform of 108–9; case study of 109–19, *111*; case study of role of principals in 168–77; centrality of school principals to 165–6, 167–8; challenges of policy implementation 115–17; characteristics of effective 86–7; current provision of 23–4; history of 22–3; institution and programme change in 106–8, *107*; rationalism as approach to 109; research on challenges facing 25; social and ideological influences 25–36; socio-historical and global context 105–6; *see also particular factors impacting e.g.* acquiescence, teacher; conditions, working; policies, education; policies, reform; resilience, teacher; teacher honour system
creativity, teacher: lack of promotion of to enhance teacher education 174
cultural dilemmas: affecting teacher reaction to curricula reform 94–5
curricula: case study of role of principals in reform of 168–77; context and expectations of principals for reform of 166–8; demands on teachers posed by reform of 6–9; dilemmas for teacher education of reform of 46–9, 87–8; features of reform of 127–9; identities and emotions of teachers during reform of 129–41, *130, 132*; impact of reform involving 46–9; implications for teacher education of reform of 100–2; purpose and teacher anxiety over reform of 90–102, *93*

data, research: collection and analysis of EFL teacher beliefs and practice 183–4; use to inform teacher development 173
degrees, university: enhancement of as part of institution transformation 113
demands, competing: difficulty for teachers to balance 56–7
Deng Xiaoping: role in revival of Confucianism driving education 33–4
departments, university: restructuring of for teacher education 114
design, research: exploring meaning of teacher resilience 149–50, *150*; on identities and emotional experiences of teachers 129–31, *130*
development and education, teacher: analyses of reform of 108–9; case study of 109–19, *111*; case study of role of principals in 168–77; centrality of school principals to 165–6, 167–8; challenges of policy implementation 115–17; characteristics of effective 86–7; current provision of 23–4; history of 22–3; institution and programme change in 106–8, *107*; rationalism as approach to 109; research on challenges facing 25; social and ideological influences 25–36; socio-historical and global context 105–6; *see also particular factors impacting e.g.* acquiescence,

teacher; conditions, working; policies, education; policies, reform; resilience, teacher; teacher honour system
Dewey's progressivism: influence on teacher education and development 27–9; interaction with other ideologies of teacher education 31–3
dilemmas, teacher: and context of education reform 88–90: reasons and nature of over curricula reform 90–102, *93*; *see also* conflicts, teacher
discussion, research: EFL teacher beliefs and practice 190–1; exploring meaning of teacher resilience of 159–61; identities and emotional experiences of teachers 138–41; reasons for teacher dilemmas in curricula reform 99–102; role of school principals in teacher development 173–7
dissatisfaction: teacher response to curricula reform 133
district, education: impact of support from on teacher identity 137
duties, teacher: impact and dilemmas of reform involving 51–6; research on impact of education reform on 45–56; *see also* lives, personal; *see also particular factors impacting e.g.* curricula; students; resilience, teacher

economies, market: role as force driving teacher education 34–6
education: challenges to traditional beliefs about 11–12; features of social and ideological influences 25–30; history of traditions and policies 4–6; interaction of social and ideological influences 30–6; *see also aspects e.g.* assessment, school; conditions, working; evaluation; curricula; programmes, educational; reform, education; schools; *see also players e.g.* teachers and teaching
education, teacher: analyses of reform of 108–9; case study of 109–19, *111*; case study of role of principals in 168–77; centrality of school principals to 165–6, 167–8; challenges of policy implementation 115–17; characteristics of effective 86–7; current provision of 23–4; history of 22–3; institution and programme change in 106–8, *107*; rationalism as approach to 109; research on challenges facing 25; social and ideological influences 25–36; socio-historical and global context 105–6; *see also particular factors impacting e.g.* acquiescence, teacher; conditions, working; policies, education; policies, reform; resilience, teacher; teacher honour system
efficacy: as factor underlying teacher resilience 150–2, *151*, 154–5
emotions, teacher: characteristics, formulation and factors affecting 125–7, *126*; coding system of for primary teachers *141–2*; research on during curricula reform 129–41, *130, 132*
English as a Foreign Language (EFL): research of teacher beliefs and practice 182–91
evaluation: impact and dilemmas of reform involving school 49–51, 58–9; impact and dilemmas of reform involving teacher 51–6; importance for policy implementation 118
'excellent teacher' 80
exhaustion: teacher response to curricula reform 134
expectations, parental: impact on teacher identity in context of curricula reform 137–8
experiences, personal: impact on teacher identity in context of curricula reform 135–6
expertise, teaching: characteristics of award in recognition of 67, 70; *see also particular awards for e.g.* teacher honour system

'face': role of teacher honour system in accounting for 74–5
findings, research : EFL teacher beliefs and practice 184–90; exploring meaning of teacher resilience of 150–9, *150*; identities and emotional experiences of teachers 131–8, *132*; impact and teacher opinion on honour system 67–72: reasons for teacher dilemmas in curricula reform 94–9
focus, institutional: case study of transformation of 112–13
fulfilment, personal: as factor underlying teacher resilience 150–2, *151*

governments, authority of : teacher honour system as enforcement of 77

happiness: teacher response to curricula reform 134
heads, school: case study of role in teacher development 168–77; centrality of in teacher education 165–6, 167–8; expectations of curricula reform and teacher education 167–8; impact of relationship with on teacher resilience 159
helplessness, feelings of: teacher response to curricula reform 132–3
honour system, teacher: characteristics 67–8, 72–3, 79–81; history and drivers for instigation of 64; implications of 78–9, *79*; research on impact and teacher opinion 64–72, *65*; role in cultivating Confucian morality and standards 73–4, *73*; role of in accounting for 'face' 74–5; *see also* 'excellent teacher'; 'special grade teacher'; *see also particular implications e.g.* authority, government; autonomy; connections, individual; professionalism, teacher; rigour, teaching

identities, teacher: challenges and tensions of education reform 9–16; characteristics, formulation and factors affecting 125–7, *126*; coding system of for primary teachers *141–2*; research on during curricula reform 129–41, *130, 132*
initiatives: case study of institution transformation 109–19, *111*; teacher education reform 106–9, *107*
institutions, educational: analyses of teacher development 108–9; case study of transformation of 109–19, *111*; *see also particular* e.g. schools
instrumental dilemmas: affecting teacher reaction to curricula reform 98–9

lives, personal: variation in teacher 13; *see also* work, teacher
lives, professional: impact of phases of on teacher resilience 156–7

management, teaching: strengthening of as part of institution transformation 114
Maoism: influence on teacher education and development 29–30
markets: role as force driving teacher education 34–6
methodology, research: education institution transformation 109–10; education, professionalism and work of teachers 45–6; EFL teacher beliefs and practice 183–4; exploring meaning of teacher resilience 149–50, *150*; impact and teacher opinion on honour system 65–7, *65*; reasons for teacher dilemmas in relation to curricula reform 92–4, *93*
methods, teaching: challenges of transition to new 11
missions, institutional: case study of transformation of 112
models: tensions of education reform models 10–11, 16–17
morality: role of teacher honour system in cultivating 73–4, *73*
motivation, teacher: impact of teacher honour system 70–1

national excellent teachers, 79–80

opinion, teacher: on teacher honour system 64–72, *65*
opportunities, development: variations in teacher 13
optimism, professional: as factor underlying teacher resilience 153–4

pain, feelings of: teacher response to curricula reform 132–3
parents: impact of expectations of on teacher identity 137–8; impact of relationship with on teacher resilience 158
policies, education: challenges for teacher development 115–17; flow of in cases of education institution transformation 110–11, *111*; history of in China 4–6; impact on teacher identity in context of curricula reform 129–41, *130, 132*; implications for teacher development 117–18; importance of evaluation and context for implementation of 118; promoting centrality of leadership of

principals 165–6; *see also particular e.g.* teacher honour system
policies, reform: case study of institution transformation 109–19, *111*; characteristics of educational 44–5; for teacher education and development 106–9, *107*; impact on teacher education, professionalism and work 46–56; limitations for solving educational problems 58–9; recent history of educational 41
political honour: characteristics of teacher award of 67–8
politics: teacher honour system as 71–2
practices, teacher *see* teachers and teaching
principals, school: case study of role in teacher development 168–77; centrality of in teacher education 165–6, 167–8; expectations of curricula reform and teacher education 167–8; impact of relationship with on teacher resilience 159
professional dilemmas: affecting teacher reaction to curricula reform 97–8
professionalism, teacher: conceptualisation of and relation to teaching 42–4; fundamentality of need for 64; impact of education reform on 45–56; resilience as factor underlying 145–61, *150, 151*; teacher honour system as cultivating 78; tensions between education reforms and 12–13; variations in working conditions and development of 13; via reflective and self-assessment 75–7
programmes, educational: initiatives for teacher education transformation 106–8, *107*
progressivism (Dewey): influence on teacher education and development 27–9; interaction with other ideologies of teacher education 31–3

quality: impact of perceptions of teacher 57; weakness as guiding principle for school evaluation 58–9
questions, research: EFL teacher beliefs and practice 182

rationalism: suitability as approach to teacher education reform 109; ecognition, professional teacher honour system as 68–9
reflection, self-: need for to professionalise teaching 75–7
reform, education: and context of teacher dilemmas over 88–90; and dilemmas facing teachers 146–7; history of in China 4–6; impact and teacher dilemmas over 46–9; international overview 85; recent history 41; tension between aims of and assessment systems 10–11; tension between teacher professional development and 12–13; *see also* policies, reform; *see also factors affected by e.g.* duties, teacher; professionalism, teacher; *see also focus of e.g.* curricula; development and education, teacher
reform, institutional: analyses of teacher development 108–9; case study of educational 109–19, *111*
relationships, workplace: impact on teacher resilience 157–9
research: and context of education reform teacher dilemmas 88–90; education institution transformation 109–19, *111*; education, professionalism and work of teachers 45–56; EFL teacher beliefs and practice 182–91; exploring meaning of teacher resilience 148–61, *150, 151*; identities and emotional experiences of teachers 129–41, *130, 132*; impact and teacher opinion on honour system 64–72, *65*; reasons for teacher dilemmas in curricula reform 92–9, *93*; role of school principals in teacher development 168–77
resilience, teacher: nature of 147–8; reasons for study of 145–6; research exploration of 148–61, *150, 151*
respect, for teachers: fundamentality of need for 64
rigour, teaching: teacher honour system as cultivating 178

sampling, research: on EFL teacher beliefs and practice 183
schools: impact and teacher dilemmas over evaluation of 49–51, 58–9; tensions between reform aims and assessment of 10–11; *see also players e.g.* principals, school; students

self-assessment: need for to professionalise teaching 76–7
self-reflection: need for to professionalise teaching 75–7
Senior Secondary Education (SSE): teacher dilemmas over curricula reform of 90–102, *93*
Shanghai: case study of role of principals in teacher education 168–77; centrality of leadership of principals 165–6, 167–8
situations, personal and professional: variation in teacher 13–15; *see also particular e.g.* identities, teacher'; professionalism, teacher
'special grade teacher': characteristics 79–80; history and drivers for recognition of 64
standards: role of honour system in cultivating 73–4, *73*
strategies: approach by principals to teacher development 173, 174; case study of institution transformation 112–13
strength, personal: as factor underlying teacher resilience 152–3
structural dilemmas: affecting teacher reaction to curricula reform 95–7
struggle, feelings of: teacher response to curricula reform 134–5
students: impact of ability of on teacher identity 137–8: impact of relationship with on teacher resilience 158
symbolic politics: teacher honour system as 71–2

teacher honour system: characteristics 67–8, 72–3, 79–81; history and drivers for instigation of 64; implications of 78–9, *79*; research on impact and teacher opinion 64–72, *65*; role in cultivating Confucian morality and standards 73–4, *73*; role of in accounting for 'face' 74–5; *see also* 'excellent teacher'; 'special grade teacher'; *see also particular implications e.g.* authority, government; autonomy; connections, individual; professionalism, teacher; rigour, teaching
teachers and teaching: case study of role of principals in development of 168–77; challenges and tensions over education reform 9–16; complexity theory in understanding 181–2; debates over respect for and whether a profession 63–4; difficulty in adjusting realigned conceptions and approaches 57; difficulty in balancing competing demands 56–7; education reform expectations of 167–8; enhancement of as part of institution transformation 113; existing research on 180–1; impact of perceptions of teacher quality 57; research study of EFL 182–91; status of in China 22; *see also* duties, teacher; evaluation; lives, personal; professionalism, teacher; respect, for teachers; schools; 'special grade teachers'; workforce, teacher; *see also aspects impacting on e.g.* accountability; assessment, school; awards, teacher; beliefs, teacher; conditions, working; curricula; development and education, teacher; emotions, teacher; identities, professional; management, teaching; policies, education; reform, education; traditions, education; *see also personal qualities e.g.* acquiescence, teacher; capacity, teacher; commitment, teacher; creativity, teacher; resilience, teacher
tensions, teaching objectives: impact on teacher identity in context of curricula reform 136–7
Traditional Confucianism: influence on teacher education and development 26–7; interaction with other ideologies of China's teacher education 33–4; purpose of cultivating morality and standards of 73–4, *73*
traditions, education: challenges to 11–12; history of in China 4–6
training, teacher: analyses of reform of 108–9; case study of 109–19, *111*; case study of role of principals in 168–77; centrality of school principals to 165–6, 167–8; challenges of policy implementation 115–17; characteristics of effective 86–7; current provision of 23–4; history of 22–3; institution and programme change in 106–8, *107*; rationalism as approach to 109; research on challenges facing 25; social and ideological influences 25–36;

socio-historical and global context 105–6; *see also particular factors impacting e.g.* acquiescence, teacher; conditions, working; policies, education; policies, reform; resilience, teacher; teacher honour system
transformation, institution: analyses of teacher development 108–9; case study of educational 109–19, *111*

universities: case study of restructuring of 109–19, *111*; degree enhancement as part of institution transformation 113; department restructuring for teacher education 114

vulnerability, teacher: and system autonomy 15–16

work, of teachers: impact and dilemmas of reform involving 51–6; research on impact of education reform on 45–56; *see also* lives, personal; *see also particular factors impacting e.g.* curricula; students; resilience, teacher
workforce, teacher: strengthening of as part of institution transformation 114

Yangtze Normal University : case study of restructuring of 109–19, *111*

For Product Safety Concerns and Information please contact our EU
representative GPSR@taylorandfrancis.com
Taylor & Francis Verlag GmbH, Kaufingerstraße 24, 80331 München, Germany

www.ingramcontent.com/pod-product-compliance
Lightning Source LLC
Chambersburg PA
CBHW050436280326
41932CB00013BA/2139
9781138580190